British Pantomime Performance

Millie Taylor

British Pantomime Performance

Millie Taylor

intellect Bristol, UK / Chicago, USA

First Published in the UK in 2007 by
Intellect Books, PO Box 862, Bristol BS99 1DE, UK

First published in the USA in 2007 by
Intellect Books, The University of Chicago Press, 1427 E. 60th Street, Chicago,
IL 60637, USA

A catalogue record for this book is available from the British Library.

Cover Design: Gabriel Solomons
Copy Editor: Holly Spradling
Typesetting: Mac Style, Nafferton, E. Yorkshire

ISBN 978-1-84150-174-1

Printed and bound by Gutenberg Press, Malta

Contents

ACKNOWLEDGMENTS

The starting point for this book was a comment from Christopher McCullough, who advised me to write from my experience about what I know. I followed his advice in the awareness of the absence of critical or analytical texts about pantomime, and the idea for this book was born.

An enormous debt of gratitude is owed to the many participants who contributed to the development of this book through conversations and the contribution of materials. I conducted interviews with the following people who gave their time, their ideas, and shared their experiences:

Dave Benson Phillips	Comedian
Gordon Dougall	Director
Peter Duncan	Comedian
Kate Edgar	Musical Director, Composer, Writer and Director
David Edwards	Production Manager
Paul Elliott	Writer, Director and Producer
Ian Good	Dame
Chris Harris	Dame and Writer
Gary Hind	Musical Supervisor and Musical Director
Chris Jordan	Writer, Director and Producer
Chris Lillicrap	Dame, Writer, Director and Producer
Ian Liston	Producer
Lorelei Lynn	Choreographer
Forbes Masson	Writer
Joanna Reid	Writer, Director and Repertory Theatre Artistic Director
Maria Taylor	Company and Deputy Stage Manager
Gerry Tebbutt	Director and Choreographer
Martin Waddington	Musical Director and Composer

These interviews were a significant contribution to the development of my ideas, even if not all the interviewees are directly quoted in the text.

Roy Hudd, Christopher Lillicrap, Paul Elliott, Ian Liston, Chris Jordan, Joanna Reid and Kate Edgar gave me access to scripts to supplement those that I already possessed (by Jack Chissick, Mark Rayment, Tudor Davies and others by Roy Hudd) and those in the public domain. Arthur Millie, archivist at Salisbury Playhouse, was an encouraging and informative host for an afternoon and contributed some photographs from his own collection as well as giving me a photograph from my own first pantomime (Salisbury Playhouse 1987). Eric Thompson, who photographed all the productions at Plymouth Theatre Royal for a number of years, helped me find my way around his collection. The wonderful results of his work can be seen in many of the illustrations attached to this book. Robert Workman, a freelance photographer, photographed many pantomimes, including the last few years at Winchester Theatre Royal and Salisbury Playhouse. These complemented the texts I had available and provide the contrast to Thompson's work. The marketing department at Theatr Clwyd sent me their photographs of the actor-musicians in *Aladdin* but have not credited the photographer, so I would like to acknowledge the work of the anonymous photographer. Thanks are also due to the marketing departments of Winchester Theatre Royal, Salisbury Playhouse, Theatr Clwyd and Plymouth Theatre Royal for allowing me to use photographs taken in their theatres.

The ideas in the book developed gradually and have been tested at conferences and in research seminars. In particular I would like to thank Peter Thomson for publishing my first article on pantomime music and the editors of *New Theatre Quarterly*, who published a version of chapter 6, as well as all the delegates who asked questions or offered suggestions at conferences in Vienna, Portsmouth and Hawaii. I also recall with appreciation the advice of an anonymous reader of an early book proposal that gave me encouragement to continue. Colleagues and friends who have offered helpful comments include Marianne Sharp, Dominic Symonds, Marie Kruger and Richard Cuming. My thanks also go to May Yao, Sam King and all at Intellect who have been instrumental in the editing and publication of this text.

Most of all, of course, thanks to my friends and family who have given me constant support.

Finally, I owe an enormous debt of gratitude to the British Academy who funded this research and the Society for Theatre Research who awarded a grant towards publication costs. Without their support and that of the University of Winchester, who gave me time to write the book, this would not have been possible.

List of Illustrations

THE PROLOGUE: WHAT'S BEHIND THEM?

Once upon a time a young musical director was employed to work on a Christmas pantomime for the repertory company at Salisbury Playhouse. 'It's *Jack and the Beanstalk* this year' she was told. She arranged popular songs and music for dance routines, discovered that percussion bangs and crashes make hitting somebody funny, and that performing twice a day is exhausting. She learnt that the fairy enters from Stage Right and the Villain from Stage Left; that they never cross the stage and they still speak in rhyme; that it is unlucky to recite the final rhyming couplet of the show before the first performance; and that comedy works using pace, rhythm and the rule of three. She discovered the excitement of an expectant packed house and the exhilaration of the entire audience joining in to shout 'It's Behind You' or compete in the songsheet, and for about fifty performances Jack climbed the beanstalk singing 'It's not where you start it's where you finish' and always won the day. That musical director was me.

In subsequent years I worked on Christmas shows and pantomimes in other repertory theatres and on commercial pantomimes for many companies. So when, some years later, I was asked 'what is a pantomime?' I thought I knew. I had become an academic by then, and was lecturing and writing about music theatre and pantomime and was assumed to have some authority, but the more I thought about it, the more I realized that there are many possible answers to that question. Certainly it is clear to a British audience that pantomime has no connection to mime or the mime sections of ballet and opera which it has in some theatrical traditions. Asking around among performers and practitioners working in the field, I got a lot of different responses: 'It's a fairy story'; 'It has to have a Dame'; 'There's audience participation'; 'Don't forget the slosh scene and the comedy'; 'Or the spectacle';

If you've got a man dressed as a woman, singing to two people dressed as a cow, about a woman dressed as a man taking that cow off to market, and the song says 'Goodbye, we'll miss you' and you as a grown adult sit there and cry, then that's panto (Chris Jordan).

Those answers seemed to identify the irrationality of pantomime and some of the constituent elements, but which of those elements are necessary for a performance to be a pantomime? Is there some combination of these and other elements that comprise pantomime, or are some of these elements dispensable? I decided to find out what was being performed as pantomime in theatres around the country and made an extensive tour during the 2003–2004 season, following smaller tours in 2001–2002 and 2002–2003. An explanation of the process by which pantomimes were chosen for inclusion is given below.

Alongside the notes of these performances, I gathered together the scripts from productions I'd been involved in, scripts given to me by contributors to this work, and the notes from many other Christmas shows and pantomimes I'd seen. But even in that sentence there is a dilemma: what is a Christmas show and what a pantomime? The creative teams and audiences plainly have some collective understanding of those terms so that audiences are able to choose one or the other for their Christmas entertainment. Creators must use the same (or similar) terms of reference as the audience in order to satisfy the audience expectations. In other words, one of the questions I wanted to explore is how are the British people collectively defining the genre of pantomime, and what falls outside that category into Christmas musical or children's show? The answers are neither simple nor straightforward for two reasons. Firstly, there are different types of pantomime created by different types of company for different audiences. Secondly, pantomime is a living form within a largely oral tradition and so is always in a state of flux. It derives from a continuous history going back over two hundred and fifty years, though the roots of contemporary pantomime are more recent, and traceable to the late Victorian age.

Originally the word 'pantomime' denoted the masked players in one-man mime performances which originated in Greece and became popular among the Romans at the time of the emperor Augustus.[1] After the rise of Christianity there was little trace of pantomime until the Italian Renaissance when the term denoted the type of performance rather than the performer in *Commedia dell'arte*. In the fifteenth century one of the principal figures was *Arlecchino*, a quick-witted, unscrupulous comic knave who became 'Harlequin' in England and was the forerunner of the hero or Principal Boy. Among the other characters was 'Pulcinella' who survives as 'Punch' in *Punch and Judy* shows. These entertainments were improvised, rumbustious and earthy, based on a broad storyline that all the players knew, and incorporating speeches and phrases from each player's extensive repertory. The older and comic characters were generally played in masks, and there is reference to music and dance in these entertainments.[2]

By the end of the seventeenth century *Commedia* was declining in Italy but was still popular in France among companies of *forains*. The popular success of these companies drew the wrath of the *Comédie Française* and the result was a Royal Decree banning the use of speech by them. It was these companies of dancing, tumbling, mute harlequins that appeared in England first in fairs and then on the stages of Lincoln's Inn Fields and Drury Lane Theatres.[3] In 1717 at the Theatre Royal, Drury Lane, *The Maid's Tragedy* was presented 'after the manner of the Ancient Pantomimes' (Frow 1985: 15). The first recorded English pantomime using the Harlequin characters was presented by John Rich in 1721 at Lincoln's Inn Fields after a performance of *King Lear* and was called *The Magician; or, Harlequin a Director* (Frow 1985: 39). The piece was topical, used satirical songs and recitatives and established the pattern which pantomime was to follow.[4] This type of entertainment was hugely popular and highly successful. John Rich put on the 1723 production of *Harlequin Dr. Faustus*. It was 'based on the legend of Faust [and] took the town by storm. Its spectacles included a fire eating dragon, a pair of disembodied legs which danced around the stage, and a transformation in which a clockwork statue changed into a live woman and the pedestal on which it stood became a chariot drawn by dogs.' (Salberg 1981: 6).

Between 1750 and 1870, the opening scenes, which contained speech in rhyming couplets, were the prologue to the moment of transformation, when, pursued by evil, the young lovers reached a point of desperation. At this moment the good fairy appeared and transformed the characters into those of the Harlequinade. There then followed a series of transformations and chases, slapstick humour and spectacular effects (Holland 1997). In 1750 the first speaking Harlequin appeared in the Harlequinade of *Queen Mab* (Salberg 1981: 7).

From the 1770s, Clown began to take over from Harlequin as the principal character, and *Mother Goose*[5] (1806) is generally regarded as a significant turning point; from then on Clown was the principal character. *Mother Goose* contained four scenes in a musical opening section using songs and recitatives, followed by the Harlequinade, which was mute. This pantomime established a style in the opening scenes that is still recognizable in modern pantomime (Frow 1985: 64). In America, the pantomime was a favourite entertainment throughout the eighteenth and well into the nineteenth centuries when it coalesced with French ballet, circus or theatrical extravaganza; the slapstick comedy moved to circus and the musical style to melodrama (Shapiro 1984: 56). Comic tunes were published separately from recitatives, and arias were used in provincial theatres. As in Britain, medley overtures were common (Chapman 1981: 809).

During the nineteenth century the opening section grew to become the entire pantomime, and principal boys appeared following a separate tradition of 'breeches parts' for women.[6] From the 1870s the tendency was growing to limit the stories to those already known; many current pantomime stories first appeared as pantomimes between 1781 and 1832.[7] Many of the stories had been known since Charles Perrault's *Histoires ou Contes du temps passé* of 1697 (Frow 1985: 109 and 122). In the 1880s, the Dame began to replace Clown as the central figure (famously played by Dan Leno) and pantomime as we know it really began (Frow 1985: 167). The elements still present in pantomime are the clowning and buffoonery, the slapstick and transformation scenes, the use of topical jokes and references, the singing and dancing, the heroic quest, and the presence of the immortals who to this day speak in rhyme.

Pantomime in Britain at the moment is a family entertainment with appeal for people of all ages, not just those taking children to the show. The story is a re-telling of a well-known fairy or folk tale along pre-determined and familiar lines. The simple structure involves a quest or journey during which the hero, often played by a woman, achieves maturity by defeating the villain and winning fame, fortune and the hand of the fair princess. Although the story is the pretext for everything that happens, and directors and producers point to the importance of the story in keeping the audience engaged, the way the story is told is an equally important feature of pantomime.

The principal driver of the pantomime (in all pantomimes except *Cinderella* where Buttons takes this role) is still the Dame, who is often the mother of the Principal Boy, played by a man dressed as a woman but not in drag.[8] The Dame functions as one of the principal instigators of the participation of the audience in the performance. She builds a relationship of complicity with the audience, and particularly the adults in the audience, through comic interaction and asides that draw the audience into awareness of the frame of performance as well as involvement with the plot. The comedian has a similar function but tends to have greater interaction with the children in the audience. The frame of performance is widely exposed principally by these two characters through reflexive references to the pantomime traditions, the rehearsal period, stage management and technicians, the band and the audience. Some reference to cross-dressing and the presence of cross-dressed actors also contributes to the reflexivity of the performance.

Music, dance, design, intertextual reference and comedy routines all contribute to the sense of artificiality and joy that the pantomime inspires. Although the story may provide an excuse for a song or a comedy routine, the event that follows does not really propel the scene forward or contribute to the narrative, but provides the excuse for entertainment. A grand ball being planned at the palace is the excuse for a decorating scene or a cooking scene, but the slapstick that follows is gratuitous as well as being (in the best pantomimes) fast-paced, slick and perfectly timed. This combination provides excellent entertainment. The arrival in an undersea world is likewise the excuse for a ceremonial procession, spectacular scenic effects or a ballet, all of which are beautifully executed with extravagant lighting and costume, dry ice or pyrotechnics, atmospheric music and a stage full of performers.

The performance is repeatedly exposed as constructed, fantastic and silly, even as some scenes are played with heightened realism to draw the audience into identification with story, quest and hero. At the same time, spectacular designs, complicated and energetic dance routines and slick physical comedy allow the audience to be amazed at the talent, craft and sheer hard work in the performance, so that even as the performers send up the genre, their ingenuity and talent are demonstrated. However, it is the artistry and wit in the play with distance as the pantomime is simultaneously played for real and deconstructed that is one of its most enjoyable facets and possibly a defining feature of pantomime.

The framing of performance and the play with distance and artifice are features that separate pantomime from children's theatre and musical theatre. The other feature, that perhaps also says something about the British character, is the inclusion of cross-dressing, saucy innuendo and double entendre; what Peter Holland (1997) refers to as the seaside postcard humour and sexuality of pantomime. The pantomime treads a fine line; it must never become blue or risqué or it would alienate the family audience it seeks to entertain, but it provides witty, saucy and silly humour which contains double-entendres, topical gags and wordplay for the adults and slapstick, physical comedy, participation and storytelling for the children.

So another definition of pantomime might be: a simple re-telling of a well-known story performed by stock characters, where the framing and sending up of the performance, the play with distance through the interaction with the audience, the physical comedy and artifice of music, dance and spectacular scenic illusion, and the implicit sexuality are equally important in appealing to a wide audience constituency.

There are four broad categories of work: Commercial, Repertory, Alternative (or fringe) and Amateur productions. These are separated to some extent by the economics of production and have resulted in significant differences in performance. Despite visiting a few amateur productions (notably at Woodstock and at Eastleigh) I decided to concentrate on professional productions as the professional world sets the parameters by which the genre is defined, followed by amateur companies. Amateur companies also have a different set of community relationships that have a significant impact on the creation and reception of the performance that sets that category apart from professional work. Within the other areas there are some similarities, but also a surprising amount of variety. In the end I visited approximately equal numbers of repertory and commercial pantomimes and any productions that appeared to be particularly unusual or in fringe venues, so covering the 'alternative' bracket. In the commercial sector I saw work in different size venues and with potentially different priorities, produced by QDos, Hiss and Boo, Eastbourne Theatres, The Proper Pantomime Company and Kevin Wood Productions. In repertory theatre there are some theatres who advertise 'traditional pantomime' while others are overtly producing Christmas shows. I picked a cross section of performances including both of these formats and some that seemed to be challenging the pantomime conventions as I perceived them. I therefore visited Nuffield Theatre, Southampton, Northcott Theatre, Exeter, Salisbury Playhouse, Theatre by the Lake, Keswick, Theatre Clwyd, Mold, York Theatre Royal, Royal Shakespeare Theatre, Theatre Royal Stratford East and Tron Theatre, Glasgow. The performances at the last two of these might be considered 'Alternative'.

Alongside performance analysis I interviewed members of the production and creative teams who put these and other performances together. I have interviewed at least one person from each of the companies or productions mentioned above. These people form yet another cross section, this time of the creative staff of pantomime, and include performers, directors, writers, musical directors, choreographers, composers and producers. Although I had opinions based on my own experiences, I wanted to discover what other creators think about how pantomime is put together and how it works. The discussions explored many issues about current trends and potential developments in the form, as well as exposing the practical realities of performance. Excerpts from transcriptions of these discussions are included in the text, allowing the practitioners to speak in their own voices alongside my analyses of scripts and performances. These are juxtaposed with historical and theoretical materials so that the subjective and the experiential are mixed with the analytical and the theoretical.

This compilation of materials and voices, the subjective and the objective, serves in some way to embody the mix of elements and genres within pantomime, in which the play with distance between audience or reader and performer is constantly shifting. However, at a broader level, I have argued elsewhere[9] that performance needs to be analysed and theorized from both subjective and objective positions and that a completely impartial analytical position is likely to remain an impossibility. Reading performance texts, especially live performances, is a phenomenal as well as an intellectual experience and the effects of both parts of that experience contribute to an understanding of the performance. I would argue that the combination of subjective and objective analysis, experiential and theoretical conception, generates new possibilities for understanding. The practical experience is viewed in new ways because it is challenged by the conceptual understandings made possible by theorizing, and the philosophical and intellectual space of theorizing is always grounded in relation to practice and its effects. For this reason this book contains both these positions. There is also the concern that for a British audience pantomime is part of the popular culture, but for most other readers it is largely unknown. This book, therefore, contains rather more description and historical framing than might otherwise have been deemed necessary.

Although the book is organized around clearly defined areas such as gender, design, dance and music, that are analysed discretely, there are several themes that run through the book. The first of these, identified above, is the play with distance and reflexivity. This can take the form of asides to the audience within scenes, even while some members of the company remain behind the fourth wall, but it is also apparent in the artifice of singing, dancing and spectacle, intertextual reference, and the play with gender.

A second theme is the use of material with which the audience is likely to be familiar developed in an oral tradition. Recognizable material might include the use of existing songs and story, stereotypical set and costume design, and even where there are discrepancies or alterations, the alterations fall within genres that are familiar and often popular. So the music score is often a compilation of known songs, but where it isn't, the style of music is easily recognizable and from a popular genre. The same is true of dance music, dance style, the structure and design of the performance, the inclusion of moments of audience interaction, comedy routines that are associated with the genre of pantomime, and the use of stock characters in pre-existing stories from popular culture. Even the performers trade on familiarity to the audience, either through their celebrity status or because of repeated appearances at a particular venue. So at the local level the pantomime is made up of a compilation of materials that are individually familiar put together in a way that has a familiar structure and form. The choice of the elements for inclusion, the exact form of each element and the interaction of those elements is what makes each pantomime unique.

The sense of familiarity in pantomime is deliberately evoked by the inclusion of material that might cause feelings of nostalgia, such as the story and the styles of music and dance, and by reference to what are generally referred to as 'the traditional elements' or 'traditional pantomime'. There is no single view of what is 'traditional'; pantomime has been present in English popular theatre since the mid-eighteenth century, and although our contemporary pantomime is clearly descended from a Victorian model it is a live form that has been constantly developing. The 'traditional' elements appear to be those with which the audience has become familiar. Although every individual might compile a different list it is likely to contain some or all of the following features: the presence of cross-dressed Dame and/or Principal Boy, the use of rhyming couplets by the Immortals, a well-known quest story, scenic transformations, singing and dancing, set-piece comedy routines, audience interaction, the songsheet and the walkdown. The inclusion of those elements appears to evoke nostalgic feelings, but the combination of elements and how they are to be incorporated will vary according to context and experience. Certainly, the idea of a tradition, relying as it does on nostalgic associations, is an important ingredient in the marketing of pantomime and in the creative development of individual pantomimes.

The marketing of pantomime as safe, nostalgic, traditional and familiar, and the consequent presence of the appropriate features in the performance reinforces the association between the event and a degree of emotional safety for the spectator. This becomes crucial because of the wide appeal pantomime must have to attract an audience from across generations and classes. There is a consequent effect on the production itself. The size of theatre and crucially the size of audience and likely box office receipts govern what can be spent on the production. Then the producer performs a balancing act judging what can be spent on star performers, other actors and dancers, production team, band, sets, costumes, spectacular transformation scenes, illusions and special effects. The economics of the production vary according to the venue size, the potential audience size and catchment area and the cost of production. Equally important is the possibility for revival of the production from one year to the next which is available to commercial producers. The economics of production is also responsible for some of the changes pantomime is undergoing in terms of the presence of comedians and slosh routines, the numbers of performers and in the scale of scenic extravagance.

The type of production also impacts on the awareness of a defined audience community present in the piece. This can exist on two levels. The audience community who are present at a particular performance are drawn into a shared experience by interaction with the performers, complicity with the comedians, topical reference and cod-corpse. The wider community within which the performance takes place includes both the local community and the shared cultural awareness of British life, as expressed in local and topical reference. These pre-existing communities tend to be more clearly defined and may have an existing relationship with the repertory theatre that presents material throughout the year, and may be less identifiable to commercial producers who arrive at the theatre for a few weeks each year. This is not a straightforward distinction, however. Through the participation, albeit controlled, of the audience in the performance and through the onstage recognition of the lived experience of the present time and place, the identity of the audience is reinforced.

The carnivalesque is a theoretical construction, characteristic of burlesque, parody and satire, in which logic or authority are subverted or transformed. It is implicit in many of the discussions that follow about reversal, transformation, the grotesque body and disruption albeit as social containment. These ideas are drawn from Bakhtin's study of the carnivalesque in Rabelais (Bakhtin [1940] 1984 and Clark and Holquist 1984). The ritual and the participation of pantomime involve the audience in seemingly subversive activity, while the laughter at physical comedy and the grotesque body as well as at topical and political humour allows the audience to laugh at the joke while becoming aware of its own subjectivity and complicity. Carnival is also the opportunity for symbolic disruption and subversion of authority, but the license for subversion for the period of carnival is granted by the authorities, thus reinforcing the social containment in the seemingly anarchic.

Within the stories of pantomime there is disruption of the accepted order as the young hero alters his status through wit, wisdom and courage, but the resolution restores the status quo, albeit with the hero in a new place within the hierarchy. This can be seen as optimistic in allowing that there is opportunity for transformation and change, or pessimistic in the continuation of the class-based materialistic society. Meanwhile the opportunities for disruptive behaviour by the actors in slosh and slapstick scenes are constrained by practical considerations of acceptable behaviour and cleaning bills, while audience participation, the anarchic opportunity to make a noise and answer back in the theatre, is signalled, directed and controlled from the stage. The possibilities for transformation are further reflected in the scenic illusions of transformation scenes and special effects, which suggest that anything is possible for this limited time. Incorporation of reference to the grotesque body and its sexuality in the person of the Dame and in the seaside postcard humour of the whole are features of the carnivalesque that are also present in pantomime. Finally, the relationship of carnival to feasting, merrymaking and to religious festivals is also apparent in the link between British pantomime and the Christmas festivities.

These themes are addressed throughout the book, but the central question that the book seeks to address is how pantomime constructs itself through its performances so that it creates a particular interactive relationship with, and potentially transformative experience for, its audiences. This requires that the experience of the performance as well as its analysis should be included. So the performance text and its contexts need to be analysed structurally and objectively, but it is also necessary to treat the event of performance as a phenomenal and subjective experience, so that the experience of attendance forms part of the understanding of the performance. There is no clear separation of the book into parts that use either an objective or experiential position, but an attempt to ground theory in experience and expose practice through theory. Some parts, such as those on music and dance, lean more to analysis, other parts, such as the discussion of gender identity, rely on theoretical frames to reconsider the practice, while others, such as the conceptualization of pantomime as a transformative experience, draw on subjective experience and observation alongside the theoretical. I have found it impossible to separate these positions in an effective way without restricting the material, but have tried to group chapters that have a similar focus or draw on the same materials. The first section provides a historical and economic context for the contemporary production of pantomime. The second group of chapters focuses on the reflexive relationship between audience and performers and the alteration of distance between them. The final part identifies some of the opportunities for distanced entertainment offered by the spectacle of pantomime.

Chapter 1 begins by providing an economic context for the production of different types of pantomime in different economic situations. The cost of production and the material conditions of culture in Britain has an effect on the presence of slosh scenes and the training grounds for developing comic routines. This is addressed in chapter 2 though the argument moves on to examine the effect of slosh scenes and chases in creating mayhem and disruption in the audience. Chapter 3 begins with the effects of the cost of production on the possibilities for transformation scenes, illusion and magic in the design of pantomime. However, the design also projects an idealized utopianism in the mix of times and places presented. The next two chapters step off from the discussion in chapter 1 of the box office appeal of particular stories to analyse the structure and interpretation of pantomime stories. Chapter 4 traces the history and development of fairy stories in a pantomime structure to identify the slow pace of change within an oral tradition and the relationship of familiarity and originality in each performance. Chapter 5 looks at the importance of quests and transformations in pantomime stories and at potential interpretations of such stories.

The next group of chapters focuses on the relationship between the audience and the performers and how distance between performers, characters and audience members alters during the performance. Chapter 6 identifies the performance frame and the possibilities for its disruption within scripted and unscripted material in many parts of the performance. Reflexive reference to the world outside the fairy story provides a separate performance level from the telling of the story, and many characters move fluidly between these levels. Chapter 7 explores the presence of cross-dressed characters, which contributes to the separation of character and performer by reducing the opportunity for identification of performer with character. Chapter 8 identifies the relationship that develops between audience and performers, generated by participation in the rituals of pantomime performance, and which can potentially offer momentary possibilities of transformation for audience members. Chapter 9 looks at the references to local, national and international events that provide a shared framework for audience and performers. Such interactions are used to signify each performance as a unique shared experience between audience and performers.

The third section of the book focuses on the parts of the performance that require a more distanced and passive engagement by the audience. Illusion and transformation in design has already been discussed, but there are other areas where the artifice of the performance allows a change of pace and the enjoyment of the wit, ingenuity and skill of the performers. Chapter 10 uses verbal comedy to highlight the fun, rhythm and musicality of comic and surreal verbal exchange. Chapter 11 looks at the combination of known styles in the music score that contributes to the familiarity and intertextuality of the performance. Music is also a feature in the signification of mood, location and atmosphere and is fundamental in the creation of a melodramatic style of acting. Chapter 12 covers similar ground in relation to dance, with the addition that dance is important for its representation of a community of dancers in a utopian vision of energy and abundance.

This leads to the epilogue which summarizes the unique combination of artifice, reflexivity and storytelling in pantomime, and the constant play with distance between audience, performers and performance brought about by this combination.

Although this book is specifically about British pantomime there are pockets of post-colonial interest in pantomime in parts of the English-speaking world such as

Canada, Australia and Hong Kong. Most interestingly, the form is alive and well and developing as a cross-cultural, bilingual form in South Africa, with productions written and directed by Janice Honeyman, and articles disseminated to the academic community by Marie Kruger. In the United States pantomime is regarded as children's theatre, despite the transfer of some of Norman Robbins' scripts in the 1970s and 1980s, and his direction of one of his own pantomimes at Iowa State University, which led to a surge of interest in the form and a New York production of his *Cinderella*.[10]

Pantomime remains the most popular form of British theatre with influences on and from other popular forms in this country and similarities to popular forms elsewhere in the world. These are not addressed here, but begin to become apparent through analysis of these contemporary performances and deserve further study. In the meantime, the pages that follow offer a way of looking at what is currently being presented as British pantomime that will, hopefully, inspire readers to review their understanding of this extremely popular form of British theatre.

Notes

1. Details about these early pantomimes and their performances are contained in Branscombe, P. 'Pantomime' in *The New Grove Dictionary of Music and Musicians* ed., Stanley Sadie. London: Macmillan 1980. Slater, W. J. 'Pantomime Riots' *Classical Antiquity* vol 13/1 1994, pp. 120–144.
2. There is a vast literature on the *Commedia dell'arte*, identifying the complexity of its development and influence which is beyond the scope of this book. A historical and critical perspective is given in Richards, K. and Richards, L. *The Commedia dell'arte*. Oxford: Blackwell, 1990. Green, M. and Swan, J. *The Triumph of Pierrot: The Commedia dell'arte and the modern imagination*. New York: Macmillan 1986 centres on its influence in the twentieth century. A practical text is Rudlin, J. *Commedia dell'arte: An Actor's Handbook*. London and New York: Routledge, 1994.
3. For a good description of the historical development of pantomime, see Frow (1985).
4. Clive Chapman (1981) describes a pantomime of the period quite extensively in 'A 1727 Pantomime: *The Rape of Proserpine*'.
5. Written by Thomas Dibdin, who was not named on the playbill, although the composer, Mr Ware, was (Frow 1985: 63).
6. For a discussion of the practice of cross-dressing in modern pantomime, see Holland (1997) and Richards, Sandra. *The Rise of the English Actress* London: Macmillan, 1993.
7. For the exact dates of several pantomimes, see chapter 4 below.
8. Gender confusion is avoided in pantomime; the Dame is clearly a man, just as the Principal Boy is clearly a woman. The cross-dressing allows comedy in the case of the Dame and fantasy in the case of the Principal Boy, as discussed in chapter 7.
9. 'Don't dream it, be it': Exploring signification, empathy and mimesis in relation to *The Rocky Horror Show* *Studies in Musical Theatre* vol 1:1, 57–71.
10. Norman Robbins worked in pantomime for many years and wrote pantomime scripts as well as other plays. He has recently published a book about pantomime history called *Slapstick and Sausages*.

1

MONEY MATTERS

Pantomime began life in the theatre as a commercial product. By the nineteenth century pantomimes and burlesques at Covent Garden and Drury Lane in particular were famous for their spectacles, illusions and hordes of extras. Most books about pantomime history concentrate on the developments in these principal London theatres, but they were followed by other theatres in London and the regions, and pantomime became hugely popular all over the country.[1] Theatre managers depended on attracting large audiences to pay for the hundreds of supernumeraries (extras) and spectacular scenic illusions. Theatres vied with each other to create the most extravagant spectacle, which would become the talk of the town and attract the largest audiences. Two things go hand in hand here; more revenue can produce greater spectacle, but the expense of spectacle relies on success and popularity. Since it is the producers (theatre managers in the nineteenth century) who take the financial risk, they must always make a judgement about the likely income from a production and assess what the outlay should be in order to ensure that they break even or make a profit. Not surprisingly producers try to assess what audiences are most likely to want to see. At the moment the most visible evidence of this is in casting, where, for example, television stars trade on their popularity in another sphere to draw the television audience in to the pantomime. Casting pantomime has always been subject to the presence of star names, from music hall through variety and later musical comedy. In the last thirty or forty years the stars or celebrities have sometimes been employed from different media including pop music, television and sport, and the transfer can be less satisfactory. However, there are other areas where the economic priorities impact on the production.

Reducing the number of dancers and musicians employed, the re-use of sets, costumes and the re-working of scripts all allow the producer to reduce the costs. At the same time the length of the run of the show and therefore the income produced is critical. Alternatively, if the show can be re-worked at a series of different venues, the costs of a production can be recouped over a number of years, which means that more can be invested in the production. It is the impact of this juggling act that underlies the different production values in commercial and repertory pantomimes. There are other differences in the perception of the audience that also impact on the two types of pantomime. Repertory theatres have subscription series and regular, often loyal audiences, while commercial producers are dependent on the production and its stars to attract the audience. Perhaps there is more pressure in this case to retain familiar material, while the repertory theatres need to present themselves as different from the commercial companies who can afford spectacular effects and well-known casts. There is a seemingly obvious correlation here, but in practice the borderlines are not clearly defined and the arguments are more complex.

During the twentieth century the regions and the London suburbs retained a pantomime tradition while that in London's West End became much sparser and finally died in the 1980s, although there was a pantomime at Sadler's Wells as recently as 1994, pantomime returned to the Old Vic with *Aladdin* in 2004 and 2005, and Mark Ravenhill wrote a version of *Dick Whittington* for the Barbican Theatre in 2006. From 1843, when the requirement for theatres to have a Royal Patent for dramatic performances was repealed, pantomime began to flourish in the regions. From then until about the 1920s it was generally local managers who produced the pantomimes catering for the specific tastes of the town and audience. This practice now continues in repertory theatres. In the first two decades of the twentieth century producers began to appear who created pantomimes for the larger cities and moved them from one venue to another from year to year. 'Partly because of economies and partly because of the growth of the syndicates which delegated their numerous pantomimes to one or perhaps two outside producers, there emerged a group of pantomime "Kings" whose activities spread far and wide and as a result to some extent pantomimes began to lose their local identity' (Salberg 1981: 61). This is the pattern that continues in many commercial productions. Commercial producers send out a number of pantomimes which they circulate from year to year, making adaptations to suit the locality.

Commercial pantomime accounts for the largest number of pantomime performances in the country and is the type of pantomime most people see.[2] Commercial producers are contracted by theatre managers to take a production to a theatre. The performance is then likely to be recreated over a number of years at different venues around the country. So, for example, QDos Entertainment Plc,[3] produced thirty-three of the biggest pantomimes in the country in 2003–4, a few of them in association with Jim Davidson and Midas Productions Plc. They therefore have the capacity to move successful productions around, though the different sizes of venues has an impact on where productions can fit. This company would expect to spend £400,000[4] on a new production. It may then take as much as ten years to recoup these costs, with the show being refurbished and the script adapted for other venues and performers. Paul Elliott, one of the executive producers at QDos, identified the difficulties and the costs:

You've got to store the production, refurbish the production, change certain costumes, sometimes you have to change bits of scenery. We used to take them out of Plymouth, which used to cost us £300,000, then spend another £100,000 to change it for Birmingham. That's why none are being built at the moment. It's all refurbish and add to, and we're making new scenes within an existing production so that it will look fresh. But it is better to spend £20,000 or £30,000 refurbishing and £10,000 or £15,000 to write a couple of new scenes than starting again (Elliott).

These pantomimes will fill the largest theatres in the country, employing a group of dancers, a band of five or more musicians as well as actor/singers, comedians and a group of children from a local dancing school. In Plymouth in 2003 there were sixteen performers onstage plus the children and eight musicians in the pit. This scale of employment is necessary to fill the stage with movement and sound at the biggest venues. The Mayflower Southampton has 2,300 seats, Birmingham Hippodrome has 1,900, and both are among those supplied by QDos productions.

> Birmingham is a better seater because it doesn't have a gallery. Southampton has a third level. Birmingham is beautifully built because it is all on two levels. In fact, I think it is the only theatre in the country where the circle is bigger than the stalls.....
> You don't have to go up a third level. People don't mind being at the back of the circle, but they do object to going up into a gallery. In Southampton it's very hard to sell the gallery. And the smallest that we're dealing with this year is St Albans and Lincoln. I still have an affection for Lincoln which holds 480 seats (Elliott).

QDos can recoup their huge costs over time but it is this sort of company who has to provide a sure-fire audience draw in order to sell the tickets. That means that, although the stories are important in selling the show, big-name stars are employed in many of the QDos pantomimes to attract the audience and create a return. In 2003–4 pantomime headliners for QDos included Lily Savage, Gary Wilmot, Brian Conley and Julian Clary. There is often a list of other celebrities on the poster and advertising material appealing to different sectors of the audience, perhaps someone from children's television or a performer to bring in 'the grey pound' and so on. This is further reflected in a script, musical score, comedy and references that will include material likely to be familiar to different age groups.

QDos is the largest company with the biggest budgets and stars, but there are many other producers who take pantomimes to a number of theatres, moving them round from year to year to recoup costs. Ian Liston at The Hiss & Boo Company Ltd describes how a production is adapted for the venue based on what the theatre can afford.

> We tailor-make all the shows to the theatre. You look at how long your run is going to be, how much money you're going to be able to take, what you want the break-even figure to be, and then you say, 'Right, for that we can do this.' So the *Aladdin* that we do this year at the Millfield Theatre in Edmonton will be a different price or a different cost to the *Aladdin* that we did at the Hall for Cornwall in Truro. That's a much bigger theatre, so we can take more money, so we can put more people on the stage, we can put special effects in, we can do all sorts of things. The cost of *Red Riding Hood* (Winchester Theatre Royal 2002–3) was about £75,000. *Peter Pan* at Barnstaple this year (2003–4) is going to cost about £165,000, 10% of that is the cost of flying the actors.

Although there is a perception that commercial companies like these are relying only on star names, many producers identify certain pantomimes that will sell whoever is performing in them. It appears to be a combination of story and star that draws the audience. Paul Elliott identifies an example of this: 'Lily Savage in *Snow White and the Seven Dwarves*. They come and see Lily Savage, but they also come and see *Snow White* ....but the impact when Savage does it is quite unique.... Yes, stars put bums on seats, but so does the pantomime'.

Opinions vary as to which stories are currently the most popular stories for pantomime, but a survey of the professional productions in 2003–4[5] reveals that, of 186 pantomimes listed, there were 38 productions of *Cinderella* and 37 of *Aladdin*. These were closely followed by *Jack and the Beanstalk* with 33 productions. Other favourites are *Peter Pan* (16), *Dick Whittington* (16), *Snow White and the Seven Dwarfs* (22) and *Robin Hood* (with or without the Babes in the Wood) (13). Less common are *Sleeping Beauty* (8), *Mother Goose* (7), *Puss in Boots* (2), *Red Riding Hood* (5) and *Goldilocks* (4). *Beauty and the Beast* had 6 productions, no doubt building on the success of the Disney film and the West End and touring productions. *Jungle Book, Pinocchio* and *A Christmas Carol* are all musical tales that appear in the Christmas slot, as is Rodgers and Hammerstein's *Cinderella* and the musical version of *The Wizard of Oz*. In fact, it is debatable whether all those listed as pantomimes are, in fact, pantomimes. As Paul Elliott commented, '*The Wizard of Oz* and those sorts of things are more musical theatre than pantomime. You've got to have elements of anarchy and participation which you don't always get in those stories. There's no audience participation in *The Lion King* or *Beauty and the Beast* – they [pantomimes] need a bit of that' (Paul Elliott).

According to Paul Elliott the best shows at the box office are *Snow White, Peter Pan* and *Cinderella*.

> Then you have *Aladdin, Dick Whittington* and *Jack and the Beanstalk*. Then you drift down to *Babes in the Wood* and *Robin Hood* which are a bit weak. *Mother Goose* is always weak, although it's the best moral pantomime of the lot.... *Goldilocks and the Three Bears* can be fun, but it has to be star led because it's an odd subject once you get the porridge. So we set it all in a circus. It's good fun, I'm very fond of *Goldilocks*. (Paul Elliott)

But perceptions vary among producers and audiences. Ian Liston agrees about *Cinderella* and *Peter Pan* but then points to the Disney influence and the increased popularity of shows like *Beauty and the Beast* that are not pantomimes at all. Chris Jordan agrees about the popularity of the big six pantomimes, *Dick, Jack, Cinderella, Aladdin* and then *Peter Pan* and *Snow White*, but doesn't regard the last two as pantomimes because of the absence of a Dame. In fact, in many productions a Dame is inserted into *Snow White* in the guise of a nurse or governess, but it is a small role that has no particular function. There is no place for a Dame in *Peter Pan*,[6] but *Cinderella*, which no one appears to doubt is a pantomime, has two Dames in the Ugly Sisters who are the villains of the piece.

However, there seems to be general agreement across both repertory and commercial fields that the story is the most important single factor in selling the show and in maintaining the audience's interest, although in the commercial field the 'star' also has an effect. The pantomimes that have generally been the key roles for principal boys, *Jack and the Beanstalk, Aladdin* and *Dick Whittington*, are variously played by men or women, again depending on the choice of star. The star role in *Cinderella* is usually either Cinderella or Buttons. The best roles for Dames are probably Widow Twankey in *Aladdin*, Mother Goose in *Mother Goose* and Dame Trott in *Jack and the Beanstalk*. The choice of pantomime can, therefore, be linked to a particular star and an appropriate character for that person to play. The difference in repertory theatre is that the story will be chosen purely for its appeal and then cast.

There is an alternative way of thinking about the economics of pantomime that is apparent in many of the commercial companies and the majority of repertory companies, and that relies on building up a sense of identity between particular performers and the venue. Paul Elliott has developed a type of repertory company at the King's Theatre Edinburgh which uses the same leading actors each year.

> Allan Stewart, Andy Gray, Grant Stott and Briony McRoberts have been in the last few pantomimes. And every year I have to write something that is going to use their talents in different ways. They're hugely talented, but on their own, people won't say 'oh I'll go down and see Allan Stewart'. Instead we say, what are we going to do this year, so now we're inventing things together, we're inventing new routines (Elliott).

For three years Ian Liston employed the same comedian, Terry Frisch, alongside the same Dame, Dougie Mounce, at the Queen's Theatre Barnstaple. The popularity of one pantomime can therefore assist in selling the following year's event. In general, however, although he employs some stars, Ian Liston believes that the pantomime story has to be a draw for the audience. This company has therefore branched out and, at Winchester, has produced two actor-musician shows by Kate Edgar and Colin Wakefield (*Red Riding Hood* in 2002, *Sleeping Beauty* in 2003), which have no star names and rely entirely on the interest generated by the title. On the other hand the company has a production of *The Wizard of Oz* with Ken Dodd recorded on video as the Wizard and they often use Roy Hudd as a writer, where Hudd's name in the pantomime title is the draw. For example, *Roy Hudd's Cinderella* played the Queen's Theatre Barnstaple in 1999–2000.

These shows are moving away from the format employed by the majority of commercial producers and begin to overlap with the priorities of repertory theatres. Without the presence of stars to attract the audience the development of an audience over several years, building on the success of previous years, becomes more important. So, for example, Ian Liston prefers to sign contracts with theatres for a number of years, so that the benefit of good reviews and word of mouth from a successful pantomime one year is not reaped by another company the next. Where his company differs from repertory theatre is in the potential for the show to be presented at different theatres in subsequent years, allowing the costs of production to be offset over a longer period.

Chris Jordan writes and directs the productions at Devonshire Park Theatre, Eastbourne. Here, too, there is an overlap with the type of pantomimes performed in repertory theatre. The theatre is relatively small and must attract an audience throughout the year by presenting touring material, but the theatre does not support a company of actors producing new productions throughout the year (as repertory theatres do). There is a strong focus on audience development in a small theatre that cannot support a bank of television stars. There is usually one recognizable name and, for several years, a regular appearance by the same Dame, Ian Good. The scripts are strong with songs, comedy and participation all developing from the story, and the performances fulfil the audience's expectations of pantomime. But, as in repertory theatre, the company produces only one pantomime and therefore cannot offset its costs over a number of years by touring the show. In *Cinderella* (2003) there were nine actors, seven dancers and four musicians as well as the children.

From the middle of the twentieth century, and especially in the 1970s, a new type of theatre developed. Repertory theatres are subsidized theatres that retain a group of actors for a season to produce a series of productions. They tend to be in smaller buildings with auditorium sizes of 400–600 seats (although the Royal National Theatre and the Royal Shakespeare Theatre operate on repertory principles but in larger theatres and with larger grants and budgets). The economics of this size means that the theatres are not financially viable because of the cost of productions and so these venues are publicly funded through the Arts Council. As funding has been squeezed, theatre managers and artistic directors have not been able to produce as many productions but must programme a mixture of their own productions with middle-scale tours and one-night performances. The result of this is that in many places the company no longer exists and performers are engaged for one production only. These theatres cannot compete directly with the commercially produced pantomimes in large venues with lists of stars so they have developed different strategies for drawing an audience. In general, this means that they have a regular, loyal audience for whom they cater, and to whose tastes the Christmas show is geared. This is particularly apparent in Stratford East, whose community is the poorest in London and the most ethnically mixed with over 100 languages being spoken in the borough. This affects the economics, as generous discounts are available funded by local authorities and regional arts boards, but it also affects the production, the design, the music, the dance and the script.

Repertory theatres employ actors, writers, directors and choreographers directly and produce their own in-house productions for the Christmas season. There are different challenges to their work than those faced by commercial producers, although the economic constraints underpin many of the production decisions. The majority of repertory theatres have between 400 and 500 seats to sell, so the cost of production has to be geared to the size of audience they can attract. The shows do not tour from one year to the next, although sets and costumes can be sold. This means that there is a much smaller time period, just three or four weeks of performances, in which costs must be recouped. In general they will have one, two or at most three band members and no dancers but will hope to employ actors who can sing and move well.

The Nuffield Theatre, Southampton employed nine actors and two musicians for *Robin Hood* in 2003, while The Northcott Theatre, Exeter employed ten actors and three musicians. Both of these companies, like most repertory companies, used children from the theatre's own youth company or children chosen at open auditions.

Theatre Clywd was exceptional in that it employed ten actor-musicians for its production of *Aladdin* (2003), and there were no children involved.

Repertory theatres are more likely to have a regular audience, since the company will produce shows for three- or four-week seasons for most of the year. The pantomime audience must be larger than the regular audience to fill the greater number of performances. So the pantomime must reach people who come to the theatre only once a year in order to fill the number of seats on offer. Therefore, there is benefit to be gained from a strategy that introduces new audiences to the theatre during the pantomime season, in the hope that they will return for other performances during the year. Artistic directors also have to consider the proximity of commercial productions which can draw the audience to see a spectacular production and well-known stars. In the event that there are other pantomimes in the vicinity, the artistic director must consider the type of production s/he mounts at Christmas to ensure distinctiveness.

There is a common misconception, of which I was also guilty, that repertory theatres use the pantomime's success to fill the coffers for the rest of the year. Unfortunately, with the rise in the cost of production, large cast, large production team and the cost of musicians, but no possibility of an equivalent rise in ticket prices, this is no longer the case. Kerry Michaels at Stratford East said that the success of the pantomime was important for audience development, but that it still made a loss. However, the pantomime makes the smallest loss of the year. Because the theatre is in the poorest borough of London very low ticket prices and many concessions are offered, but the gap is plugged by public funding and the venue is committed to the type of community theatre it offers to its dedicated audience.

At Salisbury Playhouse a small profit is still made, but each year that declines as costs rise. The most recent pantomime, *Aladdin* (2003–4) had running costs of £55k for actors, £24k in fees and £19k in royalty payments. The production cost £73k to mount, but the box office sales were very good, and the theatre made a profit of £40k-£50k. Each year Joanna Reid, the artistic director, has to reconsider whether the theatre can continue to produce pantomime or whether the team should produce a cheaper alternative. There are potential opportunities for savings in the budget, but the savings come at the cost of removing certain elements that the audience expects to see in pantomime. For example, slosh scenes need a large crew in order to clean up quickly, which increases the cost of the pantomime. The actors need a separate set of clothes that can be cleaned and dried in time for the next performance, often only a few hours away. The set needs to be mop-able and a separate floorcloth may be required.

An alternative for slosh scenes is that special trucks are built, at some cost to house particular slosh routines (especially those involving a lot of water) that can be moved away more easily, assuming the theatre has sufficient wing space. Ian Good describes his memory of a scene on a bathroom truck which he believes was developed by Arthur Askey.

[The comedian] says 'I must get ready', so he puts the shower on, and as he puts the shower on the head comes off, so there's lots of water coming down. He tries to turn it off and he can't. Other devices also malfunction so that the water keeps coming and he keeps trying to stop it, then he kicks off the tap so it all gets bigger and bigger…. The finale is a toilet – the water in the toilet shoots up the back wall, hits the top and a picture of a whale appears at the top which spurts water. (Good)

This scene took place on a complete truck that could be wheeled off with all the water contained in it. Berwick Kaler included a scene that appeared to be derived from this in *Mother Goose* (2003–4).

As Paul Harris says, 'Slapstick scenes have always been very popular in pantomimes and are loved by both children and adults. They are also fun for the actors to perform, but stage managers generally hate them' (Harris 1996: 94). Maria Taylor, who was Deputy Stage Manager (DSM) for *Mother Goose* at Plymouth (1995), explains the situation from the stage manager's perspective. It can take the Assistant Stage Managers several hours each day to prepare the slosh for custard pies etc. to the required consistency.[7] Men's shaving sticks are grated, with water and colouring being added very slowly, and the mixture whisked for hours. The stage management team would allow three hours per day to prepare the 10–15 buckets of slosh per show (they might need up to 45 buckets on a three-show day). Then, not only the set and costumes but the preparation area and the wings all gradually become covered in the mess which the stage management team struggle to keep clean and safe for dancers and children to race through (Taylor). Joanna Reid and Ian Liston both identify the cost of cleaning up as the principal reason for no longer including slosh scenes in their pantomimes, although they also point to the problem of finding people who can work the scenes well and the rehearsal time they take for performers without set-piece routines.

Physical comedy requires detailed and frequent rehearsal and the development of skills and routines over a long period which is not always possible within the constraints of contemporary economic realities. Companies that employ actors with talents in singing and dancing have to rely on verbal comedy, local and topical reference, and simple slapstick and chases. Companies who employ clowns, comedians and established pantomime performers have more opportunity to include stand-up, or to develop pantomime gags, routines and slosh scenes.

The band cannot realistically be smaller than the two or three musicians that are currently employed and the cast is already at its minimum with no chorus of villagers or dancers other than local children. Scenery is refurbished whenever possible, rather than built new, but it needs to look beautiful because it is one of the features of pantomime and so huge savings cannot be made here. Walkdown costumes and set, traditionally an opportunity for scenic extravagance in pantomime, can be cut or modified without having any effect on the story. Despite the seeming gloom of this discussion, the production of *Aladdin* at Salisbury Playhouse in 2003–4 looked beautiful and was extremely effective to the delight of the packed house.

While the commercial productions were more lavish, spectacular and comic, the types of performance I saw in repertory theatres were more varied. At Salisbury Playhouse and the Northcott Theatre, Exeter, I saw pantomimes that conformed to the expectations of a pantomime audience, but with a particular emphasis on a strong presentation of the story, verbal wit and topical reference. The performances, *Aladdin* and *Robin Hood*, attracted families who revelled in the opportunities for participation, loved the knockabout comedy and got involved in the story. York Theatre Royal's pantomime, *Mother Goose's Silver Jubilee*, also conformed to contemporary pantomime expectations, but since the same man, Berwick Kaler, has written and played Dame in a new show each year for twenty-five years, a different dynamic had been set up based on the continuity of the experience and reference from one year to the next. The audience went to see a Berwick Kaler pantomime.

At Theatre Clywd in Mold the pantomime was an actor-musician rock and roll show. It contained the story of *Aladdin* and all the pantomime ingredients, but the music was played by the actors, who were all talented multi-instrumentalists, set up in a band at the back and sides of the stage. When an actor left the performance space they moved to the next instrument they were to play. The performance culminated in a rock and roll concert.

The Nuffield Theatre in Southampton regularly produces a Christmas show that lies somewhere between children's musical and Christmas pantomime. The director, Patrick Sandford, generally retains one or two key performers that the audience identifies (notably Granville Saxton as the villain) and includes some of the comedy elements of pantomime, such as audience participation, direct interaction between comedy characters, villain and audience, and the silly wordplay, rhythm and rhyme common in pantomime. The stories presented are well-known stories but from a literary tradition, rather than the fairy stories and folk tales generally expected in pantomime. In 2003–4 it was *Robin Hood*, but in previous years I have seen (or been involved in) *101 Dalmations*, *A Christmas Carol*, *The Snow Queen*, *Peter Pan* and *The Count of Monte Cristo*. These shows have developed a house style so that audiences choose to go to these performances and know what to expect. The music is often specially composed and is sometimes based on a defined historical genre: *A Christmas Carol* used carols, *Robin Hood* used folk songs. The design for *Robin Hood* was beautiful, with a sparse and stylized single set, following the style of contemporary drama and requiring a smaller backstage team than would be required for a spectacular pantomime.

The Nuffield is an example of a theatre with direct competition. The Mayflower Theatre in the city centre, which is one of the country's largest theatres, presents a spectacular pantomime produced by QDos (in association with Jim Davidson who also starred in 2002–3). There is therefore an imperative to present something different to the commercial production nearby and to develop and maintain a loyal audience. The performances are not pantomimes; they are comic, children's musical plays which retain the fun ingredients of pantomime, but explore new territory in subject matter, design and music.

The Theatre Royal Stratford East presented *Red Riding Hood* in 2003–4. Like the performance at the Nuffield, the production appeared to be a crossover between pantomime and Christmas musical with a definite house style. It retained many of the elements of pantomime, such as a Dame, audience participation, music and magic. In this case, the gory details of eating people and cutting open the wolf's stomach were included, to the delight of the children, but there was little physical comedy and relatively little framing of the performance.

The most distant from pantomime were *Sleeping Beauty* at the Theatre by the Lake in Keswick and the Royal Shakespeare Company's production of *Beauty and the*

Beast, which were both plays with musical accompaniment. Keswick's production was probably more appealing to children and a family audience, while the RSC might appeal to a slightly more adult audience, but both told the stories clearly and beautifully without involving the audience in the development of the story.

Finally, the Tron Theatre in Glasgow presented *Cinderella* in 2003. The production used the bare bones of the story, the characters and many elements of pantomime to produce what might be regarded as an alternative version. Alternative is often taken to mean 'blue' or 'containing adult material' but that is not what I mean here. The characters and the situations had been adapted and updated to contemporary Britain, some characters had altered roles, but the derivation of the material from pantomime and of the story from fairy tale was clear. In particular the framing of the performance, the presence of cross-dressed characters and a pantomime animal (the godmother's spell goes wrong and she becomes a dogmother), the topical humour and the contemporary references confirmed this as pantomime, even though the story deconstructed and developed the story of *Cinderella.* This was still a family entertainment and played very successfully to school parties and groups of adults who each appreciated it in different ways. On the night I saw it I was struck by the number of young adults in the crowd; this entertainment was plainly popular with all age groups.

Altogether the variety of entertainment on offer for the Christmas season is vast. Although there is a difference between commercial and repertory productions because of the funding streams the companies draw on, not all the performances outlined above demonstrate a clear distinction in what they produce. In particular, some of the smaller commercial companies are using tactics that might be associated with repertory theatre; building a loyal audience and developing a house style. Rather, what is clear is that many of the differences can be accounted for by the rising costs of production but can be seen in all types of production.

The cost of pantomime is huge with spectacular design and large casts, musicians, dancers and crew. Some of the ways in which pantomime is developing result from the need to cut costs while retaining the elements by which pantomime is defined. This happens when income generation cannot be improved because of the size of theatre, the limited season and the low possibility of re-use of the production and is most common in repertory theatres. The large-scale commercial companies look to larger theatres, long runs and repetition of productions over a number of years to maintain the production of high-cost spectacular entertainments. Other companies, both commercial and subsidized, choose not to present pantomime, but still incorporate some of the elements of pantomime to produce new forms of Christmas entertainment.

All those theatres that advertise 'traditional' pantomime are conforming to certain expectations of pantomime but there appear to be separate strands to the development that might be attributed to casting as well as cost. Smaller companies are employing actor-musicians, or all-round actors and concentrating on the development of story and character with less emphasis on stand-up, physical comedy and musical extravaganzas, although all those elements are still present. Other larger companies, while maintaining the through-line of the story, have more deviations for comic routines and business, spectacular transformations, music and dance. These strands are not clearly defined, however, and it is the incorporation of all these elements in some sort of mix, to produce an entertainment that is appealing to people of all ages that allows pantomime to continue to be enjoyed in all its variety.

Notes

1. Derek Salberg (1981) traces the rise of pantomime in the regions in chapter 4 of *Once Upon a Pantomime*. Other histories of the development of pantomime are Frow, G. (1985) *Oh Yes it is!* and Robbins, N. (2002) *Slapstick and Sausages*.
2. www.its-behind-you.com has listings for the majority of pantomimes each year.
3. QDos is the result of a merger between E&B Productions, which was the biggest producer before the merger, and Nick Thomas and Jon Conway. Paul Elliott was the managing director of E&B and remains an executive producer of the new company and director of several pantomimes a year despite his retirement.
4. All figures are based on interviews conducted in 2003–4 and relate to those years.
5. These are the pantomimes listed on the website www.its-behind-you.com.
6. Marjorie Garber makes a case for Captain Hook being regarded as a sexually ambivalent role in 'Fear of flying or why is Peter Pan a Woman?' (Garber 1997: 165–185).
7. Some clowns, such as Alesis and Tweedy, always make their own slosh because the consistency is so vital to the timing of the scene.

2

Chaos and disruption in Slapstick and Slosh Scenes

As seen above, the story is a key factor in attracting audiences to the pantomime, but once there, the story creates a structure around which a variety of other features revolve, and which involve the audience in an experience of pantomime. Those features that are loosely related to the story, but which contribute to what is essentially a variety entertainment, are songs and dances, visual and verbal comedy routines. They contribute to the experience of the performance rather than having a strong storytelling function, though they follow a truthful logic. They contribute to the artifice of the entertainment which allows the audience a controlled experience of anarchy, chaos, disruption and, to some extent, danger.

Since these are not storytelling aspects of the pantomime, they may be considered dispensable in a difficult economic climate, but it is my contention (to be developed in later chapters) that without the variety, the artifice, and the entertainment, the pantomime begins to lose its links to its audience. One aspect of the entertainment that is particularly and noticeably affected by the economic climate, identified in chapter 1 above, is physical comedy, and in particular the slosh scene, though all physical routines, chases and fights could be affected. Physical comedy contributes to the sense of play in pantomime, and to the experience of the live event and is as important as the familiarity of the audience with the story and the rituals of the performance. The comedy, and especially the physical comedy, involves performers and audience in this sense of playfulness, while using routines that are known and expected; no performance is complete without a chase or a fight between hero and villain. There are certain set-piece routines and gags, such as the mirror routine, the cooking routine or the decorating routine that have been developed over many years and are imported into different pantomimes and re-worked by the comedians to fit the situation. This combination of known material re-developed, which includes slapstick and physical comedy, ensures that there is entertainment for all sections of the audience, but it relies on training and experience.

The skilfulness and trickery of physical comedy and set-piece routines come at a price. The pace and excitement of chases and slosh scenes allow the audience to be involved and stimulated by events that are real; the comedian is really getting covered in water or foam, and the cast are really tripping over your feet as they chase around the auditorium as loud, fast music contributes to the sense of chaos and anarchy. The comic slapstick and slosh scenes involve the audience in genuine moments of excitement and terror that draw them into experiencing a live and unique event and into a relationship with the comedians, but they need detailed rehearsal and split-second timing. As Kate Edgar says, 'at its most basic you have two people come in, bump into each other and fall over. Then you get that delicious gurgle – the children find it hilarious – the custard pie in the face, the absolute visual humour of somebody caught unawares and made to look silly' (Edgar). It is this moment of liveness, and the opportunity for clowns and comics to entertain the whole audience by contacting the child in all of us, that makes physical comedy a fundamentally important feature of British pantomime.

The task of creating physical comedy has, in the past, been assigned to performers with particular skills and routines, but the time required to learn and develop effective routines has had an effect on the types of routines that are still performed. The need to provide rehearsal time and special equipment for slapstick and slosh routines has economic consequences, but the effect on audiences of the fear and excitement associated with water and foam being thrown around is an important feature of pantomime's ability to entertain.

The variety of events and comedy routines in each pantomime is often the result of the skills of the performers booked, and this fact has sometimes been seen as detrimental to the coherence of pantomime. Salberg (1981) records that many people decried the introduction of Music Hall stars as 'the beginning of the end' for pantomime, but that it was only one of the many changes that pantomime has undergone. In any case a music hall performer, The Famous Turk, is recorded as appearing in pantomime at the Haymarket Theatre as early as 1749, so the introduction of performers who could bring skills or routines could hardly be counted a recent development. Nor can the predicted end of pantomime be observed. Derek Salberg identifies performances in the late eighteenth and early nineteenth centuries that included 'boxing displays, roller skating, a contortionist and feats of strength from The Italian Brothers' (Salberg 1981: 20). In the second half of the nineteenth century the pattern of using an occasional music hall performer continued, but when Augustus Harris took over at Drury Lane in 1879 the music hall performers moved from being the speciality acts to being the main attraction and playing many parts. This was the point at which the story became a vehicle for the introduction of variety acts, songs, dances and spectacular scenic transformations. Performers appearing for Harris included Little Tich, Vesta Tilley and Marie Lloyd as well as Dan Leno and many other comedians (Salberg 1981: 26).

Ian Liston describes the evolution of pantomime from the Victorian era:

[Pantomime] was very influenced by music hall and then variety, which was post-music hall, when music hall went from just shows in rooms adjoining pubs into the theatres [...]. The Christmas attractions, the pantomimes, were really just another excuse to get variety and music hall stars back onto the stage. [During the] 1930s and 1940s variety performers were the most popular stars. They were put in the guise of a pantomime character because the managers knew a box office draw, and audiences liked to see [the performers] in a different role. But all too often, the pantomimes became just like spectacular variety shows, because those acts were doing their normal act from the variety shows. Hence you've got those wonderful introductions like 'Here I am all alone, I think I'll play my xylophone.' And 'What's your dearest wish, Cinderella?' 'Oh, to hear Izzy Bonn sing My Yiddishe Momma.' And Izzy Bonn would appear and sing the song.[1] (Liston)

My argument is that the very feature that many decried because it interrupted the story was, and remains, an important element in the artifice of pantomime. The interruption, though it should be loosely related to the story, changes the pace, changes the relationship of audience to performance, and entertains. It is a moment of disruption, but it is the moment we love to groan at, and, in the case of slosh scenes and chases, it is the moment of danger and involvement for audiences and performers that increases the awareness of the liveness of each individual performance. The wit, ingenuity or bare-faced effrontery and energy with which clichéd routines are performed and the story interrupted has become a key feature of the artifice and entertainment of pantomime.

This aspect of the artifice of pantomime is dependent on experienced variety performers and so there are particular issues about its continuation and the consequent development of pantomime into the future. The use of performers who bring set routines and comedy material to pantomime continues in some parts of the commercial world, but is declining. I remember being a rehearsal pianist in the mid-1980s for a pantomime starring Terry Scott, who came into rehearsal, identified the routines he would perform and then left for the coffee room. The pantomime rehearsal time of six days (plus technical time) for these productions was therefore adequate.

Maria Taylor, DSM for *The Legend of Mother Goose and the Golden Eggs* at Plymouth Theatre Royal in 1995, recalls seeing Jack Tripp and Roy Hudd discussing the routines they would include in the performance, giving her information about the props that would be required, but not rehearsing the routines. The script for the performance identifies the routines and provides a prop list but then simply announces that 'Billy and Mother Goose do the mirror routine plus dance at end' with an instruction about music for the band to play. Towards the end of the rehearsal period, one lunch time, they performed the Mirror Routine perfectly to remind themselves of the sequence and so that others could see it and time it for cueing. The DSM remembers her astonishment that the accuracy and timing were so precise given that the routine had not been performed for almost a year (Taylor). Figure 1 shows a photograph from this routine, which can also be seen on the video of *Babes in the Wood* at the Theatre Museum Covent Garden. The important feature of this routine is the absolute accuracy and timing so that the pretence that there is a mirror present is credible to the victim of the gag, until gradually, slight discrepancies cause suspicion, and attempts by the characters to catch each other out reveal the truth.

In other scripts from the early 1990s there are places where 'Dame's spot' or 'Comic's Spot' is all that is included, such as 'Enter Sarah. Own Material' in *Dick Whittington* (Elliott and Davies 1991: 1-3-17). In other places particular routines are specified, such as 'Shopping Routine' to describe the routine and material the

Figure 1: Jack Tripp and Roy Hudd performing the Mirror Routine in *Babes in the Wood* (Plymouth: E&B Productions, 1991). Photograph by Eric Thompson

comedian should flesh out for the opening spot for the Dame, which would incorporate the give-aways, or '7x13=28 routine' both in *Robinson Crusoe* (Davies 1990–91: 1-1-10 and 1-2-19). Figure 2 shows a different mathematical gag in

Figure 2: Alderman Fitzwarren proving that Dick never does any work in *Dick Whittington* (Plymouth: E&B Productions, 1992). Photograph by Eric Thompson

which Alderman Fitzwarren demonstrates that Dick Whittington is lazy by proving that he doesn't work a single day in the year. Scripted versions of many of the best-known routines have been gathered together by Paul Harris in *The Pantomime Book* (1996), but they still rely on the performers to develop, personalize and contextualize the basic material.

In some scripts routines are written out in full, such as *The Legend of Mother Goose and the Golden Eggs* (Hudd, Plymouth 1995) in which the Numbers Game is written out in full. In the same script, as identified above, the routines for Tripp and Hudd were not notated, demonstrating that scripts are adapted according to the experience of the performers. Tudor Davies, another experienced writer, director and Dame, performed all these roles in *Jack and the Beanstalk* at Plymouth Theatre Royal (1998–9). Since he was directing the pantomime he was able to write 'Comedy milking routine Jack and Simon' in the script (Davies 1998: 26), knowing that he would be on hand to direct the routine. Figure 3 depicts a moment from a similar comedy milking scene at Salisbury Playhouse, at the point that Daisy has just successfully produced a can of Carnation Milk, and astonishment at this fact is shared with the audience.

Figure 3: Daisy is a clever cow in *Jack and the Beanstalk* (Salisbury Playhouse, 1999). Photograph by Robert Workman

Although some Dames and comedians, and especially those in commercial productions, arrive with their own material or provide additions to the written script, others are provided with material by writers which they can use or replace according to agreement. The vast majority of scripts I have seen while working in pantomime and in the course of preparing this book, and certainly all the rep scripts, have included most of the material for comedy spots. This is especially true when an actor rather than a comedian is employed. On other occasions there is a co-writing credit for the comedy star, and many alterations are made in rehearsal; the script is far from sacrosanct. The problem with this is that when performers arrived with their own material and routines a six-day rehearsal period was adequate to mount the show. With the movement towards an integrated musical theatre style and fewer known routines, more rehearsal is required but this still doesn't allow for the problem of delivering, developing and personalizing physical comedy for actors trained in a literary theatre. The exclusion or reduction of slapstick routines and slosh scenes that would need detailed rehearsal may be a partial response to this situation.

Finding performers with the skills to develop this type of physical comedy, who are also a box office draw can be a problem. All the producers I spoke to clearly cared about the product they were offering to the public, even while they were forced into a competition for audiences that used television profile to increase the box office takings. The problem is that the television performer may not have sufficient (or indeed any) stage or pantomime experience. There is a misconception that pantomime performance is easy, which may stem from the good-humoured comedy interactions and cod-corpsing that provide the performance frame, or from the fact that children laugh when a custard pie is thrown. The end result of this is a reduction in the number, variety and sophistication of slapstick and slosh scenes and a consequent development of the pantomime towards a less physical type of performance.

> We don't have the clubs any more, we don't have variety. It doesn't exist. We don't have the comics that are up and coming. We're not making stars as we used to, and so you haven't got the people of experience who are stars to do it (pantomime). So you rely on television stars who sometimes can't do it. They're fine actors in *Eastenders* or whatever, but can't deliver the sort of varietyesque thing you need. Now there are people around who can, but they're multi-purpose actors, and I think those should be encouraged. (Elliott)

Until the last twenty years or so, the training ground for pantomime included the last vestiges of variety and music hall, but largely consisted of an apprenticeship in pantomime itself. Now the training grounds are street theatre and circus. In the past, young performers could learn by working with performers who were topping the bill in pantomime around the country. A young actor might start as a broker's man or Chinese Policeman with simple chases and knockabout comedy and observe the comic and the Dame in action and learn the routines they performed. The youngster would then graduate to comic roles before arriving at the pinnacle as Dame or Ugly Sister.

Ian Liston recounts an experience working on a slosh scene with Charlie Cairoli.

> It was very funny, but my goodness me, it was worked out with years and years of knowledge and experience and precision. It was quite an astonishing scene to watch and it never varied, it was exactly the same every night. (Liston)

Norman Robbins describes Ken Wilson's slosh scenes with Lauri Lupino Lane:

> the special mix, devised by the Lupino family, was prepared for each performance and unlike modern 'slosh' only went where it was intended to go. In addition, each 'mishap' appeared to happen by accident; there was none of the 'your turn, my turn' about this act; the timing was perfect. By the time the scene finished, the pair were almost invisible beneath the quaking and glistening multi-coloured foam while the audience were helpless with laughter. (Robbins 2002: 212)

Ian Good remembers watching Charlie Drake and Norman Wisdom doing the decorating scene. Roy Hudd and Jack Tripp have a series of routines that are no longer performed now that Jack Tripp has retired, that drew on their own early years in variety. Their kitchen slosh was last performed in *Mother Goose* in Plymouth 1995 but was recorded on video at Covent Garden Theatre Museum from the 1994 production of *Babes in the Wood* at Sadler's Wells. This process of apprenticeship has all but disappeared.

Many repertory theatres incorporate a pantomime into their season, but the employment patterns are different to those in commercial performance. Actors are still sometimes employed for a season, playing roles in a number of types of performance, including the pantomime.[2] They are likely to be multi-skilled performers, but unlikely to be comedians or to have developed routines. Slapstick and slosh routines and physical comedy, as well as songs and dances, therefore need more time for development and rehearsal. The three-week rehearsal period allows time for the development of new, but basic material, chases and comedy business. This system puts pressure on the comedy performers to come up with material quickly, whereas the old pantomime routines had been honed in variety over many years.

Joanna Reid explains that some young actors find the timing of pantomime gags and routines difficult because it is unlike anything they have done before.

> Sometimes actors don't know how to play it and you actually have to go 'Do this – beat – in you come – beat' and you have to do it exactly the same or else it won't work. Some of them get it brilliantly and some of them don't. Then you just have to teach it. You have to say 'You need to see it – beat – look – beat – back again' and they'll pick it up eventually in performance. (Reid)

Having worked their way up in repertory pantomimes, learning styles of delivery, comedy timing and audience interaction, the performers may be employed by commercial companies. Performers can also learn the skills of audience interaction in children's theatre, and clowns learn and develop knockabout and physical comedy routines in circus. These performers are bringing new blood and developing new routines in pantomime, although they cannot command the status, billing or remuneration of celebrities.

The physical comedy scene that is most threatened by the lack of apprenticeship opportunities and the financial imperatives is the Slosh[3] scene. These are physical comedy or slapstick scenes that involve at least two actors and often the crew or stage management operating equipment that makes a mess. The scenes involve all sorts of comedy; verbal, visual, slapstick and knockabout, but can be classed together because of the wet or dry mess they make. The mess might include paste for decorating, soap for washing, dough and eggs for baking, make-up for beautifying oneself or water in a bathroom or other scene, all of which ends up on the actors, the set and the floor, and occasionally the audience.

Certain scenes are associated with particular pantomimes, although they can be interchangeable if the situation arises within the plot. The make-up and hairdressing scenes are generally reserved for the Ugly Sisters in *Cinderella* (see figure 4 which shows a photograph from a hairdressing scene) and the laundry scene for Widow Twankey and Wishee Washee in *Aladdin*. Figure 5 shows the set of the Laundry Scene at Salisbury Playhouse with the washing machine that can produce soapsuds and the mangle through which one of the Chinese Policemen will be squashed flat. Tumble Dryers are often used to spin and shrink a person; the size of the dryer in this photograph suggests it would be practical to use it for the gag. Other slosh scenes are fairly interchangeable.

Figure 4: Ugly Sisters in the Hairdressing Scene *Cinderella* (Plymouth: E&B Productions, 1990). Photographer Eric Thompson

Many slosh scenes are performed by the Dame and the principal comic. The Dame has the higher status of the two and often stays relatively clean for the majority of the scene as all the slosh is aimed at the comic, no matter how much he tries to avoid it. However, there is always a comeuppance when the Dame receives her due and the status is reversed. As Dave Benson Phillips puts it, 'The comic cops it most because he's there just to laugh at, he's the fall guy. The Dame often seems on top and gets the pay-off – the biggest bit of slosh at the end'.

This is not true of all slosh scenes; for example, there is a bathroom scene described in chapter 1 above, in which everything breaks so that water is pouring everywhere, that can be performed by a solo performer. The laundry scene involves the two comics and sometimes Aladdin washing and mangling the Chinese Policemen, so often as many as four performers are involved. However, by far the majority involve the two comics in a competition with the lower status comic trying to reverse the roles and wreak comic vengeance on the higher.

In another group of scenes the slosh happens by accident as the two comics fail to carry out a simple task. The kitchen scene is an example that demonstrates how the comic misunderstands instructions because of the double meaning of many

Figure 5: Potential for comedy business in the Laundry Scene in *Aladdin* (Salisbury Playhouse, 2003). Photograph by Robert Workman

words in aural delivery. These leads to silly confusions as, for example, the comic brings on 'a little flower' instead of 'a little flour', he kneads the dough with his knees and both performers end up using the dough as a cleaning rag. The decorating scene incorporates both of these strategies. The scene develops from what might be read as understandable mistakes, such as paint landing on the comic's head and the Dame painting the comic's face with paste, into a tit-for-tat response culminating in both being covered in paint and paste. This interaction is part of the topsy-turvy world of pantomime where roles are reversed and status is challenged, and where the comics can respond in childlike ways to the fact that the simplest tasks and tools become dynamite in their hands.

The other area of play in slosh scenes is the threat to the audience of involvement in the game. Comics will increase the excitement and tension of the audience and build the threat to their colleague by delaying the impact in order to ask the audience, verbally or by a look and gesture, if they should throw the egg or the custard pie, as in the following extract from *The Legend of Mother Goose and the Golden Eggs*

We then have the Kitchen slosh scene.
At the end, enter the Squire. He leans on the table and falls about laughing at the
  mess. Billy picks up big trifle.
Billy (to audience)   Shall I?
(Hudd 1995–6: 1-4-3).

The audience is often involved in encouraging the mess and devastation and this increases the involvement of the audience in the game and the excitement when the target is hit. Even more exciting is the threat posed to the audience members as the comics turn on them as in figure 6. There is fear and excitement as a comic walks towards the audience weighing an egg or a bucket in his hand. Having seen that all previous buckets have contained water or paste the audience expects this to be the same and shrieks in horror. The egg is usually blown, the bucket may contain confetti and the fear and excitement are released in laughter. What the slosh scenes are playing with here is the taboo of acceptable behaviour. It is not acceptable to make a mess, to play with food, to get dirty, to throw custard pies or to wreak havoc on your friends and colleagues. So excitement is built up for the audience as these taboos are challenged in a safe and permissive environment. The audience feels safe in its seats until threatened through the fourth wall, and suddenly the play becomes more dangerous and exciting, even while most people secretly know that the audience will not really be attacked (the theatre couldn't afford the cleaning bills).

Interestingly, I have seen several pantomimes recently in which there was no slosh scene, but chases with water pistols were carried on through the audience or the pistols were aimed at the audience so the effect of the threat and excitement were still present but without any real reason or good visual comedy. These moments were considerably weaker than good slosh scenes because they don't develop from the plot or follow a truthful logic with wit, ingenuity and skill, but they stem from the

Figure 6: Asking the audience what to do next in *Jack and the Beanstalk* (Salisbury Playhouse, 1999). Photograph by Robert Workman

same desire to cause the excitement and fear that slosh often invokes, and don't require the rehearsal and development time. They are therefore considerably cheaper.

Slosh scenes are visual comedy, but visual comedy or slapstick also includes many other types of physical routine that involves bumping, hitting and tumbling. The slapstick developed from the sword of the French harlequinade to a 'thin, double-lathed baton which could be used either to beat other characters unmercifully, making a maximum amount of noise whilst causing the minimum amount of pain, or act as a signal for the off-stage workers to effect a scene change.... Slapstick comedy took its name from the style of chaotic activity it inspired' (Robbins 2002: 36). In the early days of the Harlequinade, traps were used during chase sequences. 'Thus did the Demon King "shoot" into view; Harlequin dive through the wall or the clock-face; and Clown get "hammered into the ground"' (Frow 1985: 151). The characters of the harlequinade would perform acrobatic tricks tumbling into and out of windows and doors and appearing out of traps, all to escape the pursuer. Traps are much less common these days and certainly are not used within acrobatic chase routines, though they are still used within illusions or for special entrances and exits. However, the use of a star trap out of which the villain is shot up on to the stage has made a re-appearance in the work of Peter Rowe who has directed Rock and Roll pantomimes at Ipswich and Theatr Clwyd. The acrobatics have also disappeared from pantomime, except in speciality trampette acts such as those of The Acromaniacs, but chases and fights are still a feature of most pantomimes. The chase generates excitement by creating mayhem and noise and upsetting the audience from its passive perusal of the pantomime. Again, the audience becomes involved in a real event that intrudes into its space and challenges its safety.

Slapstick humour is accompanied by bumps and thumps played by the percussion to accentuate comics getting hit or falling over. These sorts of sound effects moved into early films with such comedians as Laurel and Hardy, Charlie Chaplin and Buster Keaton and are still present in many action films and cartoons where the framing of an effect with a percussive sound removes it from realism and renders it painless, or heightened, or comic. Figure 7 shows a simple device often used in the schoolroom scene, but that can be used elsewhere; a bench with legs spaced unevenly. Whenever the comic on the stable side stands up the victim's weight tips the bench and dumps the victim on the floor. A sequence ensues as the victim tries to get to the other side of the bench to dump his tormentor on the floor. The audience enjoys the battle of wits between the performers, but also feels the pain of the victim who repeatedly lands on the floor accompanied by appropriate percussion effects. Figure 8 shows a moment of conflict in which the size of the truncheon would suggest a painful blow, but the shape and design, the reaction of Roy Hudd and the sound from the pit all make this sort of violence appear cartoon-like and comic. The Broker's Men or Chinese Policemen and the Dame and comic are the principal participants in this sort of comedy business requiring punctuation from the pit.

The Broker's men are a pair of characters who, with the other comedy characters, undertake comedy business and chases through the auditorium. They always get

Figure 7: The School Room Bench in *Sleeping Beauty* (Plymouth: E&B Productions, 1989). Photograph by Eric Thompson

everything wrong and delight the children with their ability to withstand accidents. Although these characters are not mute, they are the characters who most clearly make the link back to the physicality of the harlequinade.

One alternative to a chase onstage or through the auditorium is the crossover. This involves a series of characters crossing the stage in sequence and may include a visual gag to complete the sequence. Crossovers can happen on the way back from the ball in *Cinderella,* on arrival in Morocco after the storm in *Dick Whittington,* racing from the Giant's castle to the top of the beanstalk in *Jack and the Beanstalk* or at just about any time in *Aladdin.* A recent innovation in chase scenes is the introduction of comedy films. The advantage of this is that the possibilities for the chase become limitless and don't rely on the detailed rehearsal and precision of slapstick and other set piece routines.

Figure 8: Cartoon pain never hurts in *Babes in the Wood* (Plymouth: E&B Productions, 1991). Photograph by Eric Thompson

Robinson Crusoe (Davies 1990: I-5-33) contains the following:
The Eye of the Storm
This scene consists entirely of a front projected high speed boat race seen from the stern. BILLY is in his small lifeboat and manoeuvres it in keeping with the picture on the screen. We go through a few comic high speed journeys:
1. Power Boat
2. Up Regent Street and round Piccadilly
3. London to Brighton train journey
4. Back to power boat, reverse into forward motion and crash into rocks
BLACKOUT. (Guildford 1992)

The camera and therefore the audience joins the performers on rides so that the effect of sudden changes of direction is felt by the audience amid screams of terror. At York Theatre Royal (2003) the film followed the characters running through the city to interested looks from passers-by before breaking into a pop concert and going onstage to interrupt the band and singer at another city venue. The use of the city located the pantomime clearly in the present-day world of the audience and the juxtaposition of the Dame and comic in a different type of performance (a pop concert) and the interaction with the musicians and concert audience of that event was disconcerting and bizarre adding to the sense of playfulness, topsy- turvydom and surreality. The crossover and the filmed chase are effective in creating the sense of movement from one place to another, involving comedy, wit and ingenuity. However, their effect is different from the mayhem and noise of chases through the audience or the fear and excitement of slosh scenes.

Fight scenes have a similar effect to chases in whipping the audience to a state of excitement with noise and involvement. Although fights have moments of heroic swordplay or fisticuffs, as in figure 9, they also contain visual gags, swords getting stuck, toes getting stamped on or villains getting tickled. The upshot is that although the fight is played 'for real' with energy and conviction it is still not serious, but a cartoon fight that the hero is bound to win. Like the chase sequences, the effect is to rouse the audience to vocal involvement cheering for the hero, led by the hero's supporters and supported by loud, fast or heroic music. Many drama schools teach

Figure 9: Bonnie Langford as Jack fighting the Giant's Henchman in *Jack and the Beanstalk* (Plymouth: E&B Productions, 1993). Photograph by Eric Thompson

stage fighting, but even so, the cost of a good comedy fight director and the rehearsal time to perfect the routine means that fights are often quite short and simple.

As well as the noise and excitement, audiences love the silly visual comedy because the Dame and other comedians draw the audience into the comedy through looks and asides. Tony Allen describes mugging as 'sharing exaggerated little cameos of their own feelings with the audience via looks, double takes and visual asides' (Allen 2002: 29). The comedians communicate with the audience wordlessly, breaking the fourth wall with no more than a look or a raised eyebrow. The more expert and experienced the comedian, and the more the audience has become attuned to her/him over the course of the performance, the less the comic has to do to raise a laugh. Figure 10 shows how comics share discomfort with the audience at every opportunity, maintaining eye contact in the most awkward of poses so that the audience has a perspective from which to share in the comedy.

The principal features of physical comedy are: that truthful logic is developed out of the story to a surreal or fantastic conclusion; that status between the performers or between performers and authority figures is challenged in competitive routines

Figure 10: Sharing the situation with the audience in *Sleeping Beauty* (Plymouth: E&B Productions, 1989). Photograph by Eric Thompson

and sequences; that the pantomime world is a dangerous place and everything comedians touch will, in some way, cause mayhem; and that the audience is involved in the comedy by a complicitous look from the Dame, the question 'Shall I' while holding a bucket of water, or the physical presence of performers within the auditorium. All these features suggest that the performers are behaving anarchically, breaking the fourth wall, challenging status and creating grotesque or extreme situations. However, the appearance of anarchy is tightly controlled and familiar. As soon as a plank appears on the stage the audience knows the sort of comedy routine that will take place and equally that no one will be hurt. The audience is moved to scream with fear, excitement, laughter and, most importantly, recognition. The story provides a loose thread to which moments of physical comedy are attached. They have a purpose in providing fear and excitement, but also in providing variety and entertainment that contrasts with the storytelling aspect of pantomime.

There is a safe combination of familiar routines and expected rituals with riotous activity and playfulness that is seen in pantomime. 'Play is understood as the force of uncertainty which counterbalances the structure provided by ritual. Where ritual is predictable, play is contingent. But all performances, even rituals contain some element of play, some space for variation. And most forms of play involve pre-established patterns of behaviour' (Bial 2004: 115). The pre-established patterns in pantomime comedy consist of tightly rehearsed routines for the performers, and the expectation of familiar routines and types of comedy by the audience. The element of play involves the comedians in following truthful logic to an extreme point that involves anarchy, excitement, competition and the disruption of status. The play for the audience comes from the fear of being doused in egg, water or slosh, even as it becomes complicitous in the anarchy and competitiveness of slosh and the mayhem of slapstick and chases. Just like going on a roller coaster in order to experience controlled fear and excitement, the pantomime provides the experience of anarchic physical comedy and the live enjoyment of seeming out of control.

Notes

1. These stories may be apocryphal, I've heard them from many sources but haven't been able to trace the productions in which they might have occurred.
2. This pattern has been changing following the funding crisis in regional theatre that means that many theatres cannot afford to produce a whole season of plays, but must buy in middle-scale touring productions. Actors are therefore employed for a single production. The effect is to save money over the season because of the reduced production costs, but to increase the costs of the single production because performers are paid for rehearsal, whereas under the old system actors would rehearse one production while still performing the previous one.
3. Paul Harris calls these scenes 'splosh' scenes (Harris 1996: 94).

3

Fantasy and Illusion in Design

The second feature of pantomime that, as discussed above, is subject to the effects of a changing economic climate is the spectacular scene and costume design and the potential for scenic illusion and transformation. As noted above, the building costs are enormous, and for smaller theatre companies, and those who cannot spread the costs over several years, they can be prohibitive. Joanna Reid talked of repainting sets from one year to the next at Salisbury Playhouse, but suggested saving money on extravagant walkdown costumes and slosh sets. The Nuffield Theatre in Southampton uses a single contemporary theatre design for its Christmas musical, as did Theatr Clwyd for its actor musician version of *Aladdin*. In both cases, the approach to design was also appropriate to the concept of what was presented. In the case of *Red Riding Hood* at Stratford East the design was mostly based around large props and objects, again a way of reducing costs, but befitting the style of production. A different approach was taken at the Old Vic for their lavish production of *Aladdin* which created the same scenic illusions as 'traditional' pantomime with cloths and flying sheets and a huge staircase for the walkdown, but with some unexpected moments of scenic transformation such as the opening cloth being pulled into a box and the castle growing on an inflatable base.

However, it is not the economics of presenting colourful and ornate designs that concerns me here, as much as the function of design in the experience of pantomime. The importance of transformation for the hero will be established later, as well as the potential for short-lived transformation of the audience. Here the emphasis is on the importance of illusion and transformation in sets, costumes and stage machinery that supports the idea set up in the stories that anything is possible and nothing is as it seems. The magic and illusion that is presented in particular moments of transformation support the idea of pantomime as excessive and outrageous fantasy, but so do the colours (which tend towards pastels or bright clashing colours with glitter and spangles), and the scale (which is larger than life) and the style (which suggests cartoons or fairy story illustrations with clear outlines and enormous depth of perspective). What is being presented visually is a fantasy that is idyllic, often bucolic, and certainly distant from the lives of the audience. This awareness of distancing from reality prefaces the discussions of distancing between audience and performers later, but here the focus is on distance that promotes a sense of idealized beauty and utopian imagery that is removed from the everyday, but with contemporary references. This movement in time and place, to a world that is distant, but that could be read as a version of the present mirrors the potential interpretations of the story, as a social or moral fable for those who choose to read it that way, or as illusion and entertainment for other audience members.

The words illusion and artifice can be read negatively as terms that imply trickery and deception, but they are also at the root of storytelling, which creates images and illusions that disappear, but potentially leave a mark of their presence in the minds of audiences. It is in this second sense that I speak of the illusion and the artifice of pantomime, but, of course, the first reading of the terms is also present. The makers of pantomime use tricks and deception to create an illusion that entertains, that draws its audience into another world that is a magical utopian transformation of our own world.

The stage design for the vast majority of pantomimes maintains the proscenium stage, with its links to the pictorial illusions of nineteenth-century romanticism. These pictorial illusions of reality, known initially as 'scènes à l'italienne', were feats of romantic perspective painting first seen in the English Playhouses in the late eighteenth century. Spectators were removed from the stage of the Theatre Royal Drury Lane and the actor retreated behind the picture frame allowing the visual spectacle to triumph (Mackintosh 1993: 20–21). This type of romantic scene painting inspired the suspension of disbelief that followed in the late eighteenth century. Before then the actor and audience had shared space on the stage and acknowledged each other's presence, but in the mid to late eighteenth century the actor retreated behind the picture frame in all performances except the pantomimes produced by, among others, Christopher Rich at Covent Garden (Mackintosh 1993: 21). The continuation of the acknowledgement of the audience's presence, despite the romantic illusions created in the scene painting, remains a feature of pantomime that I will return to later. However, the grandeur and style of the visual spectacle, as well as the increasing size of the theatres, also had an effect on the acting style which became a visual rather than an aural performance, using gesture and spectacle.

Philippe Jacques de Loutherbourg was engaged by Garrick as a scene designer at Drury Lane in 1771. There he 'wasted his talents on trifling pantomimes' and was rarely offered the opportunity to engage in 'legitimate drama'. Nevertheless, his 'illusionistic realistic scenery made its entrance on the English stage' (Nagler 1952: 399).

> [Loutherbourg's] backdrops were marvels of picturesque perspective painting. He used cloud effects and transparent scenery and gave flexibility to the wing and border lights by using filters of colored silk.[....] In 1785, when O'Keeffe's pantomime *Omai* was produced at Covent Garden, Loutherbourg made use of the sketches which John Webber had painted in the South Seas while accompanying Captain Cook on his last voyage. (Nagler 1952: 399)[1]

John O'Keeffe, the Irish actor and dramatist who produced *Omai* paid tribute to Loutherbourg's talents in his *Recollections*, while the critic of *The London Magazine* wrote:

Loutherbourg planned the scenery. He had previously invented transparent scenery – moon-shine, sunshine, fire, volcanoes, &c. as also breaking the scene into several pieces by the laws of perspective, showing miles and miles distance. Before his time, the back was one broad flat, the whole breadth and height of the stage. (Nagler 1952: 399)

Other significant innovations and inventions were the introduction of the moving diorama in the early nineteenth century, gas lighting in 1817 which allowed the audience's attention to be directed to particular events, and improved audibility,[2] and in 1881 the introduction of electricity. The raked stage began to be replaced at the end of the nineteenth century by the flat stage, which allowed the introduction of revolves, hydraulic stage lifts and new flying systems.

Important illusionist scene painters of the nineteenth century were Clarkson Stanfield and William Beverley, who, according to Gerald Frow may have been responsible for the transformation scene that remains in contemporary pantomime (1985: 154). By this time (mid-nineteenth century) the transformation was no longer the transformation of characters from the first part to the Harlequinade, but a scenic display. In the post-war period in Britain, Oliver Messel resumed a career that had been interrupted by war and influenced the new-romanticism that led to a painterly approach to scenic design, using cloths, cut cloths and flats arranged to create pictures bound by a frame (Goodwin 1989: 17). Despite the new direction that theatre has subsequently taken, pantomime retains its links to the scenic illusion and to the machinery of the romantic and neo-romantic periods. Ian Liston still owns and uses cloths painted by Oliver Messel in some of the pantomimes of The Hiss & Boo Company, and Messel's influence can be widely seen.

The other significant influence on contemporary pantomime comes from the mechanical effects and spectacular designs used in large-scale musicals such as *Evita* (1978), *Phantom of the Opera* (1986), *Beauty and the Beast* (1994) and *The Lion King* which opened in 1997 (in Minneapolis) and arrived in London in 1999. This is comparable with the development of many other parts of the pantomime, which simultaneously maintain continuity with the past, producing nostalgic familiarity, but incorporates influences from contemporary popular culture.

Figure 11 shows a frontcloth for *Aladdin* at Plymouth Theatre Royal in 1994 (E&B Productions Ltd). In it the influence of illusionist scene painters is still apparent in the sense of depth that takes the eye from the forestage to the trees in the far distance. The cloth gives a sense of a vague historical period; a time that is not the present. It contains a grand palace entrance in a specific, exotic, geographical location; China, though the China presented is a cross between a Victorian image of the exotic East and an idealized bucolic idyll. Also noticeable is the false proscenium, decorated with Chinese geometric designs reinforcing the sense of exotic location and theatricality throughout the entire performance.

Figure 12 shows the Cave Scene from the same production. This demonstrates the use of cut cloths and trucks to increase the sense of depth. This scene allows many entrances, principal of which is the central raised entrance down which Aladdin will enter. The presence of the false prosceniums allows downstage entrances while the trucks and flats mask upstage entrances. In both these designs the principles of

Figure 11: Frontcloth for *Aladdin* (Plymouth: E&B Productions, 1994). Photograph by Eric Thompson

illusionist scenic painting are apparent, but there is no sense of 'realism'. There is theatricality in the raised central entrance for the hero, the false proscenium and the use of trucks and cut cloths that create romance, illusion and fantasy but not realism. This is utopian imagery of other times and places that creates a fantasy world and clearly signifies escapist performance. The use of colour supports this reading, with idyllic pastels predominating in both cases.

Smaller theatres have smaller stages and less space or economic opportunity for scenic extravagance, but the principles of creating depth and fantasy and providing multiple entrances and peepholes remains the same. Figures 13 and 14 show the opening sets for *Babes in the Wood* (2000) and *Aladdin* (2003) at Salisbury Playhouse. The similarities between the sets, which in any case are repainted from one year to the next, are clear. The false proscenium created by the trees in figure 13 and the arches in figure 14 contain entrances. These are a reference to proscenium entrances that disappeared from many commercial theatres in the early nineteenth century and add to the number of possible entrances in the design and therefore to the possibilities for chases and comedy business. There are many

Figure 12: Inside the Cave *Aladdin* (Plymouth: E&B Productions, 1994). Photograph by Eric Thompson

entrances and peepholes at ground level and above; on the castle walls at the back and Stage Left and in the tree Stage Right in *Babes in the Wood* and through the windows in similar locations in *Aladdin*. As Lorelei Lynn said when discussing the design of pantomime sets,

> It is all the spangles and the bright lights, it needs all the twinkles on the sets and everything. I like these magical sets that do things and have windows that suddenly appear. I think they ought to be like cut-out books, Christmas sets. That's what I remember from childhood. (Lynn)

This suggests the importance of the illusion of spectacle and transformation alongside the total lack of realism to create a fairy tale, other-worldly place that nonetheless gives suggestions of geographical and historical setting; *Babes in the Wood* represents an idealized medieval England, in *Aladdin* it is an exotic English-China with English joke names on the shops and glitter on the roofs and curtains. The sense of fun is apparent in the use of the joke names in both sets, but also in the cartoon-like outlines, the romantic trees and the sloping roofs.

Figure 13: Opening Set for *Babes in the Wood* (Salisbury Playhouse, 2000). Photograph by Arthur Millie

In *Babes in the Wood* the ground rows behind the central entrance extend the illusion of distance at the back, with a tree trunk at the front providing a useful seat and pulling the eye forward. The proscenium is not at the front of the stage so that the designs can extend out into the audience, with, for example, in *Aladdin*, the trelliswork at the side of the stage and decorating the pit rail and the painted steps and stage. This means that although there is a proscenium, much of the action can take place on the forestage, the steps into the audience, and even in the auditorium. This provides a continued sense of contact between audience and performer framed by the illusionistic setting. The proscenium and the pit separate the actors and audience creating a distancing effect and artificial formality in the design, but the presence of the forestage and the steps into the audience allow the performers to alter their relationship with the audience, or step into the audience for chases and other interactions. This continues the sense that performers and audiences acknowledge each other's presence and share a space and an experience that dates from eighteenth-century theatre design and practice.

Figures 15 and 16 show the same design principles which include perspectival depth, multiple entrances and exits, bright colours, contemporary references and a sense of fun, but the designs are more angular and modern with the lacquered effect and geometric patterns in figure 15 (*Sleeping Beauty* 1989) and the psychedelic imagery and metallic cogs/suns for the scene above the clouds in figure 16 (*Jack and the Beanstalk* 1993). They offer large open spaces, grand designs and stronger

Figure 14: Opening Set for *Aladdin* (Salisbury Playhouse, 2003). Photograph by Arthur Millie

colours. These two demonstrate the influence of the large-scale designs for musical theatre in the removal of the quaint and cosy décor of the majority of pantomimes. However, they retain a sense of nostalgia through reference to well-known imagery as well as a sense of the spectacular and the fantastic. All this relates very neatly to the idea that familiarity and nostalgia are prized, but that progress is constant as a result of contemporary influences and references that introduce fun and topicality. Overall, however, the pantomime set always retains the suggestion of an idealized other world.

Another key feature of pantomime is the use of magic and surprise. So, at Salisbury Playhouse, glove puppets appeared to dance on the pit rail during the overture, the sets contain many nooks and crannies for unexpected appearances. However, pantomime also provides the opportunity for large-scale scenic transformation and magical illusion. The early pantomimes relied on stage machinery and spectacular tricks which were developed from the work of designers and technicians in Renaissance Italy such as Sebastiano Serlio and Nicola Sabbattini. The style had been introduced into Court Masques in England by Inigo Jones. Little had been seen of such tricks in the public theatres when the Puritans closed them down in 1642, and the revival when the theatres re-opened was on a much smaller scale (Frow 1985: 149). By the eighteenth century, spectacle was rare in the theatre except in opera and pantomime. Rich's machinist, Sam Hoole, contributed mechanical

Figure 15: *Sleeping Beauty* (Plymouth: E&B Productions, 1989). Photograph by Eric Thompson

serpents, while Drury Lane's Alexander Johnson constructed flying chariots, cars and banners. He was also famous for wickerwork birds and animals, including a stuffed elephant (Frow 1985: 150).

From the earliest pantomimes scenic extravagance and stage machinery were important features. A description of John Thurmond's *Harlequin Doctor Faustus* (1723) appeared in 1724, which includes the following description:

> [Faustus] enters [....] pricks his Finger with a Pin, drops the blood into a Pen, and signs the Contract. Immediately, Thunder and Lightning follow, and Mephistophilus flies down upon a Dragon, vomiting Fire: Faustus seems supriz'd, and runs from the Spirit, who lays hold of him and embraces him; and after several Actions of Courtesy from the Spirit, he seems to be pleas'd, and he receives a Wand from him, which gives him the conjuring Power. (Nagler 1952: 347).

The use of flying is clearly derived and developed from the early court masques, but is not the only scenic extravagance in the early pantomimes. Garrick's biographer described the origin of the English harlequinade, produced by John Rich at Lincoln's Inn Fields in the early eighteenth century, as follows:

Figure 16: Above the Clouds in *Jack and the Beanstalk* (Plymouth: E&B Productions, 1993). Photograph by Eric Thompson

By the help of gay scenes, fine habits, grand dances, appropriate music, and other decorations, he exhibited a story from Ovid's Metamorphoses, or some other fabulous writer. Between the pauses or acts of this serious representation, he interwove a comic fable, consisting chiefly of the courtship of Harlequin and Columbine, with a variety of surprising adventures and tricks, which were produced by the magic wand of Harlequin; such as the sudden transformation of palaces and temples to huts and cottages; of men and women into wheel-barrows and joint-stools; of trees turned to houses; colonnades to beds of tulips; and mechanic shops into serpents and ostriches. (Nagler 1952: 345–6)

This sort of scenic transformation was made possible through the use of specially built illusions. The following items are included in a list of theatrical properties and scenery at Covent Garden in 1743:

Cottage and long village, Medusa's Cave and 3 pieces, Grotto that changes to Country house. Inside of Merlin's cave, outside of ditto, dairy, Hermitage, Clock

Chamber, Farm Yard, Country House, Church, town, chimney chamber, fort, Rialto, Harvey's hall, Othello's new Hall. Hell transparent and 2 pieces, Inn Yard, Arch to Waterfall, Back of Timber Yard, Short Village, Second Hill, front of timber yard, garden, short wood. (Nagler 1952: 352)

In this list, the 'Grotto that changes to a country house' allows the possibility of transformation, while the 'Arch to Waterfall' points to the use of water in scenic display. Frow describes other trick changes such as 'a box into a table, splendidly furnished; a Baggage Waggon into a Stage Coach'. The transformation of a post-chaise into a wheelbarrow, a trick from Grimaldi's time is explained as follows:

The chaise is to be merely a profile but when the door opens a piece of hanging canvas is to give the appearance of substantiality. On entering, Pantaloon is to stand in a wheel-barrow. When he undoes a brace, the upper part of the chaise will be hauled up while the lower sinks through a cut in the stage and into the cellar leaving the wheel-barrow exposed (quoted in Frow 1985: 151).

It is generally agreed that the transformation scene as we know it began in 1849, when William Beverley devised a scenic effect for J. R. Planché's *The Island of Jewels* at The Lyceum (Salberg 1981, Frow 1985). The London Illustrated News reported that 'The concluding scene – the discovery in the midst of an unfolded colonnade of palm trees, seven nymphs supporting the Crown jewels on a cushion – is indescribably magnificent' (Salberg 1981: 168). Gradually the pantomime opening had become the complete pantomime, which made the transforming of figures from the story into the Harlequinade unnecessary. However, rather than disappearing, the spectacular display of transformation scenes became more important in maintaining the prestige of pantomimes. The scenic transformation still occurs in contemporary pantomime, generally as the climax to Act One, though there may also be other opportunities for scenic display, magical illusion and visual excess in the pantomime.

The most well-known transformation in contemporary pantomime is the magical creation of Cinderella's coach and horses from the objects and animals in the kitchen, and the transformation of her costume from rags to riches. While part of this transformation occurs, as with all magical illusions by distracting and drawing focus, there is a wonderful piece of stage machinery that has been used at Exeter's Northcott Theatre and at Eastbourne Theatre on different occasions to complete this illusion. The section of the script for Eastbourne (Jordan 2003: 41) begins with the Fairy Godmother's spell with musical underscore:

Now Finbar and Freddy [frogs] both under my charm
Shall footmen become with a wave of my arm.
By the power of magic that rat shall appear
As a Coachman with silver-white horses to steer
Drawing a coach made of crystal and gold
Cross a sky full of dreams where adventures unfold.
Now spirits with fancies and sorcery spin
Unleash the magic. Let the journey begin.
(*there is a crash and the transformation Ballet begins*)

The spell is cast by the Fairy Godmother and Cinderella appears beautifully dressed in her ball gown. Then the Fairy signals with her wand and the outline of a coach and horses is drawn in light on the blackcloth. The cloth rises to reveal a spectacular coach and horses. In the middle of the ballet the Fairy Godmother gives Cinderella the warning that she must be home before midnight still accompanied by underscore music. Then the final stage of the transformation occurs. Cinderella climbs in to the coach, and, with smoke disguising the machinery, the front section of the coach and horses rises off the ground and the horses' legs start moving as though they are galloping through the air. The rig then appears to move forward before spinning round as though to head out into the audience. It is a spectacular effect drawing enormous rounds of applause.

Other companies, especially where there is room and budget, still use live ponies to pull the coach, but the important moment is always the moment of revelation and surprise. This occurs at the appearance of the coach and at the magical transformation of Cinderella's clothes. These events, one of scenic display the other of magical illusion, draw gasps of amazement from the audience.

The use of water was also a feature of spectacular transformations. Stanfield's diorama of 1829 used 39 tons of 'real water', while as early as 1753 Garrick had introduced a 'cascade of real water' into his pantomime. Water remains a feature in some pantomimes, either in slosh scenes such as those described above or in transformations. The most common place for using water is in the transformation to the Pool of Beauty in *Mother Goose*, which might have a fountain or a waterfall, but equally might be created with lighting effects. Most other underwater scenes are the result of storms at sea and since the entire auditorium is transported to an underwater world, scenic effects are used rather than water.

In *Dick Whittington* the two opportunities for transformations are the Dream Sequence in which Dick, lying asleep downstage, dreams of the future in which he appears behind a gauze upstage. This often occurs as the climax to Act One, but the second place for a transformation, which sometimes marks the climax to Act One and is sometimes halfway through Act Two, is after Dick and the Fitzwilliamses are reconciled and set out on a ship for Morocco. King Rat casts a spell to conjure a storm that wrecks the ship. The following is the version written by Paul Elliott and Tudor Davies for the Yvonne Arnaud Theatre Guildford in 1991.

King Rat   Come winds of north and blow the ship off tack
Come crashing waves and pound the prow
Come wrack the sails with stinging rain and icy blast
Come thunder, lightning, tear into the mast
Oh God of thunder – listen unto me!

(*There is an almighty crash of thunder and flash of lightning, King Rat by this time is screaming fit to bust*).

Commit this ship to the bottom of the sea!

(*The mast breaks rigging falls to the deck.*)

King Rat   Ha ha ha ha ha ha

(*Dick falls overboard and is seen drowning as the curtain falls*).

(Elliott and Davies 1991: I-10-34)

Various parts of the ship are built so that they can crack and fall, while the body of the ship may break or rock.

The scripts contain no explanation of the stage machinery required to carry out the magical tricks, but flying either alone or on some sort of machine is a regular feature. In *Jack and the Beanstalk* (Rayment Redhill, 1997) the Dame and Dick fly to cloudland in a balloon, in *Peter Pan* flying is a key feature. *Aladdin* sometimes includes a flying carpet as in the following end to the scene in the cave:

> With a gesture of his arms the cave begins to transform, Aladdin begins to sing. Musical Number.
> Gold and Jewels appear and dance a transformation ballet.
> Aladdin exits and re-appears in a change of costume. The genie says there is just one thing left to do. At the end of the number he casts a spell and Aladdin flies out of the cave. (Jordan Potter's Bar 2002)

Within transformation scenes such as these there are occasionally opportunities for magicians to introduce special tricks, such as in figure 17 from *Dick Whittington* (Plymouth 1992). However, in general, magic tricks and illusions are incorporated into the transformation or into the events of the story. The use of small, hand-held magic tricks is sometimes a feature of a particular pantomime, such as *Red Riding Hood* at the Theatre Royal Stratford East. In the fairground scene the Wolf appeared as a magician doing his tricks. The use of magic tricks then became a theme of that pantomime. Similarly many fairground scenes in *Babes in the Wood* or *Robin Hood* include the use of magic tricks and small-scale illusions.

The surprise of transformation and illusion contributes to the scenic extravagance and supports the fun of pantomime. In addition, the transformation of settings reflects the transformation of the hero, and as we will see later, the potential for transformation of the audience. At the same time festive laughter 'keeps alive the sense of variety and change' (Clark and Holquist 1984: 301). This sense of fun in transformation and illusion pervades pantomime. An illusion is created that anything is possible and anything can happen.

UV (Ultra-violet) sequences are another special feature of pantomime during which the audience can simply sit back and enjoy the colour and excess and, even though the setting of the ballet is suggested by the story, the story takes second place. Most common among UV scenes are underwater scenes in which various creatures dance across the stage. In *Dick Whittington* (Elliott and Davies Guildford 1991) the Spirit of the Bells saves Dick from the shipwreck by casting a magic spell that allows him to survive in the underwater world of King Neptune, which of course features an Underwater Ballet with UV sea creatures manipulated by the children.

Figure 17: A Speciality Act *Dick Whittington* (Plymouth: E&B Productions, 1992). Photograph by Eric Thompson

During the song a SEA HORSE flies in and Dick mounts it. King Neptune and the Babes bring on a huge cloak which they fix to Dick's shoulders. The sea Horse goes up and the cloak fills out completely covering the stage (II-1-2)

Jack and the Beanstalk (King's Theatre Edinburgh 2003) used UV for the growing of the beanstalk, which was surrounded by dancing flowers and butterflies. *Mother Goose's Silver Jubilee* (York Theatre Royal 2003) contained a UV mopping sequence after a scene that required Dame, comic and an audience member to throw buckets of water. *Cinderella* (Eastbourne 2003) used puppets in UV for the rat, mouse, pumpkin and frog that were transformed into the flying horse and carriage to take Cinderella to the ball.

The sense of visual fun can be seen in figure 18 in which there is an excess of decoration in the scenery. But here, too, is the fun of the dancing pantomime cow whose costume is designed to allow for tricks and gags but to present no illusion of reality whatsoever. The same is true of the Dame and Principal Boy pictured here. There is no historical period or geographical location suggested by the costumes, but rather a play with conventions and stereotypes. The Victorian nurse, mother or governess is

Figure 18: Daisy the Cow in *Jack and the Beanstalk* (Plymouth: E&B Productions, 1993). Photograph by Eric Thompson

the model for the Dame costume with excessively large sleeves and a silly hat. The spots and stripes contribute to the fun of excessive decoration. Many of the costumes the Dame or Ugly Sisters wear also make reference to contemporary fashion, such as lycra aerobics outfits at Eastbourne (*Cinderella* 2003) or a mini-skirted air hostess outfit for flying on a balloon in *Jack and the Beanstalk* (Redhill 1987). This adds a contemporary reference and sense of parodic fun to stereotypical outlines.

The principal boy is treated more seriously. This is plainly a girl, with patches sewn onto the tunic to represent poverty. This costume has a distant affinity with medieval or Tudor tunics as seen in cartoons and storybooks and also with Harlequin's tunic. Other characters wear a combination of outrageous, brightly coloured costumes. Male dancers wear tights and tunics, male comics wear the same or replace the tights with mid-calf-length trousers with stockings and buckle shoes. The principal girl and dancers wear mid-calf-length dresses with flared skirts, aprons and frills. Almost everyone wears a hat or headdress to complement their outfit. The characters can be clearly identified by their costumes and form part of a defined pantomime whole, but the whole canvas contains such a variety of images that no one historical period is identifiable.

Occasionally, in particular productions, the costumes imply a particular period of history, such as in *Mother Goose's Silver Jubilee* at York Theatre Royal, where the villagers of Ebargum appeared in post-WWII working-class outfits with the girls in curlers and scarves. This setting allowed time continuity to be maintained during the later incorporation of an aerobics routine on the wings of a plane. Such continuity is not often a feature of pantomime, which can include dance, music and costume from all periods of history.

Location is more identifiable through costume, though the costume is always an outrageous travesty of the original; costumes for *Aladdin* define the location by parodying Victorian ideas of Chinese dress, Dick Whittington's trip to Morocco allows the possibility of parodying Victorian British and 1930s Hollywood film imagery of Sultans and their harems. However, the unity of the dancers' costumes contributes to the sense of community of the group, and the similarity with the principal's costumes, despite the range of eras, gives a sense of completeness. These people all belong to the same, rather bizarre world.

The unreal, abundant world of pantomime is reflected very effectively in the set and costume designs. Despite the painted perspectives, the scenic design makes no attempt at 'naturalism' but instead presents a brightly coloured fantasy world of spectacle and illusion. The costumes are equally fantastic, but also highly coded, drawn from Victorian pantomime, fairy story illustrations and, more recently, cartoon imagery. There is no clear sense of a historical period; the design places pantomime in an 'other' time and place or an 'everytime' but with strong contemporary cartoon-like references. The most important scenic feature in the pantomime, however, is spectacular illusion, with the transformation scene often providing the climax to Act One and the walkdown set drawing applause for its magnificence.

The costumes and scenery contribute to the perception of pantomime as both familiar and nostalgic, but containing reference to contemporary popular culture. There is thus a play with time, linking the present and the past in an idealized 'other' time and place. The costumes conform to expected stereotypes which are parodies of costumes from a range of historical periods, thus presenting a bizarre community that could exist in 'anytime' and in the present. This allows the possibility to read the pantomime as an escapist adventure and entertainment that provides a brief respite from real-life concerns, or it could be read as an allegory for the possibility of individual transformation and personal growth. The beautiful idealized scenic design, the transformations and the illusions provide escapism to an 'other' world that is, at the same time, an idealized reflection of the present; a place where transformations and magic are possible. All together, this means that the design promotes the sense that pantomime is simultaneously distant and present, familiar and surprising, and always excessive.

Notes

1. Pictures of the wings and backdrop for *Omai* designed by Loutherbourg are kept at the Victoria and Albert Museum, London. Copies are reproduced in Nagler 1952: 400.
2. It has been proven that hearing and seeing both contribute to audibility, as hearing is almost always supplemented by lip-reading, as well as understanding of facial gesture and body language.

4

FAMILIARITY AND NOSTALGIA IN AN ORAL TRADITION

Although the pantomime contains a variety of ingredients, the story is one of the most important factors that affects the pantomime box office. It is not the only thing people mention when asked what constitutes British pantomime, but it is a common factor; a story of good overcoming evil, a story that is already familiar and a story that involves gods and villains and a little bit of magic. During interviews with theatre practitioners, Gordon Dougall talked of the importance of the story, audience participation and the relationship with the audience; Chris Jordan talked of the story and the Dame; Paul Elliott talked of the importance of drama and sincerity in telling the story; Ian Good described the story as the most important thing, but also mentioned the presence of good and evil, and the magic and beauty of pantomime. But the pantomime story cannot just be any story; there are three features that appear to be fundamental. First, the story should be recognizable 'and the enjoyment comes out of that recognition factor' (Kate Edgar). This fact has led in the last century to an increased concentration on a small number of very well-known pantomime stories as identified in chapter 1. Second, the story should contain a quest or a journey alongside a love story that is thwarted and finally resolved. As Joanna Reid says,

> the audiences prefer [adventures] and they sell – especially the quest; the sort of adventure where [the characters] go and search for something and achieve something. In *Aladdin* there is the quest for the lamp and then to find and save the princess. In *Jack and the Beanstalk* they've got to get money for the rent and then kill the giant to save the princess. In *Cinderella* she has to find her man [perhaps the least clearly a quest], *Dick Whittington* heads for London seeking his fortune. (Reid)

The moral tales or fables and those stories without a clear, strong direction, or the sense of a quest such as *Humpty Dumpty*, *Goldilocks and the Three Bears* or *Puss in Boots* have disappeared over the last half century or are generally doing so. Third, the story must allow for transformations and reversals. Transformations can be magical scenic extravaganzas or changes in the status and position of the hero. Both these possibilities for change need to be included; 'you need the hero's fortunes to be reversed in some way' (Joanna Reid), 'Pantomime is magical, pantomime is about magic' (Gerry Tebbutt). Quests and transformations, and their potential interpretations, will be explored in the next chapter. Here I will concentrate on the first feature of the pantomime story, that it is familiar, and that the familiarity is maintained, developed or challenged through an oral performance tradition. This allows the audience to feel familiarity with the story, knowledgeable about pantomime, and nostalgic for what they regard as 'the pantomime traditions' which provide a continuous unbroken thread from one generation to the next.

Since Pantomime must have a familiar story, the derivation and longevity of these stories and their incorporation into cultural mythology, whether as pantomime or in some other form, is important to the sense of familiarity and recognition that is a feature within pantomime performance. Some stories, such as *Cinderella*, can be traced back to a folk tradition of storytelling. Folk tales became fairy tales, at first as refined adaptations for the court of stories told by governesses, nurses and servants in the second half of the seventeenth century. From the seventeenth century onwards, fairy tales became very popular and were appropriated by the upper classes and written down, converting them from dynamic infinitely changeable tales into single authored versions. Educated writers converted the tales into a 'literary discourse about mores, values and manners so that children would become civilized according to the social code of that time' (Zipes 1988: 3). Stories from the European literary tradition reflect the ethics of a male-dominated Christian society, in which they were designed to 'instruct and amuse' (Zipes 1988: 9). Despite the fact that the stories had become authored, there are still different versions of the same story reflecting different authors, societies and eras. For example, *Cinderella* appears in versions by the brothers Grimm as *Aschenputtel* and Charles Perrault as *Cendrillon*. These versions have significant differences in the events of the story and in how the details of the story are worked out. Marina Warner identifies a Chinese version of the story written down in around AD 850–60. She remarks that 'the story was taken down from a family servant by an official, and the way it is told reveals that the audience already knows it: this is by no means the *Ur*-text' (Warner 1995: 202).

Exploring the differences between versions of stories can reveal facts about the author, storyteller or society. Pantomime, which still relies on transmission by performance and whose stories and structures are passed on verbally and visually, continues to develop, drawing on material and conventions from society. The changes in pantomime are, therefore, a reflection of the way society is developing as well as a response to the economic situation. Laurence Coupe argues that the interpretation of the stories is also a reflection of the codes of society, and the desired perfection or utopia at the end of the pantomime is a projection and selection of what the viewer perceives in our own society (Coupe 1997: 182).

Given this argument, there is a surprising amount of consistency in fairy stories from all over the world. There are two theories that have been proposed to account for this similarity. The first, known as monogenesis and diffusion, is that there is an originating tale of each type from which all others are descended, altered through migration and oral transmission. To many folklorists this is an inadequate explanation for the similarity of tales where there is no discernible path by which the stories could have travelled. Vladimir Propp summed up the problem when he asked: 'How is one to explain the similarity of the tale about the frog queen in Russia, Germany, France, India, in America among the Indians, and in New Zealand, when the contact of peoples cannot be proven historically?' (in Tatar 2003: 64). Propp appeared to favour a theory of spontaneous generation of the tales, the breeding ground being the human psyche. As similar situations and events occur everywhere, the symbolism of fairy stories, in which the actions provide a means of understanding life and society, is likewise similar. This theory is also open to dispute since literature in general is far more varied, failing to display the structural similarities of fairy tales.

In response to this Roman Jakobson has suggested that the cultural conventions of fairy tale and the censorship of the audience both play a part in limiting the freedom of the storyteller (Tatar 2003: 64–66). The fundamental difference suggested between literature and folklore is that each draws on different symbolic codes, that for folklore being that the tale is told in 'public and set down by custom' (Tatar 2003: 81). Tatar concludes that 'the study of fairy tales tells us something about the way in which the mind draws on the double movement of language between literal meaning and figurative expression to fashion stories that dramatize psychological realities' (Tatar 2003: 92), meaning that physical action represents the psychological development of the character and subsequently ourselves. Finally, of course, the principal events of the stories and the structure remains, but the social differences are overlaid in the details of the renewed stories.

Although little can be known about the individual tellings of such tales, Jack Zipes argues that the re-telling was 'intended to transform a specific oral folk tale (and sometimes a well known literary tale) and designed to rearrange the motifs, characters, themes, functions and configurations in such a way that they would address the concerns of the educated and ruling classes of late feudal and early capitalist societies' (Zipes 1988: 6).

Laurence Coupe argues that 'realising that myth is always going to be open to change, we must participate in the operation'. He then quotes Marina Warner:

'I believe the process of understanding and clarification… can give rise to newly told stories, can sew and weave and knit different patterns into the social fabric and that this is a continuous enterprise for everyone to take part in' (Warner 1994: xiv in Coupe 1997: 189).

Zipes' arguments explore the political function of stories, while Marina Warner and Bruno Bettelheim point to the understanding of folk tales in personal psychological development. The essential feature here is that the stories were adapted quickly and easily to reflect the relationship of narrator and audience and the configuration of society. The stories were interpreted by the listener in ways that were appropriate to the individual and the society. In the same way, pantomimes are adapted for the time and place of performance, as well as for and by the teller of the tale. Continuous development of the form can be observed in response to the prejudices, opinions and mores of the day. Modern pantomime derived from a Victorian model that adapted stories to suit the patriarchal capitalist society. Pantomime continues to develop in response to the cultural norms of society with the inclusion of topical and political references, references to the media and the inclusion of contemporary music and dance. The stories and characters also become shaded by reference to contemporary culture. The fox-hunting scene in Cinderella, if present, rarely shows the prince being involved in hunting; it is no longer politically correct.[1] Principal girls and fairies have become more feisty, black and Asian performers are now employed in all roles, and some versions of pantomimes reflect the cultural diversity of our society in music, dance and casting.[2] The presence of female principal boys is challenged in response to a desire for clearer heterosexual relationships in a family entertainment.

Of the most popular pantomime stories, *Cinderella*, *Red Riding Hood*, *Jack and the Beanstalk*, *Snow White* and *Sleeping Beauty* are based on fairy stories recorded by Charles Perrault and/or the Grimm brothers. *Aladdin* is based on a story from *The Arabian Nights* also known as *The Thousand and One Nights*. In pantomime it has an Oriental setting, but takes on the values of Victorian Britain. *Dick Whittington*, *Babes in the Wood* and *Robin Hood* are based on historical legends, and *Robinson Crusoe* is an eighteenth-century political satire. *Peter Pan* is the most recent addition to the pantomime listings as the play was not written by J. M. Barrie until 1904. Some versions of the pantomime are based on the play with additions and exclusions, but others take influences from Disney's film *Peter Pan* (1953), the Broadway musical (Comden, Green, Bernstein, Styne et al. 1954) or the later Disney film *Hook* (1991).

These stories form the basis of pantomimes which have developed into quite formal theatrical structures. V. C. Clinton-Baddeley (1963) has traced the earliest performances of several pantomimes as follows:

Robinson Crusoe	1781 (written by R. B. Sheridan based on Daniel Defoe's novel)
Aladdin	1788
Cinderella	1804 (the fairy's role was transferred to Venus in this production)
Mother Goose	1805 (the story was almost unrecognizable in comparison to contemporary versions)
Dick Whittington	1814

Norman Robbins (2002) identifies the derivation of other pantomimes including:

The Babes in the Wood	1827
Beauty and the Beast	1852
Jack and the Beanstalk	1819
Red Riding Hood	1803
Sleeping Beauty	1822

In these early versions the stories presented were often quite different from what we would now expect, but gradually pantomime versions have become standardized so that there is now a high degree of predictability about the story content, the scene structure and even some of the routines contained in contemporary pantomimes.

Both *Cinderella* and *Aladdin* became standardized following versions by Henry J. Byron in the second half of the nineteenth century that gradually influenced other writers. The version of *Cinderella* that still provides the basis of today's pantomimes is derived from Byron's 'Fairy Burlesque Extravaganza' of 1860–61 at the Royal Strand Theatre called *Cinderella! Or the Lover, the Lackey, and the Little Glass Slipper* in which the character of the sisters is established, the older sister is played by a man, and Prince Poppeti by a woman (Clinton-Baddeley 1963: 10–11). The kitchen scene that is still present in most productions, now between Buttons and Cinderella, was present as early as 1830. It was the same servant who insisted Cinderella should try on the slipper. By 1910 the kitchen scene had become established as an important moment in the plot and in the relationship between Cinderella and Buttons, and from this point it was generally Buttons who brought Cinderella to try on the slipper.[3] Thus the pantomime versions of stories in contemporary use are largely based on a Victorian model.

Pantomime has largely been part of an oral tradition of continuous development, with much of the business of pantomime passed on from performer to performer rather than scripted and published. Chris Jordan is writer and director of the pantomime at Devonshire Park Theatre, Eastbourne. Asked for the sources he used when writing a new version of a pantomime, he explained:

> I was brought up on pantomime, so since I was five I've been going to pantomime. Your earliest memories of seeing those shows tend to become your definitive idea of what they should be. When I wrote *Jack and the Beanstalk*, a story that I knew least, I went to see about five *Jack and the Beanstalks* and I sat and made notes of how each one had used the story and told the story. Then I did a bit of research on the Internet about the *Jack the Giant Killer* story..... I also use the Ladybird books. The Ladybird books are basically the fairy tales (Chris Jordan).

He is also aware of the influence of the writers of pantomimes in which he performed. Like the other pantomime writers, Jordan includes some new material and gags alongside the routines that are expected in each pantomime. For example, Jordan's Genie in *Aladdin* was an Elvis type character, an innovation, but he retained the slapstick laundry scene and the mangling of one of the Chinese Policemen. In *Cinderella* a new introduction was an aerobics scene for the Ugly Sisters, but he maintained the long stocking and the false leg gags in the slipper-fitting scene, as well as the lines 'I can't get my foot in the Crystal slipper' to which the response is 'You couldn't get your foot in the Crystal Palace'. In this way pantomime incorporates new material and topical reference alongside tried and tested, even hackneyed, but familiar gags.

Cinderella is probably the most formulaic of all the pantomimes, since not only the story but quite a lot of the comedy business remains constant in different productions. Rather than an opening prologue between good and evil the Fairy Godmother opens the pantomime. Her main function is in the transformation scene at the end of Act One during which, by the power of magic, a pumpkin becomes a coach, rats, mice, lizards and frogs all variously become horses, footmen, or coachman, and Cinderella's appearance is transformed. There is no supernatural evil character in the pantomime, instead the stepsisters take on this role playing grotesque and outrageous characters. This is different from most other pantomimes in which the cross-dressed Dame character draws the audience into a relationship of empathy and complicity. The Ugly Sisters vie for the affection of any man they see with outrageous flirtation, costumes and make-up. Their principal comedy scene is in Act One when preparing for the ball. This may be a slapstick make-up scene or a hairdressing scene. This is followed by an important scene in which any sympathy the audience has for the Ugly Sisters is removed as the Sisters give Cinderella her invitation to the Ball and then force her to tear it up. They have a second comedy scene in Act Two when dressing for the prince's visit to try on the slipper, and a set-piece routine in the 'Trying the Slipper' scene in Act Two.

Cinderella is friendly and popular and is usually seen interacting in song and dance with the villagers, helping an old woman (the Fairy Godmother in disguise) collect wood for her fire and saving a fox from the hunt. Her father is Baron Hard-up,[4] whose character varies and whose relationship to her stepmother ranges from being engaged to being a widower. The stepmother rarely appears. Buttons has become established as the comedy character with whom the audience is expected to empathize. His unrequited love for Cinderella is most clearly developed in the kitchen scene just before the Fairy Godmother arrives to transform Cinderella into Princess Incognita for the Ball. Buttons discovers Cinderella crying instead of preparing for the ball and tries to cheer her up by creating a make-believe ball from the objects in the kitchen; the tablecloth as a dress, a colander as a tiara, a fourteen-carrot necklace. They sit on the table with stools for horses and imagine riding off to the ball, where they dance together. This scene is important because it anticipates the events of the transformation scene to come, and because it is the clearest exposition of the relationship between Cinderella and Buttons. The Prince's part is the least important in the piece, he is little more than a means of transforming Cinderella's fortunes, but demonstrates the patriarchal values that see a woman transferred from father to husband. As with all pantomimes the plot ends in the marriage of hero and heroine which is represented as the walkdown[5] and follows the songsheet.[6]

However, in some versions of the fairy tale the Ugly sisters cut off toes and heels so that their feet will fit into the slipper. In other versions of the story the Ball is a three-day affair, dresses for which are provided magically at Cinderella's dead mother's grave. As Cinderella leaves the Ball on each occasion she hides first in a dovecote then a tree, each of which her father destroys. All of this would be difficult on stage and within the confines of two acts, the first of which usually ends in a transformation and the second in a wedding, and might have been considered unsuitable for children or a family audience. Therefore, there is an expected version of the tale, associated with the live performance of pantomime (and, of course, the Disney film) that is, in fact, removed from some versions of the fairy story.

I stress the way characters and stories have developed within a pantomime tradition, as opposed to the literary tradition, because, although pantomime has become standardized, it is part of an oral tradition with no defining 'original' or 'authentic' scripts, characters or structures. Rather there are versions of stories, versions of routines and gags, and likely scene structures and combinations of characters.

Aladdin first appeared as a pantomime in 1788 at Covent Garden (Robbins 2002: 143). However, it was about 80 years later that several versions of *Aladdin* combined to provide the precedent for the twentieth-century versions. *Aladdin and his Wonderful Lamp: or the Genie of the Ring* in 1856 was closely followed by Byron's burlesque *Aladdin* (1861) produced at the Old Strand Theatre with the 'cheerful Widow Twankay [sic]' (Robbins 2002: 144). Byron's version includes the main characters and structures that are still present in contemporary pantomimes including the presence of Widow Twankay played by a man, and, to continue the reference to tea, Pekoe as the Vizier's son played by a woman. The second influence on Byron was the scenic extravaganza produced by Charles Farley at Covent Garden in the first half of the nineteenth century. Farley's production was not pantomime, but a spectacle with beautiful scenery, called a 'Melo-Dramatick Romance' *Aladdin or The Wonderful Lamp*. It contained Abanazar and three slaves: a dumb slave, a slave of the lamp and a slave of the ring. It was produced in 1813 then revived in 1826 and 1836 (Clinton-Baddeley 1963: 31). Two of the slaves or genies usually survive in contemporary versions; the slave of the lamp and the slave of the ring.

Aladdin is portrayed in Grimms' *Nursery and Household Tales* as a 'headstrong and incorrigible good-for-nothing' (Tatar 2003: 88) who lives with his mother Widow Twankey[7] and his brother Wishee Washee. Together they run the Emperor's laundry in old Peking, which provides the setting for much of the physical comedy. The pantomime is notable for the opportunities it provides for chases, slapstick and slosh scenes either in the laundry or in the streets, which incorporate the two Chinese Policemen, most commonly known as Ping and Pong.[8] The Eastern setting provides the excuse for extravagant sets, bright colours and magic spells. The laundry provides the setting for a slosh scene which usually culminates in either the vizier or one of the Chinese Policemen being threaded through the mangle and coming out flat. The transformation occurs in the Cave as the jewels are revealed. There are other opportunities for magic or transformation in the journeys to and from the Cave, Peking and Abanazar's lair which are sometimes conducted on a flying carpet.

From this description the common features of the majority of productions can be deduced, and audiences arrive with a similar set of experiences and expectations. In the majority of cases, and especially in those productions that advertise themselves as 'traditional', an attempt will be made to fulfil these expectations and to give the audience the experience they expect. This reinforces the set of expectations for future generations, though, of course, the particularities of each telling of the story vary.

There are exceptions from the continuous development from the Victorian model, but these rely on the community consciousness of pantomime. That means that the writers assume a common and widespread knowledge of the pantomime versions of the stories and of the pantomime conventions so that the differences between what is being presented and the expectations of pantomime are highlighted. This is, of course, dependent on the fact that pantomime is the most popular form of theatre entertainment in Britain, with the widest audience constituency, so that although there are regional variations there is a common understanding of the genre.

The most interesting example that I have seen of this subversion of pantomime, based on thorough and complete reliance on its structures and patterns, was an 'alternative' version of *Cinderella* at the Tron Theatre, Glasgow (2003–4), written by

Forbes Masson and directed by Gordon Dougall. This version subverted the elements of the tale, relying on the audience's knowledge of the story in its pantomime version, and the pantomime conventions. The story is set in the basement of the tenement where the family live and where Ella works. Prince Charming had disappeared on the eve of his marriage to Ella; he was thrown into a furnace by the stepsisters to stop Cinderella from inheriting the family fortune, which will happen when she marries. Dandini has become the principal villain of the piece, along with the sisters, and Buttons, for once, and in contrast to the pantomime versions, gets the girl. The ball has become a *Pop-Idol* type television game show to which Ella is sent in a rocket ship by her 'Dogmother' (half woman, half dog as the result of a failed magic spell) at the end of Act One. In this version the structure of the commercial pantomime is maintained but the events are updated, even to the extent of using identifiable pantomime characters with new roles and characteristics (such as conflating the skin part with the inept Fairy Godmother).

This version of *Cinderella*, and this pattern of subversion, is very unusual but is particularly interesting here because it demonstrates the assumptions on which it is based. These are that every member of the audience will be completely familiar with the events of the story of *Cinderella* as it is told in pantomime and contemporary film, and will therefore recognize and be amused by the deviations from the predictable patterns. Secondly, it relies on knowledge of the pantomime conventions in telling this story, including the cross-dressed Ugly sisters, the timing of events in relation to the two-act structure with a transformation before the interval, the use of magic, the use of music, dance and audience interaction. The comedy of this version relies on familiarity with a long-standing tradition, both in terms of the story and in terms of its use in the live performance of pantomime.

There are other examples of this sort of subversion, in which particular literary versions of tales are foregrounded over the pantomime tradition. *Sleeping Beauty* is not one of the most common pantomimes. It normally begins with the Queen's wish for a child, followed by the christening and the thirteen fairy godmothers' wishes for the child (twelve good and one wicked). The first act culminates in Sleeping Beauty's finger pricking and the beginning of her sleep. Act Two therefore brings us a new protagonist and a different quest, as the prince attempts her rescue. This pattern was followed at the Theatre by the Lake in Keswick (2003).

A very different version was premiered at Winchester Theatre Royal the same year, called *Sleeping Beauty...the whole story*. The intention in this case was to return to a literary version by Charles Perrault. In this production the first act ended, as expected, with the princess falling asleep, but the second act was set in the 1950s and followed Perrault's version of the subsequent events (though obviously in a different era). Briar Rose (the name given to Sleeping Beauty) is rescued by the prince and taken home to his kingdom. She is not welcomed by her new mother-in-law, who attempts to cook and eat Briar Rose's baby daughter. The mother-in-law is eventually thrown into the oven herself before everyone lives happily ever after. This version contains some pantomime elements, including a female grotesque as a villainous mother-in-law (played by a woman), audience participation, a transformation at the end of Act One, and a songsheet at the end, but the story takes a new direction and lacks certain pantomime elements, notably a cross-dressed

Dame. Attempted cannibalism is introduced, a feature of many of the early written fairy tales that were later sanitized for a family audience.

This version, like others that have returned to a literary text, is interesting for the reinstatement of the gory elements. These performances retain some of the contemporary conventions of pantomime but differ from the commercial performances and challenge the more widely known Victorian or Disney versions of the tales by incorporating specific events from a particular literary version, usually by Charles Perrault or the Grimm brothers. Other examples of this are *Cinderella* in Westcliff-on-Sea (2001–2) or *Red Riding Hood* at the Theatre Royal, Stratford East (2003–4). This latter production used the Grimms' version as a source and became very gory in the second act when a scene was played inside the Wolf's stomach, before he was cut open onstage for the rescue of Granny and Red. Finally, the wicked wolf, still with his stomach gaping open, was banished.

These few examples demonstrate that while the majority of repertory and commercial pantomimes tend to present similar versions of the tales with alterations in how they are told, and advertise the product as 'traditional', a minority of smaller companies and repertory theatres are exploring or updating the stories and featuring this fact in their publicity. As the content is developed, the pantomime structures may need reworking, but there is a continuation of the contact with, and awareness of, the pantomime conventions and a reliance on familiarity with the pantomime stories. This fact demonstrates the continuity with the past and the possibilities for gradual development relying on both familiarity and originality within the pantomime tradition.

Pantomime stories appear to be moving in several different directions. The majority show a gradual development building on an oral and visual history of pantomime performances. A small minority are looking back to an earlier literary source but incorporating some of the features of pantomime, and a very few others take the story as a piece of shared knowledge to which they refer in creating a new version based on the bones of the story and the conventions of pantomime. Not surprisingly, given the similarity in story and structure from one pantomime to the next, the characters and their actions also have a high degree of conformity to accepted patterns. When people are asked what a pantomime is they usually mention some of the features discussed above, but they also list the types of characters that are present, and they are generally aware of the function of the character in the story and the pantomime.

> You've got to have good versus evil, you've got to have the Good Fairy or whatever and either a King Rat or the Demon King, or Abanazar the wicked uncle....And then you've got to have the comedy evil and you've got to have the comedy good. Then you've got to have the straight hero type and the straight heroine type, and they've got to go through trials and tribulations before Jack wins the girl. (Liston)

Pantomimes generally include six principal characters. These are the Dame, the hero, a supporter of good (a fairy or genie) and a supporter of evil (a demon or his henchman), a heroine and a second comedy character, the Silly Boy (either a brother of the hero or son of the Dame who is usually briefly taken in by the villain). After these six there is a selection of other characters as required to develop the plot and provide the comedy and other entertainment. These often include the father of the heroine, a henchman of the evil character and a comedy duo or broker's men. Other characters such as Neptune, King of the Sea might be introduced during transformation scenes or other spectacles to provide singing or dancing roles for particular stars. They, like the speciality acts, dancers and children, remain incidental to the action.[9]

In the majority of pantomimes the relationships between characters are also fairly standardized. The Dame, a descendant of Clown in nineteenth-century pantomime, is often the mother of the hero (*Jack and the Beanstalk*, *Aladdin*), but Dames might also play a nurse or governess to the heroine (*Sleeping Beauty*, *Snow White*) or the children (*Babes in the Wood*). The hero always falls instantly in love with the heroine, a love which is reciprocated. The hero and heroine are descendants of Harlequin and Columbine of the *Commedia dell'arte*. The principal girl is the lovely, virginal heroine often kidnapped by the baddie and rescued by the hero. The hero is assisted in this task by an immortal figure, the Fairy. The Dame often has another son, a comedy character, who is a dim-witted boy, played by a man and often enlisted or outsmarted by 'Evil' (Simple Simon in *Jack and the Beanstalk*, Muddles in *Snow White*, Wishee Washee in *Aladdin*, Idle Jack in *Dick Whittington*).

The relationships of characters to each other and the balance of actions vary in each story, but applying Propp's 'seven spheres of action of the *Dramatis Personae*' gives an understanding of the role of each character within the plot (Propp 1968, p. 79).

Russian Folk Tale	Pantomime
The Villain	The Villain. King Rat in *Dick Whittington*, Fleshcreep and the Giant in *Jack and the Beanstalk*, Abanazar in *Aladdin*, the Wicked Queen in *Snow White*. The Ugly Sisters in *Cinderella* are less clearly villainous though they serve this function.
The Donor	The Fairy gives a magical gift or other protection.
The Princess and her Father	Princess/ Principal Girl and her Father. Alice and Alderman Fitzwarren in *Dick Whittington*, Princess Jill and the King in *Jack and the Beanstalk*, Princess Jasmine and the Emperor in *Aladdin*, Cinderella and Baron Hard-up have a slightly different, and more varied, relationship. Snow White's father is dead.
The Hero	Principal Boy. Jack, Dick, Aladdin, Prince Charming. Cinderella and Snow White might be regarded as the heroes of their stories as they are the centre of the action and the characters who change state.
The Helper	At different times, the Fairy or the comedy brother or Dame fulfils this function. In *Jack and the*

	Beanstalk Dame and Dick arrive in the skies to help rescue everyone, in *Cinderella* Buttons is instrumental in Cinderella's appearance to try on the slipper, in *Dick Whittington* Tommy the cat fulfils this function, freeing the shop and Morocco of rats and helping fight the villain. In those pantomimes with a female hero the Prince falls into this category.
The Dispatcher	The reason for the hero's departure generally comes indirectly from the villain (a kidnapping or theft), but may be encouraged by the Dame or the princess's father. In *Dick Whittington* the Dame and Simple Simon are hypnotized, in *Jack and the Beanstalk* and *Aladdin* the impetus comes from the King / Emperor demanding his rent.
The False Hero	The villain disguises him/herself and dupes the comedy brother into helping him, or tricks the Princess into his power. In *Aladdin* the hero is tricked into the cave, later the Princess is tricked into giving up the lamp. In *Jack and the Beanstalk* Jack is tricked into accepting the beans.

It is apparent through this breakdown of actions that characters can be involved in several spheres of action, either with respect to different characters or at different times, and the reverse is also true, that a single sphere of action can be carried out by several characters. Only the hero is clearly in one category alone,[10] although the heroine may also be.

Good characters and evil characters are clearly separated and identified, although some good characters are tricked into betraying the hero. It is only after the tale is completed that some evil characters may be magically altered to be good or choose to reform rather than be banished (they are generally not killed in pantomime). There is no room for complexity or development of character because the tale is told through action and each character has a role in delivering the action of the story. The identification of the audience and the action of the story revolves around just one character, the hero. As we will discover in relation to comedy and participation in the framing of the story, the audience enters into conspiracy and empathy with the comedy characters, Dame or Silly Boy, but in the story itself, the hero must excite the audience to identify with her/him and win the day. The principal boy and girl are still the last to enter at the walkdown as the focus of the story remains on the hero's quest, the successful achievement of which is demonstrated in that moment.

The importance of this reading of the actions undertaken by characters in the story is that it demonstrates that there is clarity of intention, and that characters are clearly demarcated and archetypal. Within a dynamic world, Frye defines an archetype as 'a symbol, usually an image, which recurs often enough in literature to be recognisable as an element of one's literary experience as a whole' (Frye 1971 in Coupe 1997: 170). The fact that it is possible to identify the characters by their type

(Dame, principal boy or girl etc.) rather than by a character name, and that they are clearly recognizable and largely interchangeable between pantomimes, makes it possible to classify them as archetypes. But the fact that they also fall so easily into Propp's formulation demonstrates that their types and functions are paradigmatic within literary culture.

Although the central intention of each character is to develop the action of the story in relation to the hero, there are also particular relationships between the characters which are only partially determined by their function in the story. For example, the relationship between the Dame and the comic or the Dame and the Principal Girl are not directly related to the plot, but they support the representation of family life. Dave Benson Phillips describes the relationship between Dame and Comic as follows:

> The mother goes 'I know you're silly but I love you'. That has to be believable [....] the relationship between boy and mum has to be love, but it's like feeling love for this bumbling idiot. (Benson Phillips)

The comedy characters attempt to create a credible family unit, despite being heightened or grotesque characters in the midst of incredible events. On the other hand each of these characters has a part in the structure of the pantomime event as Ian Good describes:

> I see the role of the pantomime Dame as to bring the characters together. So, for example, in *Jack and the Beanstalk*, Jack very rarely comes in contact with Simple Simon because they've both got different things to do. It's basically facilitating all these characters meeting each other, ... I think in a good book, [the Dame won't just] come on and tell a gag and disappear again, she actually facilitates the meeting of these characters and the moving on of the story. (Good)

Dave Benson Phillips describes the role of the Silly Boy character as

> To be silly, to be the audience's friend and link to the show.... He is the slightly pathetic, the failure son... who doesn't get the girl. But ....you've got to show you're the people's friend and everybody kind of likes you and that you possess the talent for something, but ultimately, you're not going to get the girl. (Benson Phillips)

What these descriptions reveal is that although the action centres round the hero, with whom the audience is expected to identify, the comedy characters build a relationship with others to reveal the details around the story, and with the audience to link them to the telling of the story. So we see several functions for the characters in addition to the dramatic functions of Propp's categorization. These include the creation of a community of support for the hero and the establishment of a relationship with the audience that draws them into a sense of community with the performers and the performance.

Pantomime is an example of a theatre form that still retains its oral tradition, though, as was argued above, the loss of training grounds outside formal theatre training, and the cost of slosh and physical comedy, music and dance are causing change. For producers and performers pantomime has to change as a result of economics; for audiences the changes are gradual and therefore possibly less noticeable. This may be the result of the reliance on fairy tale structures and archetypal characters that remain constant though open to changing interpretation. Each person's expectation is constantly modified by each experience and each re-working for the participants and the audiences. Each production adds to the body of experiences and to the development of the tradition, demonstrating the way 'tradition' provides a genre or framework that is recognizable and familiar, but is also live and dynamic, so that each creator modifies or influences that tradition, using familiar and recognizable patterns that are constantly developed in terms of their own structures and in response to the influences of culture, economics and society.

Notes

1. It will be interesting to see what transpires in this scene in future productions of *Cinderella* now that hunting with dogs is banned in the UK.
2. This is particularly apparent in South Africa where multilingual, multi-racial pantomimes have developed since the end of apartheid. For more information, see Kruger 2000 and 2003.
3. Clinton Baddeley has traced the development of the character Buttons to the comic servant, a stock theatrical character, who was called Pedro when played by Joseph Grimaldi in Cinderella in 1804. The appearance of Buttoni occurs in Byron's version of 1860, but doesn't appear widely until 1921.
4. Many of the names are subject to change. The Baron's name usually refers to his impecunious state. The Ugly Sisters generally have comic names.
5. Each of the characters walks downstage and bows to the accompaniment of singing and sometimes dancing. The last to enter are the happy couple whose entrance is presaged by three cheers. There usually follows one last chorus, the rhyming couplets and the curtain.
6. The songsheet is community singing by the audience led by the comedians in which the words of a song are flown in on a cloth and a competition is engaged in between different portions of the audience. It is the opportunity for participation and a convenient way of keeping the audience occupied while the final set is prepared. The comedians generally invite a group of children onto the stage to chat or lead the singing.
7. This is the normal spelling in contemporary pantomime.
8. A common convention in pantomime is to have a comedy duo who perform slapstick comedy and chases. Sometimes the principal comic is one of the duo, but not in *Aladdin*. The term Broker's Men is sometimes used as a generic term for such comedy duos, although it refers specifically to debt collectors who chase the hero or his mother and are often seen in *Cinderella*. The Robbers in *Babes in the Wood* have the same function.
9. Neither *Cinderella* nor *Snow White* conforms to this pattern. In these two pantomimes the story is told from the heroine's point of view, making her the principal protagonist, and neither contains a strong quest.
10. Maria Tatar describes the critique of this formulation by Claude Lévi-Strauss and other structuralists and the subsequent development by A-J Greimas. She then explores the development by Eleazar Meletinsky in which the hero stands in contrast to all the other characters as the only 'pure' role, the only role that does not overlap with any other spheres of action (Tatar 2003: 67ff).

5

Quests and Transformations in Pantomime Stories

Having focused on the familiarity of stories developed in an oral tradition in the last chapter, this chapter returns to the other two features deemed necessary in a successful pantomime story: the quest and the potential for transformation. The structure of pantomime stories follows that of the fairy tales on which many are based. A pattern that is common to fairy stories was identified by Vladimir Propp and further developed by Tzvetan Todorov through the study of many Russian fairy tales. However, it applies equally to many heroic adventure stories or quest stories and can be seen applied to pantomime below. The five stages of the fairy story according to Todorov are

1. the opening situation of equilibrium
2. the degradation of the situation
3. the state of disequilibrium
4. the search and recovery
5. the re-establishment of equilibrium (Todorov 1990: 29).

This pattern moves away from and returns to a stable position, in an arch-like structure in which stage 1 reflects stage 5 and stage 2 reflects stage 4.

The way the pantomime version of the story is structured is influenced by the practical requirements of a two-act performance on a proscenium stage with stage cloths, flats and picture book design. This has led to a pattern of performance using frontcloth and full stage scenes in alternation finishing each act with a full-stage spectacle. The standard structure now includes the prologue, the introduction of characters in turn in a long opening scene, musical numbers and comic routines often as frontcloth scenes, transformation scenes, an interval, a songsheet and the walkdown finale. Such features provide a framework within which the plot is structured and tension is built and released. Other comedy routines, small scenes and songs are played out as required by the plot or the timing of the evening, on frontcloth or half stage, allowing the crew to carry out scenic transformations.

A   Prologue or opening scene between the immortals – a frontcloth scene.
B   Opening chorus of villagers in a song and dance routine, often fronted by the heroine – full stage.
C   The comedy character's opening spot – full stage.
D   The hero's opening number / spot – full stage.
E   The Dame's opening spot – full stage.
F   A plot event such as the introduction of a McGuffin,[1] which requires action from the hero – A new scene and set.
G   A supernatural event or transformation scene which leads to a change of circumstances (and often the interval) – full stage.
H   Opening of Act Two is often a dance routine or UV ballet – full stage.
I   Everyone gathers in the new place
J   The Duel and resolution – full stage.
K   The Songsheet – frontcloth.
L   The Walkdown or Wedding – full stage.

There may be other spectacular numbers or transformations, song and dance routines, comedy chases, fights, audience participation and comic routines, but these will be placed as appropriate to the story, the dramatic timing of the events in the plot, and the requirement for the practicalities of scene changes. The events listed above are likely to occur in every pantomime at least once. Some, such as transformations and gatherings, may occur more than once.

These two sets of requirements; the fairy story with its transformation of fortunes and the practicalities of live dramatic performance with dance, design and music have all coalesced into a coherent and familiar pantomime structure. The pantomime opens with a prologue for good and evil often spoken largely in rhyme, which anticipates the quest or the difficulty that is the catalyst for the story. This is followed by the opening number for the villagers, and sometimes the principal girl, which presents a happy and stable situation. Here the opening equilibrium of happy village life has been preceded by the immortals who predict the potential degradation of the situation. Although the scene is happy and carefree, the potential for disaster is apparent, which sets up a dramatic tension between what the audience and the characters know. So the characters are in the state of equilibrium, while the audience is prepared for change.

Each of the characters is then introduced with an opening spot the ordering of which follows the order of importance on the playbill. Once everyone has been introduced, the plot can begin. During this phase, short scenes will be played out, introducing the King or the Broker's Men, identifying the evil that is feared and allowing the villain to expose his plan. An example is that the King's rent collectors threaten the Dame and her family with eviction for non-payment of rent, forcing the family to take extreme measures such as selling Daisy the Cow in *Jack and the Beanstalk*. In *Dick Whittington* a theft occurs and Dick is believed guilty and sent away. Aladdin discovers he will never be able to marry the princess without a great fortune and so goes with Abanazar to the cave. In all cases, the first signs of disequilibrium appear.

The next major event will move the situation further into disequilibrium; something will be stolen (the lamp in *Aladdin*, the Goose in *Mother Goose*) or the princess kidnapped (*Jack and the Beanstalk* and *Aladdin*). This is followed by the search and recovery, which begins with the transformation scene just before the interval when a journey will be undertaken by the principal boy, followed in Act 2 by the other principal characters (up the Beanstalk in *Jack and the Beanstalk*, to Morocco in *Dick Whittington*, to Abanazar's lair in *Aladdin*). The transformation is the opportunity for scenic extravagance and a big song and dance number which is usually the climactic culmination of the first act. Dramatically, the moment of disequilibrium occurs before the interval, so that the hero begins his heroic journey from a position of disadvantage before the interval. This creates tension which will be resolved after the audience returns. It is a similar device to that used in adventure series and Saturday morning cinema of the 1960s and 1970s, which always ended an episode with a cliffhanger moment, leaving Batman and Robin or Tintin in a potentially fatal trap. In Act 2, the heroine is rescued and any stolen objects recovered thanks to the hero and the rest of the principals. There is usually a chase and a fight before the villain is defeated, the hero and heroine return to the palace to be married and to live happily ever after, and equilibrium is restored.

One reading of this structure is that the equilibrium of the state, represented by the happy villagers, is restored, but with the hero or heroine in a new place within it. Economic and emotional success is secured for the hero within the hierarchy from which he came. The stable structure of the form allows the exceptional hero to move forward, but the form, like society, does not change. The two halves of the structure are reflections of each other, an arch-like structure, where the journey away from, and back to, equilibrium are mirrored to reflect the stability and fixity of society. Alternatively, although the stable form reinforces the ethics of the society in which the story is set, in this case, a capitalist society with Christian morals, it could also be read as opening up the possibility for transformation, change or renewal. The movement of the hero into a new position in society and the destruction of the potential for disequilibrium create the possibility of a new society. According to Laurence Coupe in his analysis of Northrop Frye's writings in *Myth*, the secular scripture of romance does not reflect an existing cosmos, but creates it. 'Symbols and narrative patterns recur, and the more one recognises them, according to Frye, the more one is able to infer a vast quest-myth at work. The quest is for totality, for completeness, for perfection' (Coupe 1997: 170). Read in this way, there is a utopian possibility in the structure of pantomime stories that creates a sense of permanent possibility and freedom.

What has become apparent from this analysis is the very high degree of conformity to familial similarity both in the structure of the story and in the structure of its pantomime version. Some of the features of performance, such as the prologue, the opening scene, the transformation, the frontcloth comedy scenes, the songsheet and the walkdown, have come to be regarded as conventions of pantomime. These exist alongside the structural features of the story which allow for the possibility of change and transformation, and the importance of both community and individual in the success of the adventure.

The importance of quests becomes apparent by studying a structural map of several pantomime versions.

Dick Whittington (Elliott and Davies, 1990)
A, B, C, E, D, F (the theft of money which is blamed on Dick), G (the dream sequence and the decision to return and clear his name), H, I, G (the storm on board ship orchestrated by King Rat), I, J, K, L.

Dick Whittington (Hudd, 1998)
A, B, C, E, D, F (the theft which is blamed on Dick) G (the dream sequence and decision to return), H, I, G (the storm), I, J, K, L.

Robinson Crusoe (Davies, 1990)
A, B, E, D, C, F (all sign up for a voyage) G (a storm which leads to an underwater ballet in which) F (a treasure map is given to Robinson), H, (non-supernatural dangers, chases and rescues follow), I, F (more exchanges with the treasure map), I, J, K, L.

If one substitutes trying on the shoe for the Duel, *Cinderella* fits into this structure (Cinderella defeats the Ugly Sisters). *Snow White* does not conform to this structure, although it contains Todorov's five elements, which is interesting in light of the fact that many people argue that it is not a true pantomime.

Robinson Crusoe relies on one external McGuffin, the treasure map, which is a repeated source of movement and interest. In *Dick Whittington* the story has separate catalysts; in the first half there is the accusation of theft and Dick's exile, then in Act Two, the trip of the main protagonists to Morocco to make their fortune. More events occur in *Dick Whittington*, but the focus on a single quest in *Robinson Crusoe* makes the adventure appear stronger and slightly more coherent. However, the focus on Robinson's quest is perhaps less apparent in performance because of the amount of comedy business, song and dance that fills the pantomime and the events of the quest are less easily attributed to Robinson's valour. On the other hand, there is always some difficulty about how Dick Whittington comes to be forgiven or the plot to discredit him is revealed, and the pantomime can appear as two separate journeys.

The same separation into two quests is apparent in *Aladdin*; the first half of the story culminates in Aladdin's return with his fortune, and the Emperor's blessing being given to the marriage of Aladdin and the Princess. A second adventure follows as Abanazar tricks the Princess into giving him the lamp so that he can kidnap her with the power of the lamp. All the protagonists then go on the journey to rescue her.

In both *Dick Whittington* and *Aladdin* the first journey is made by the hero alone and in the second he is helped by the other characters. This is also true of Jack who goes alone to sell the beans and journey up the beanstalk. He is only later followed by the others. The fact that the most popular pantomimes have two parts to the quest, thus giving a new focus in the second act, rather than using the second act simply as a time of fight and resolution, might be a significant factor in their continued popularity. The second quest which requires the assistance of the family of helpers also introduces a sense of the community working together to transform the status quo. One of the utopian features of literature as argued by Frederic Jameson is the expression of collectivity, through which a community is able to affirm itself (in Coupe 1997: 177). So for the first time there is a sense of the popular pantomime stories as utopian both because of the possibilities they suggest for individual transformation and for the possibility of affirmation of collective action and community.

The idea of adventure, a quest or a journey has been seen to be particularly important in pantomime. The hero sets out in search of something that has the potential to change his life and with which the audience can identify. According to psychological interpretations of fairy tales, the journey represents the development of the psyche to a new self-understanding and the quest for an object represents the internal quest for maturity of the hero. The audience identifies with the hero in the action and can learn the importance of growth, change and development. I'm not suggesting that pantomime writers and producers have the psychological growth of the audience in mind when planning their pantomimes, but that the reason certain stories, and particularly stories containing quests, journeys and happy endings, continue to resonate is because they appeal to the audience on more than one level.

In all the quest stories the hero undertakes a life-changing journey to a distant place through which he will achieve maturity. The quest becomes a rite of passage from one life stage to another. The journey can represent the physical journeying of merchants in a historical period, and the fact that marriage was not possible without sufficient income to support a wife and children. The journey also represents Dick's journey from adolescence to adulthood. His growing maturity and psychological development are rewarded with happiness represented to a patriarchal capitalist audience by wealth and marriage, and finally the possibility of transformation provides a utopian possibility.

Laurence Coupe talks about the importance of falling into, sailing across or being recovered from the sea in many classical myths. One could draw parallels, as Coupe does, with the idea of death followed by new life or with baptism in Christian ritual. Journeys across the sea and the destruction of boats by storms created by demons are a fairly common feature of pantomimes, thus linking gods and humans in the affairs of men. Robinson Crusoe and Dick Whittington both survive shipwrecks with magical help that enables them to breathe underwater before re-surfacing, reborn to make their fortunes. The imagery in *Mother Goose* also relates to Christian baptism as she bathes in a pool of water. However, since the pool was provided by the evil demon she turns into a glamorous version of her former self but with the cardinal sin of vanity. Her finer self is revealed only when, with the help of the good fairy and her family, she recognizes and discards her vanity. In alternative spiritual traditions water is assumed to represent the emotions, so in the journey through water there is not only the re-birthing of the body, but the cleansing of the emotions.

Other journeys undertaken by pantomime heroes involve the elements of air and earth as well as journeys into deserts and forests. I know of no baptisms of fire within the pantomime canon, though villains are sometimes punished by being thrown into fires or ovens (note the Christian symbolism of hellfire). Jack climbs the beanstalk and arrives in a land above the clouds. He is journeying to an unknown land which is a rite of passage in itself, but journeying into the sky carries symbolism too. There is the Christian symbolism of rising to a heavenly place from which the giant/Lucifer must be banished. There is also the symbolism of air as the intellectual cleanser, so

Jack must use his wits and his intellect rather than brute force to attain maturity. As Marina Warner reminds us, 'This trick from the Odyssey is literally one of the oldest in the book. The hero who lives by his wits survives in countless hard luck, Puss in Boots-style stories' (1994: 25). This is particularly important to boyish pantomime heroes, who are not only signified as young, but are often played by women, which highlights their youthful, androgynous lack of physical power.

Aladdin travels through the air as a result of the magic spells of the genies, travelling on a magic carpet, but first of all he is buried in the cave, in the bowels of the earth where Abanazar leaves him at the end of Act One. Again the symbolism of rebirth is plain, and again the escape/rebirth is accomplished with supernatural help. Aladdin has a second quest in Act Two; to rescue Princess Jasmine who has been stolen by Abanazar and imprisoned in his lair, another cave. Through Aladdin's intervention and the deployment of his magical assistants, Princess Jasmine is also rescued from a death in the earth and reborn to her new married life.

Red Riding Hood, *Snow White*, *Babes in the Wood* and *Sleeping Beauty* all contain journeys into forests. In the dark forest the traveller feels lonely and lost. She has forsaken her connection with home and is moving into a dark, dangerous and unknown territory. The symbolism of the impenetrable forest signifies the unconscious. However, in all cases there are places of safety and helpers to guide the hero. Red Riding Hood arrives at the dubious safety of her grandmother's cottage, where she must use her wits to defend herself, defeat the wolf and save her grandmother. This is often finally accomplished by the huntsman who becomes the hero of the piece through demonstrating that he can survive in the woods. Snow White is safe in the house of the seven dwarves, but still succumbs to her stepmother's trickery thereafter to be rescued by the Prince. The pattern that emerges is that the forest contains the dangers of the world or the unknown perils of the unconscious, and the hero/ine must use her/his wits in a mature way to survive outside the safety of the home and assimilate all sides of her/his personality. In both these cases, outside help is needed to save the female protagonists. The same is true of the Babes in the Wood who are protected by the animals of the forest before being rescued by Robin Hood, another male hero who has arrived at maturity and awareness of his unconscious so that he is able to survive in the woods.

All of the pantomime stories can signify the personal and sexual development of the main protagonist.[2] *Jack and the Beanstalk* and *Red Riding Hood* are stories particularly noted for their sexual or phallic imagery. Bruno Bettelheim, in a Freudian reading, relates the cow's inability to give milk to the separation of the child from the mother, Jack's journey up the beanstalk to the development of his own sexuality and the destruction of the giant to the Oedipal fantasy of killing the father. At the end of the story, in chopping down the beanstalk, Jack gives up phallic and oedipal fantasies and chooses to live in the real world. In *Little Red Riding Hood* there are many Freudian anxieties in the imagery which associates the Wolf with images of the father and then puts Red Riding Hood in bed with him. However, the principal sexual imagery is the oral imagery of the wolf's mouth which has been interpreted as an allegory of the child's aggressive feelings towards the mother's breast (Géza Róheim in Warner 1995: 182) and the orality involved in eating one's victims. Warner challenges this by suggesting that the orality might also be interpreted as revealing language or oral knowledge. The final part of the tale, when Red Riding Hood is cut from the wolf's stomach has images of pregnancy and birth, which bring back the idea of the adventure as a process of rebirth for the hero.

The three objects Jack steals from the Giant represent what he needs in life. The bag of gold is a finite resource, which soon runs out. The hen lays golden eggs, which signifies the production of goods and thus permanent financial security. The third item, the harp, is not necessary to economic satisfaction, but it represents the desire for beauty and art and may be considered a necessity for a happy and fulfilled life (Bettelheim 1976: 191).

Bruno Bettelheim develops a Freudian interpretation when he says that fairy stories speak to the unconscious and preconscious mind allowing the id, the ego and the superego to develop (Bettelheim 1991). The child sees life as dangerous, like the physical threats in the story. The stories allow the child to externalize the dangers she fears and overcome them. Maria Tatar suggests that the hearer recognizes cultural references and connects it to her own lived experiences (Tatar 2003: xv). The form and structure of the stories offers imagery which represents the psychological struggles that a child goes through in achieving maturity, but can also represent the ongoing struggles throughout life. In this way the stories are variously interpreted by people at different stages throughout their lives. For example, the struggle of a child to achieve maturity, a complex psychological development, becomes the journey of Jack up the Beanstalk and into the frightening and unknown territory of the Giant, or Red Riding Hood's journey into the woods, or Aladdin's exploits in the cave. As the hero overcomes the dangers on his journey, so the child identifies with the possibility of growth and change. Since there are always new obstacles to be faced and new difficulties to overcome in life, the stories remain relevant in adulthood. They provide a material example of the possibility of achieving new understandings and states of being. This assumes identification with the hero, who struggles against severe difficulties and always emerges victorious at the end of the quest.

In order to speak easily to the whole audience community, the interpretative codes in the character constructions are fairly easy to decipher, 'Kings and Queens as a rule represent parents; a prince or princess signifies the self. A deep, impenetrable forest symbolizes the dark, hidden depths of the soul' (Tatar 2003: 80). Other elements of the tales are disputed. For example, Bettelheim follows the Freudian argument that 'the wicked stepmother acts as the Janus face of the good mother, who can thus be saved and cherished in fantasy and memory, split from the bad mother' (in Warner 1995: 212). The idea is that as the child grows apart from the mother but continues to love and be dependent on her the child identifies different aspects of the relationship with the mother that are physically represented as two separate people.

On the other hand, Marina Warner argues that social history has to be read into the interpretation of fairy and folk tales. So the absent mother, generally through death in childbirth, was a common reality until relatively recently. In the contemporary world the split family through divorce is more common and step-siblings an everyday reality. Warner argues that in many cases it was the social reality that was expressed in the familial relationships of fairy tales and that continue to be relevant to audiences. In the majority of pantomimes the Dame is now a poor, single mother or widow struggling to bring up her sons alone and often on social welfare. In the case of Cinderella there is not only the relationship with a stepmother, but there is also step-sibling rivalry. This can be read either as a social reality that is replayed, or as a device to distance the sibling relationship allowing the expression of animosity and jealousy against a sibling. The child identifies with Cinderella as her feelings of self-worth develop with the knowledge that she will one day be discovered by her prince (which need not imply only marriage, but adulthood, confidence or success).

In most of the stories outlined above there is the requirement that change takes place in the position of the hero; Cinderella achieves happiness through marriage to the Prince, Aladdin wins wealth and the hand of Princess Jasmine as a result of defeating Abanazar. Other pantomimes contain reversals of fortune as Jack defeats the Giant to save the village, rescue the Princess and earn a fortune, and Dick Whittington becomes Lord Mayor of London. According to Northrop Frye's classification of narratives *Cinderella* falls into the *low mimetic mode* as the hero (or in this case heroine) 'is superior neither to other men nor to his environment...we respond to a sense of his common humanity' (Frye 1971 quoted in Coupe 1997: 161). This opens the possibility that the audience identifies with the hero and consequently with the possibility for change and transformation or, as Frye says when describing the Cinderella archetype, 'the incorporation of an individual very like the reader into the society aspired to by both, a society ushered in with a happy rustle of bridal gowns and banknotes' (Frye 1971 quoted in Coupe 1997: 162). Most other pantomimes follow this mode of potential transformation for the principal character, but the stories also contain a quest followed by the hero, such as Aladdin, Jack or Dick. Quest stories fall into the paradigm of 'hero myth' identified by Laurence Coupe (1997: 3) in which the protagonists are human but inspired (or fathered) by a deity. The majority of pantomime heroes, like Aladdin, have supernatural assistance to defeat a villain with supernatural powers and complete the quest.

It is also notable that in all the examples above there is more than one opportunity for scenic transformation and any number of opportunities for scenic extravagance, with magical transformations, storms, undersea worlds and exotic locations. Such transformations of position and fortune might be regarded as carnivalesque in the Bakhtinian sense of the word. Historically, carnivals were the opportunity for symbolic disruption and the subversion of authority, and the term carnivalization describes the subversion of authority and the introduction of alternatives within literature (Bakhtin 1981). In pantomime there are liberating and potentially transformative experiences within the audience participation and comedy (they will be discussed later), but significantly the stories contain the liberating influence suggested by the possibility of change and transformation. Laurence Coupe shows how mythology 'carries with it a promise of another mode of existence entirely, to be realised just beyond the present time and place' (Coupe 1997: 9). This has a clear relationship to design and scenic illusion in pantomime, with its sense of the exotic 'other' place, the transformative potential, and the presence of utopian possibilities in the creation of 'everytime', 'everyplace' and 'everyman'.

Bettelheim describes the positive effects of fairy stories on children's moral education. However, there is significant complexity in the way this occurs, since the role models fairy stories and pantomimes provide are not ideal. Jack kills the Giant, Aladdin is presented as a lazy good-for-nothing and Snow White repeatedly disobeys the dwarves' instructions. The events of the stories provide no consolation either, as vengeance is regularly practiced on the wicked. The family values the stories espouse are equally extreme containing wicked stepmothers and sisters, mistreatment of siblings, and girls are readily given to any wealthy man in marriage. However, the polarization of good and evil draws attention to moral values in an easily comprehensible way. Good wins, punishment is visited on the bad. The fact that pantomime or fairy stories always end happily demonstrates the possibility that even the meekest can succeed. The punishment of evil provides an incentive to goodness but also demonstrates the linking of justice, punishment and revenge.[3]

Jack, who steals from the Giant but rescues the princess and the villagers, is rewarded, Red Riding Hood who disobeys her mother's instructions learns from her mistakes and survives, the lazy Aladdin achieves wealth and fame, again justified by journeying into the unknown, defeating evil and rescuing the princess. The encouraging conclusions of the stories provide hope from the despairs of life. Justice will prevail against unfair treatment, and correct action will produce good results, the small and meek can triumph over the rich and powerful.

Many of the features discussed above can be seen in *Cinderella*. It presents a moral tale that good deeds will be rewarded (helping the old woman leads to the magical trip to the ball and consequent marriage to the Prince). It also shows that feelings of low self-worth, demonstrated physically by Cinderella's place by the hearth, can alter. People can identify with the transformation from low self-worth to high self-confidence and feelings of self-esteem. The ball might represent the step into the unknown that is rewarded with success and greater self-confidence. Alternatively, one might read the removal of Cinderella from acting as a servant in her family home to being the chattel of another man as a demonstration of the plight of women in a patriarchal society, while the desire for money and the link between money, marriage and happiness demonstrates the capitalist values (as well as the patriarchy) of the Victorians and our contemporary society.

It is important in all these potential readings that the stories are sufficiently distanced from real contemporary experience to allow various interpretations rather than a single didactic presentation. The place of the events is always an 'other' world and the events are in an 'other' ill-defined time. Exotic locations are common, and costume and design refer to many ages of history and mythology to create an 'other' time that both is, and is not, now. This is a feature of the history of folk and fairy tales which were first passed on in an oral tradition before being written down. The writer interpreted the stories in relation to contemporary events so that they contained influences and references to social and ideological norms. Now stories continue to develop and change providing an intertextual interaction between social history and the myth. In this way, fairy stories and myths reflect their societies and contribute to the sense of order in that society.

Myths and fairy stories need telling and retelling and will always be open to interpretation from a societal and an individual perspective. What they carry within them is the trace of the many retellings and re-interpretations that have preceded this moment, which includes Christian and pre-Christian imagery and symbolism,

Freudian and Jungian psycho-analysis and the political and social history of our culture. Each subsequent telling will build on all the previous experiences in a continual process of re-creation. As Coupe says, 'we may come to see that it is the task of myth constantly to imply, but always to resist, completion' (Coupe 1997:197). I would argue that the same could be said for pantomime which recreates stories that have become mythologized within our culture. Moreover, within pantomime it is not only the stories that are presented both as familiar and different, but the pantomime conventions and many other areas of the performance rely on the same dialectic 'of same and other, of memory and desire, of ideology and utopia, of hierarchy and horizon, and of sacred and profane' (Coupe 1997:197).

Notes

1. A McGuffin is an object that acts as a catalyst for events, such as the lamp in *Aladdin*, which can produce the genie, be stolen and recovered, or the treasure map in *Robinson Crusoe*, which is also the subject of everyone's interest and desire.
2. There are interpretations of *Jack and the Beanstalk*, *Cinderella*, *Snow White* and *Sleeping Beauty* in Bettelheim (1991). Other theorists such as Zipes and Warner, while accepting some parts of Bettelheim's arguments, argue that context and social history must be read more strongly into the interpretation.
3. Many pantomimes do not include the vengeance that is apparent in fairy stories; it is not politically correct. Rather, villains are magically made good, made to marry the Dame or banished.

6

PLAYING WITH DISTANCE IN PANTOLAND[1]

Fairy:	Back, grisly monster, to your lair!
Fleshcreep:	Always the same – it isn't fair!
	Just when I'm getting into my stride
	She enters from the other side
	And always in the nick of time
Fairy:	Of course I do – It's Panto time! (Chissick and Horlock 1987)

Having discussed the contexts and stories of pantomimes I will move on to consider the performance of pantomime. Significantly, the stories are not told simply or using 'realistic' conventions as they might be in children's theatre, but are told from a distanced position by performers who take part in the telling, who enjoy and are aware of the pantomime conventions and who refer to the world of the audience as well as the world of the story.

Pantoland is not the place where the story of pantomime takes place; that might be Nottingham or Peking or the Village of Much Giggling. Pantoland is the theatrical world where the performers exist 'as themselves' and from which they tell the story. It exists while the characters/performers are performing within the confines of the theatre and the performance time. Within pantoland both performers and audience remain aware of the pantomime conventions, the audience, stage management and musicians. As I mentioned above, performers acknowledge the shared space of the theatre and the other people present within it. Within pantoland performers can refer to rehearsals and other performances of this or any other pantomime and to the world outside the theatre. But pantoland is a mythical place where, despite the performers giving an impression that the audience is seeing their 'real' character, they are still performing. It is a place where everyone is always having fun, despite reminding us of the hard work they're doing repeating the show: 'it's this twice-daily, that's what it is!' (Dame in *Babes in the Wood* Sadler's Wells 1994). And Panto-time is the time framework of performance, season and convention in which, like Brigadoon appearing out of the mist, pantoland comes briefly into existence.

Pantoland is a performance frame within which the story is told by performers who become characters in a story, but who also exist as comic or anarchic personas who comment on the story, the performance, the perceived world of the performers and the audience's lived reality. Some performers and some characters can manage the interchange between the two worlds more effectively than others. However, this play with distance through the exposure of the performance frame, the revelation that the performance is constructed, and the implication by the performers that it is not well-constructed but that they're having fun, provides a continuous reminder that the pantomime is fantasy performance and a constant disruption of the distance between audience and story.

In pantomime there are many events that occur throughout the performance and through which the frame is revealed. The first occurrence of framing the story is at the start of the performance when the immortals appear. In many cases the Fairy is the first to appear, and she introduces the fact that a story is about to be told. She carries out the same function as the 'Once upon a time' of British fairy story tradition,[2] or 'There was and there was not, there was a boy….' which is one of the formulaic beginnings favoured by Armenian storytellers (Carter xi). In pantomime the opening scene frames the story in the same way that these formulaic openings do, but it also sets out the rules of the event. There is usually a little audience participation so that the audience knows what is expected of it, there is usually a brief reference to the plot that is about to be disclosed, and there is usually some comment about being in a theatre or about pantomime itself.

In *Jack and the Beanstalk* at the Queen's Theatre Barnstaple Lettuce, the fairy welcomed the audience to the theatre:

> Welcome mortals, boys and girls
> It's that special time of year
> When here at the Queen's Theatre
> It's your chance to boo and cheer (Hudd 2002–3).

The fairy godmother in *Cinderella* at Eastbourne began:

> Oh my goodness gracious, it surely can't be
> Hundreds of faces all looking at me.
> I hope I remember how I should respond
> 'Cos it's been a while since I took up the wand (Jordan 2003–4)

Cinderella's Fairy Godmother concluded the opening scene by introducing the pantomime itself after a brief opportunity for audience participation:

> That's perfect then, thank you so much for your time
> Now we can start off this year's pantomime
> It begins in a forest in a clearing that's there
> Where someone important is taking the air (Jordan 2003–4).

The frontcloth then flies out to reveal the village where Dandini and the chorus are discussing the royal hunt and the story begins.

In both cases the opening words are about being in the theatre with some reference to the show that is to follow. Hudd immediately reminds the audience that it is expected to take part in the events to come, while Jordan leaps into the fiction by introducing a facet of the fairy's character with the reference to the fairy's wand and some likely ineptitude. Both demonstrate awareness of the event and the presence of the audience. Hudd does this by direct speech, 'Welcome, boys and girls', and by mentioning the place, the Queen's Theatre. Jordan accomplishes the same effect with the words 'hundreds of faces all looking at me' which demonstrates awareness of the audience, and then at the end 'now we can start off this year's pantomime' shows awareness of the genre. In a similar fashion, Abanazar opened *Aladdin* at Salisbury Playhouse with the words 'Wake up fans, settle down, pay attention, the pantomime's started....' (Reid and Thomas 2003–4). These are all extended and less formulaic versions of 'Once upon a time' setting up the frame within which the story will be told.

At the end of the performance there is a concluding speech that draws events to a close which, in storytelling produces some wonderful verbal flourishes. 'I was there and drank mead and wine; it ran down my mustache, but did not go into my mouth' recorded at the end of 'The Armless Maiden' (Carter xi) tells the listener that the tale is over, while also implying an authority to tell the tale, but subverting that with the suggestion that he didn't swallow the drink! Armenian storytellers finish with 'From the sky fell three apples, one to me, one to the storyteller, and one to the person who entertained you' (Carter xii) which implies thanks for the story but fails to suggest truth. In pantomime the walkdown/wedding and the final couplets[3] serve the same function; closing the performance with the equivalent of 'and they all lived happily ever after'. The physical action of the walkdown is a clear sign to the audience of the end of the performance, and the presence of the lovers in their wedding costumes signals the future happiness of the young couple. After all, in pantoland marriage can only bring joy and happiness, but the frequent presence of other couples such as Dame and Emperor getting married to each other challenges the fantasy of the happy ending.

In many pantomimes the final set of rhyming couplets follows the walkdown and completes the frame opened by the immortals at the start.

Roy Hudd's *Jack and the Beanstalk* concludes with:

Jack	Our story now is over
Jill	And so goodbye to you
Baron	I'll leave you with a cheerio
Stink	And I'll have one last 'Boo'
Audience	Boo!
Jill	We hope that you've enjoyed our show
Lettuce	And you've all had a ball
Jack	So now we all would like to say
Foxy	Merry Christmas one and all (Hudd 2002–3).

At Potters Bar *Aladdin* closed with:

Pong	So now our story's over and that villain is no more
Genie of Ring	Although it took two genies to settle up the score

Princess	The Opera House is gleaming thanks to all Aladdin's money
Emperor	Next month I'm due to play the lead in Mozart's *Don Giovanni*
Wishee	Now we've got the royal seal I'm big in smalls you see
Genie of Lamp	And I've got myself a little place in Memphis Tennessee
Abanazaar	Now I am a goody, no longer do I tiff
Twankey	And he's bringing out a Christmas song with squeaky clean Sir Cliff
Aladdin	We've had a great adventure that's been filled with song and laughter
	Now prince Aladdin and his bride
All	....!⁴(Jordan 2003–4)

In these speeches the focus of the writers is apparent. Hudd gives the audience one last opportunity to join in while saying goodbye and reminding the spectators of their everyday lives with the reference to Christmas (or New Year later in the season). Jordan refers to events in the story and winds up loose threads with one-line gags while completing the frame in a traditional fashion 'our story's over' and 'happily ever after' (implied in the blank line to be filled in on opening night).

Figure 19: Fairy Bow Belles in *Dick Whittington* (Plymouth: E&B Productions, 1992). Photograph by Eric Thompson

This sort of framing of the story in the style of fairy stories is just the tip of the iceberg as far as pantomime is concerned. The references to the audience and the pantomime above are reflexive reminders of genre and place, but there are a whole range of devices used in pantomime that reflexively remind the audience that it is attending a performance while at the same time continuing to tell the story. In a performance there are many elements that can be referenced as a reminder of the act of performance, the performer (rather than the character) throws attention on her/himself, the script, the rehearsal, the theatre space or the performance itself. The reminder of the presence of performers and actors in the room together draws attention to the materiality, the liveness of performance and brings awareness of the potential for disruption. Reflexivity necessarily involves the audience in play with distance, as the distance from identification with the story is increased. Instead the audience is allowed to share in what is signified as a unique experience and is drawn into the perceived anarchy of the performance world, or pantoland, that is revealed.

A simple device that frames the story is direct address to the audience by the performers. The performer has to step outside the pretence of a coherent 'real' onstage world in order to acknowledge the audience's presence. The immortals constantly do this, especially when encouraging the audience to boo and cheer, as in figures 19 and 20, which show the Fairy and the villain in direct address to the audience. The comedy characters also address the audience directly, and in some pantomimes other characters address the audience too. For example,

Figure 20: Villain addressing the audience in *Jack and the Beanstalk* (Salisbury Playhouse, 2004). Photograph by Robert Workman

Figure 21: Les Dawson throwing sweets to the children in the audience during his opening spot in *Dick Whittington* (Plymouth Theatre Royal: E&B Productions, 1992). Photograph by Eric Thompson

Aladdin is likely to rely on the audience to tell him to rub his magic ring or to point to the magic lamp. In order to give the audience license to speak to him it is likely that he will have had some earlier interaction with the audience. The effect

Figure 22: Des O'Connor speaking to a child in the audience in *Cinderella* (Plymouth Theatre Royal: E&B Productions, 1990). Photograph by Eric Thomson

of this interaction is to involve the audience as a co-conspirator in the telling of the story.

Most important of participatory moments are those where the plot cannot be completed unless the audience takes part as required. These can be created in any pantomime and are also apparent in many children's musicals, but the best known are those in *Cinderella* (telling Buttons where the Ugly Sisters have imprisoned Cinderella) or in *Peter Pan* (clapping to show they believe in fairies and saving Tinkerbell's life).[5] Other opportunities for audience involvement occur in the opening spots of several characters during which they address the audience and call for participation. Figure 21 shows Les Dawson during his opening spot in *Dick Whittington* in 1992 'doing the giveaways' or throwing sweets to the children in the audience, each item accompanied by an appropriate gag. The interaction of audience and performer draws attention to the performance space and the presence of the audience and so acts reflexively to distance the audience from involvement with the story, to draw the audience into an attachment with the comedy character and to create the opportunity for this to be a unique performance. This is especially true in figure 22, in which Des O'Connor is speaking to a child from the audience. The performance is unique because of this particular interaction, but the interaction clearly breaks the performance frame physically as well as metaphorically as O'Connor lies in front of the band on the pit wall in close contact with the audience.

At other times the physical world of the pantomime expands to include the band in the pit, who the performers speak to. During the shooting of water pistols over the audience in Eastbourne the band members put up umbrellas to protect themselves from the water. The 50p gag, performed in 2003 at Birmingham Hippodrome, included the musical director from whom the comic borrowed 50p (in Manchester it was £5). In *Dick Whittington* at Plymouth Theatre Royal the musical director was asked for the key. His mistake about whether that meant the key to the shop or the key to the song was followed by a commentary on the joke: 'and it's not even funny!' At Stratford East Uncle Robert[6], the musical director in the pit, was repeatedly referred to, while at Guildford the band were introduced with the comment 'I like the simple things in life, musicians' before a series of gags about each of the musicians in turn.

On some occasions, and generally as the pantomime wears on, the comedian and percussionist will often start having a game in which the comedian attempts to catch the percussionist with the wrong stick or instrument, or by fluffing the cue for an effect. Martin Waddington describes it as follows:

> You have to have an elephantine memory for what an actor's going to do in his routine, not to miss things and to be consistent. Then, of course, the actors turn round and take malicious delight in trying to catch the percussionist out, and that becomes a joke in itself. We had the joke with the sausages. In the kitchen scene the sausages had a life of their own, and the actor hit them back down, only he sort of half-hit them, and poor Graham (the percussionist) had to decide whether he was going to make the rim-shots or not. And the audience loved that. To them it's a glimpse behind the scenes, a glimpse of the relation between the actor and the musician and the fun that we are having in the show. (Waddington)

Kerry Michael director of the pantomime at Stratford East commented that while he was happy to have characters address the audience directly and to include the band as part of the pantomime world, he preferred that performers did not extend their ad libs to include the backstage world. This appears to be a minority position as references are made to all sorts of activities in the backstage world. For example, at the Tron, Glasgow (2003–4), the audience was asked, 'Would you like to hear a song? Well, I'm going to sing it anyway to cover the sound of the set being changed' (*Cinderella* 2003). At Sadler's Wells the audience was encouraged to join in with the song 'If you're happy and you know it clap your hands' with the comment 'Everyone will join in. At least we hope they do because they've got a lot of scenery to shift up here' (*Babes in the Wood* 1994). More subtle was the comment at Stratford East (2003) where the appearance of the words for the songsheet (which was sung at a moment of crisis to progress the story rather than at the end of the performance) prompted the comment 'Why doesn't that surprise me'. This was an indirect reference to the presence of the backstage world which could be interpreted as the magic of pantoland and didn't disrupt a child's belief in the fantasy world.

In most performances the presence of crew and Deputy Stage Manager (DSM) sitting in the wings and cueing set changes, lighting and sound cues are often referred to. Dave Benson Phillips at Birmingham Hippodrome commented from the stage to the wings, referring to the audience, 'We've got a funny bunch today'. The most common gag is that a member of crew or stage management hands something to a performer, allowing their hand to appear within the proscenium arch. The performer then says 'Look at that, a stage hand!' Another device is for things to appear to have gone wrong providing a comedy moment. At Manchester Opera House a ringing phone appeared but kept on ringing after being picked up so that Brian Conley could shout, 'I've picked it up now', while Berwick Kaler at York Theatre Royal drew attention to the DSM by pointing out to her that 'It's all right, they [the audience] know you're there'.

In these examples the pantomime world includes the backstage area and the people in it and audience and performers share in the conspiracy that the audience is suspending its disbelief in relation to the story that the performers are telling. The audience and the comedian are joined in laughter about the inadequacies or simplicity of the stage machinery. Often the stage management and crew are the recipients of jokes and detrimental comment (which they have no choice but to take in good part). In some of these cases the usual position of the performer speaking to the audience supported by all onstage is reversed as the performer and audience are joined in a complicitous act of laughter towards the production. This is an effective device as it reflexively reveals the frame surrounding the story, it causes laughter and it starts to create an impression, however illusory, of what the performers' world is like. It sets up the two myths of pantomime: that the performance is rubbish and anyone could do it; and that the performers are having great fun simply enjoying themselves in a free-flowing anarchic way. Both of these features were particularly apparent in *Mother Goose's Silver Jubilee* at York Theatre Royal. Berwick Kaler, playing the Dame but also the man who had written the script, repeatedly referred to the pantomime as 'rubblish'. The sense of chaos and things going wrong is linked to the fun of pantomime and often to cod-corpsing.[7]

Onstage awareness of the pantomime conventions (such as audience participation, presence of the immortals, rhyming couplets, thigh-slapping principal boys and extremely fortuitous coincidence) is demonstrated in many cases. At the end of the first scene David Leonard as the villain at York Theatre Royal (2003) raged at the DSM, 'I don't like fairies, I don't like rhyming couplets and I don't like being first on'. The conventions are referred to more directly, for example, by Julian Clary, at Birmingham Hippodrome (2003), who told the audience, 'You're required to join in, no one knows why but it passes the time'. At York Theatre Royal (2003) Jack said of the Principal Boy, 'It really is a pantomime and to prove it here comes a handsome stranger' and no principal boy can slap her/his thigh without appearing to ironically refer to the pantomime convention.

A pantomime convention that is frequently referred to in asides is the cross-dressing of dame, ugly sisters and principal boy.[8] 'Well, that's what I call a man' was said of the Principal Boy at York. Other comments might be 'Look at the legs on him!' or 'He's a manly man!' The Dame asides that draw attention to her gender often occur when she is being seduced. For example, on Elizabeth Wood's video *The Pantomime Dame* we find the exchange:

Seducer	Marry me, you'll get a surprise
Dame (to audience)	Not half the surprise he'll get

A final example from *Aladdin* at the Yvonne Arnaud Theatre 1992–3 draws ironic attention to the cast size as Wishee Washee calls, 'Entire populace of Peking come hither' and is joined by five dancers and eight children. This is similar to the possibly apocryphal story from *Ali Baba and the Forty Thieves*, which is said to include the line: 'You four come in and all you others wait outside'. To enjoy these references the audience is required to know the story and the pantomime conventions so that it feels included in the gag and the pantomime world. In all these examples the important thing is the complicity between audience and comedian, who steps out of the story to become a watcher of the pantomime, conspiring with the audience in commenting on the performance, revealing the frame of performance and increasing the distance between audience and story.

In other examples the pantomime world extends again to encompass the script and the rehearsal period. A frequent comment is 'It wasn't like that at rehearsals'. At Plymouth Theatre Royal the line 'I'll look for Alice and you can look for Dick' brought a laugh which was followed by the comment 'the next line was cut at rehearsals'. At Manchester Opera House, 'I must go and look at my script' provided an exit line, while during the ghost scene at the Anvil, Basingstoke, one character asked, 'How did you know it was me' to which the reply came, 'It was in the script'. Slightly more subtle was the following sequence in *Cinderella* at Eastbourne:

Marj [Ugly sister]	Invitations? Not invitations to a Royal Ball?
Cinders	Yes. How did you guess?
Marj	Well, you being called Cinderella was a bit of a clue (Jordan 2003–4).

In all of these the audience is being reminded that the performance is written, rehearsed and performed many times, but in the final example reference is also made to the widespread knowledge of the story within our culture. This reveals one of the features of pantomime; that the story is known and no pretence to originality in the story or the conventions is made. It is in the framing of the story and the comedy that the performance is signified as unique.

Finally, the time frame can be further extended to include reference to other pantomimes by the same performers at the same venue in other years. This plays on the continuity of casting that is a feature of some pantomimes, where, for example, a particular performer will be advertised as 'Back by Popular Demand'. This was particularly apparent at York Theatre Royal's 2003 production in which Berwick Kaler asked the audience, 'Do you remember him from last year?' with reference to a chorus member, who was then singled out for the rest of the performance.

These examples demonstrate the variety of devices used in pantomime to keep the two worlds, that of the story and that of the theatrical presentation, simultaneously in focus throughout the performance.[9] But why is this important? Well, first because the story is not presented simply and directly, as it might be in a performance for children alone. The constant play with the performance frame might be one of the significant factors in defining pantomime and separating it from other forms of Christmas entertainment. There is reflexivity in other forms of theatre, especially musicals (for example, the show within a show of musicals like *Cabaret*), and there is often direct address and narration (as in *Into the Woods*), but there is rarely the degree of exploration of the performance frame that there is in pantomime.[10]

Any theatrical occasion involves the audience in awareness of at least two simultaneous levels of 'reality'. In Karen Gaylord's analysis the outer frame of performance includes promotional material, the type of venue, previous experience of venue and genre and the knowledge of expected behaviour within the theatre. This provides the frame within which the individual audience members suspend their disbelief and engage with the performance that takes place within the playing space. The inner frame demarcates the playing space (Gaylord 1983: 136). As Susan Bennett remarks, 'it is the intersection of these two frames which forms the spectator's cultural understanding and experience of theatre' (Bennett 1997: 2). While some forms of theatre (particularly naturalism in the twentieth century) attempt to reduce awareness of this frame, many forms of theatre, including pantomime, explore the frame of performance, demonstrating theatre's lack of verisimilitude and reminding the audience of the outer frame.

Bertolt Brecht encouraged the audience to distance itself from identification with a story in order that it should maintain a conscious and intellectual engagement with the events presented. The audience was expected to be aware of the performer demonstrating the role and telling the story, rather than believing that the actor *was* the character. 'The peculiarity of the artist watching himself, which is an artistic and ingenious act of self-alienation, prevents the total identification of the spectator.....and brings forth a wonderful distance from the events' (Brecht quoted in Fischer Lichte 1997: 36). But the tradition of the creation of distance in comedy performance began much earlier. Clowns are renowned as characters who have played with the performance frame for comic effect throughout many ages of theatre. The transition from Clown to Dame as principal character and driver of pantomime in the 1880s makes a link between Clown and Dame that is still apparent in pantomime performance. John H. Towsen remarked that clowns often step out of the play and comment upon it 'appearing to be as much a part of the audience as of the drama' (Towsen 1976: 31). He goes on to say that the clown was both a popular comic actor taking part in the drama and a fool free to ignore dramatic conventions. In pantomime the comedians are characters in the story and are free to step out and comment on it, and they are also free to comment on the conventions of performance. The immortals have less freedom, though they do interact with the audience.

Daphna Ben Chaim discusses the way twentieth-century performance has experimented with the distance between audience and performer in *Distance in the Theatre: The Aesthetics of Audience Response* (1984). Although pantomime does not fall into the categories of performance discussed, some of the issues are relevant. She suggests that the emotional distance between performer and audience is reduced by a semblance of reality and increased by separation from reality. 'The aesthetic tension between these two opposing tendencies constitutes distance and provides the conditions for the variability of distance' (Ben Chaim 1984: 67). In pantomime the distance varies as some performers, generally the comics, speak directly to the audience, while others, the hero and heroine and the minor characters, maintain the illusion of a fourth wall even when soliloquizing in speech or song and facing directly out front. This is particularly true of the comics, the villain and the fairy who constantly negotiate between interacting with other characters, direct speech without participation and the moments of participation. There are moments of playing 'truth' and moments of interaction, moments when the audience is drawn into the story and moments when it is distanced by comedy and participation.

But the issue of emotional distance is more complex in pantomime than the formulation above suggests. It may be true that the audience feels closer to the story in moments of 'realism' and further removed in reflexive moments. But at those moments when identification with the story is distanced, a new relationship is established with the performer who appears to be revealing her/himself as a co-conspirator with the audience through direct speech or interaction. The distance increases between audience and story, but decreases between audience and comedy performer. It is this complicity between comedian or Dame and audience that gives the audience a sense of being part of an anarchic world in which the performance is simultaneously mocked and enjoyed, in which the world of the performers is revealed to be one of fun, laughter and accidental success, in which perfectly timed comedy routines are perceived to be fortuitous and unique to that performance. The performance frame in pantomime is revealed not only to distance the audience from the story, but to draw the audience into complicity with the comedians in the perception of the performance world, pantoland, as unique, original, anarchic and fun.

The single most important element in contemporary pantomime is generally agreed to be the narrative drive of the story. However, despite the importance of the story, just as in fairy stories and in many forms of theatre before the rise of 'naturalism' in the twentieth century, there is a theatrical frame within which the story is told. Although the events of the story are acted 'realistically' by characters who play the truth of each situation, albeit in a heightened fashion, there are constant reminders throughout the performance that the pantomime is a theatrical artifice, not least the set and costumes. This is similar to fairy tales, where

> the form of the fairy tale is not usually constructed so as to invite the audience to share a sense of lived experience. The 'old wives' tale' positively parades its lack of verisimilitude (Carter xi).

Although producers, writers and directors stress the importance of the narrative drive in keeping the interest of both children and adults, and producing empathy with the hero, the interest for many people is not in what happens, which they already know, but, as in folk tradition, how the story is told. The inclusion of the audience as co-conspirators in the comedy and as vocal participants in the action makes them complicit in the telling and provides an experience different from most other theatre or television experiences with which the audience might be familiar.

Finally, an image is presented of the world of the performers that is fun, anarchic, sometimes hard work (references to the number of performances), and that the performers are spontaneous and witty, but that they are just ordinary people like the audience members. Revealing the world of performance draws the audience into this world, the world of pantoland rather than that of the story, to share in the fun. Of course, pantoland is also a construct, a fiction, but it provides an experience of involvement and the illusion that the 'real' performer is revealed.

Notes

1. A shorter version of this chapter was first published in *New Theatre Quarterly* (2005). I am grateful to the editors for permission to publish this extended version.'
2. I refer to the traditions of storytelling and fairy and folk tales because many of the stories of pantomime are drawn from such tales. Some of the elements of storytelling, notably the framing of performance and the idea that it is not the story, but the telling of the story that is important, are apparent in pantomime.
3. This is one of the features generally included in pantomime when each character contributes to the brief epilogue, but which is now sometimes replaced in commercial pantomimes with a curtain speech by the star.
4. One of the traditions of pantomime is that it is unlikely for the final line of the final couplets to be spoken before the first performance. It is therefore not always included in the script, sometimes the whole speech is withheld, on other occasions it is written but not spoken. It is apparent from the rhyming scheme what the words should be: 'live happily ever after'.
5. Opportunities for and effects of audience participation are discussed more fully in chapter 8.
6. The musical director is generally one of the pantomime 'family' referred to by their first name with status and familiarity conferred by the prefix Aunt or Uncle. For many years I was Auntie Millie to pantomime audiences. However, it is still rare to find women musical directors especially in commercial pantomime.
7. Corpsing is the act of laughing inadvertently during a scene onstage. Cod-corpsing is when such moments that sometimes occur by accident are planned, in the case of pantomime they are often extremely entertaining.
8. This will be addressed more fully in the chapter on gender and cross-dressing below.
9. I also notice in re-reading this chapter that the number of references to Berwick Kaler's work at York Theatre Royal is instructive. That pantomime, one of the funniest I've seen, is packed with reflexive references. The link between effective comedy, complicity between audience and performer and reflexivity is worthy of further study.
10. *A Funny Thing Happened on the Way to the Forum* and the stage version of *The Rocky Horror Show* might be an exception to this rather sweeping generalization. Based on the use of audience participation, framing and cross-dressing either of these could be argued to share this feature of pantomime.

7

Is She or Isn't He? Gender and Identity

I'm a love lorn woman, which is, I'm a widder
To be disposed of to the highest bidder.
I'm not a new lot, truly, but every particle
Is perfectly sound. I'm a genuine article.
(*Puss in Boots* 1882 quoted in Robbins 2002:169)

One of the areas where the play with distance, or the lack of pretence at 'realism' is most clearly apparent is in the presence of cross-dressed characters. The quotation above is typical of pantomime dames, men dressed as women who make no attempt to create an illusion of womanhood. They lay claim to being 'genuine' or 'womanly' as an ironic statement that contradicts the facts that are plain for the audience to see. Dames present themselves as love-lorn, or nowadays, sex-starved, with a very high opinion of their own charms, but they are always at least middle-aged and becoming aware that their charms are fading and that they may remain lonely. This gives rise to the desperation that figures in the dame's comedy interactions with other men. This feature of the dame has been constant since 'she' became a regular feature of pantomime in the 1880s. A 1922 dame in *Robinson Crusoe* introduced herself: 'I'm Mrs Crusoe, a lonely widow, as you can plainly see. With not even a gentleman lodger to keep me company' (Robbins 2002: 188) while in 2002 Widow Twankey proclaimed:

> Now I've been very sad since the death of my husband Willie Twankey......Yes, I've had this ring on my finger since my husband died and I haven't had it off since. Now that I'm back in the marriage market I owe it to the men of Potters Bar to look my best at all times. (Jordan 2002: 7).

Similarly, Widow Twankey in Salisbury explains her loneliness and sadness through comedy:

> Oh dear dead Mr Twanky! [*sic*] He went off to the big launderette in the sky 10 years back and I miss him like a spin wash misses the rinse cycle, like fluffy towels

miss fabric conditioner! But life goes on and I'm looking for a new love to push the buttons on my tumble dryer. Any takers? (Reid and Thomas 2003: 12).

The presence of cross-dressed characters is a useful and constant reminder of the performance frame. The characters are clearly represented with two genders, one in pantoland and another in the story. So the pantomime dame refers through innuendo or irony to 'his' maleness within pantoland asides and comedy, while the maternal dame playing truthful loving scenes with 'her' sons exists within the story. The dame's relationship with the audience is clearly that of a man in a dress, but one who indulges in a pretence of complicity with the 'girls' in the audience and flirtation with the men. Both men and women can identify with, and laugh at, aspects of the grotesque character being presented, while sympathizing with the single mother bringing up her children.

There is generally less reference by the principal boy to 'his' gender, except through physical gestures of outdated, melodramatic machismo, though others, especially the comics, refer to 'him' and 'his manliness' in ironic terms. At the same time the princess falls in love with 'him' and the dame refers to 'her son' within the story. More important in the presentation of the principal boy is the absence of manhood, so that the character can be read comically as a girl in drag, sexually as an available woman, transformatively as a youth approaching maturity (which links to the idea of transformation in the stories of pantomime), positively as a role model for both girls and boys, and androgynously as neither male nor female but as an asexual innocent.

There is a long history of cross-dressing in the theatre, that will be traced briefly below, but the question of why these anachronistic remainders of the Victorian age are still so important in pantomime performance is the fundamental one here, especially as the presence of the female principal boy is threatened by male stars. I will argue that there are many reasons for the continued presence of cross-dressing in pantomime, not least that the performance frame, which has been shown to be important both to the comedy and to the audience interaction with the performance, continues to be exposed through their presence. Other reasons for their continued presence relate to the balance of casting that would be male dominated without the female principal boy, the positive active role for a woman in the case of the principal boy, and the opportunities for comic confusion opened up by both cross-dressed characters, but particularly the dame. But both these characters have a further function in adding to the confusion of reversals and transgressions that links pantomime with the anarchic fun of the carnivalesque. Finally, the fact that gender identity is infinitely variable and complex and that it is culturally performed can be exposed by these representations that tend to extreme characterizations of both male and female.

The pantomime dame is a comic character, bawdy, vulgar, vain, quick-witted and irrepressible, but the character must be based on truth to elicit sympathy and identification from the audience. It is usually played by a comedian or comedy actor who has extended his comedy by cross-dressing, rather than by a drag artist attempting to hide the fact that he is a man. The dame connects with the audience on two levels: as a mother figure talking about family problems and social issues;

as a man pretending to be a woman to an audience who sees through the pretence and shares the joke. This type of performance has become an accepted part of British pantomime, in which the pantomime dame replaced the clown in the latter part of the nineteenth century and continues to this day. The character is generally that of a working-class woman, often struggling to make ends meet. There is the opportunity for physical comedy and pathos as well as social comment and the offering of 'girlish' confidences. The function of the dame in contemporary pantomime is to drive the story, create the comedy and to interact with all age groups in the audience, but also, as discussed above, to draw the audience into a complicitous relationship in the creation of comedy and telling the story.

Roger Baker, in *Drag* (1994), identifies the appearance of the female impersonator as a comic figure at the end of the seventeenth century. There was not a consistent or continuous tradition of female impersonation until the middle of the nineteenth century, but there is a separate tradition of the characterization of elderly or middle-aged women as figures of fun that can be traced back centuries, whether played by men or women. Mrs Noah in the Chester cycle of the Mystery Plays[1] might be seen as a precursor of the pantomime dame. The character provides a comic sub-plot to the story, in which she is represented as a nag, a busybody and a gossip. She takes part in noisy knockabout comedy and was probably played by a man since women were officially banned from the British stage until the late seventeenth century. These characters play broad comedy that anticipates the tradition of nagging wives and mothers-in-law who still inhabit stand-up comedy, situation comedy and pantomime, but they also indulge in physical comedy.

Roger Baker argues that many female characters of the Restoration period, such as Lady Wishfort in *The Way of the World* (Congreve 1700) and Mrs Malaprop in *The Rivals* (Sheridan 1775) follow in this tradition (Baker 1994: 162). Victorian examples might include Lady Bracknell in *The Importance of Being Earnest* (Wilde 1895) and Katisha in *The Mikado* (Gilbert and Sullivan 1885). Meanwhile, in nineteenth-century pantomime, the clown was still the central character, although the clown sometimes disguised himself as a woman in the Harlequinade (Pickering 1993: 58), but audiences did have the opportunity to see pantomime dames. Pickering cites an actor by the name of Harper who played the cook in *Dick Whittington* in 1731. Samuel Simmons played Mother Goose in 1806, a performance in which Joseph Grimaldi appeared, and in 1814 Grimaldi played Queen Rondabellyona (Pickering 1993: 57) and later Dame Cecily Suet in *Harlequin Whittington* (Baker 1994: 166).

The marked change began in the music halls in the second half of the nineteenth century as comedians such as E. W. Marshall introduced drag numbers into their music hall repertoire (Baker 1994: 168). Since comedians performed several spots in a show, often as different comic characters, playing a scene in drag afforded them the opportunity to increase the variety of what they offered. In the mid-nineteenth century dame figures sang popular, comic or pathetic songs, often making fun of the marital dilemmas of middle-aged women. These performers didn't present themselves as youthful or glamorous; generally they used a bonnet or grey wig with a pinafore or shawl as props for the act. They also allowed their trousers to be seen, making plain that they were men performing as women. The main difference between these routines and those that appeared in pantomime was that they were for different audiences. At the time the music hall was for a working-class audience, while pantomime included a middle-class family audience.

Although the appearance of comedy dames in pantomime was quite widespread from the 1860s, it was not until 1881 at the Theatre Royal Drury Lane that Augustus Harris booked Arthur Roberts as Mrs Crusoe in *Robinson Crusoe* (Baker 1994: 169), and the practice became firmly established. In 1882 *Sinbad the Sailor* had Herbert Campbell as Mrs Crusoe and Vesta Tilley as Captain Tra-la-la (Baker 1994: 174). Dan Leno, who is often regarded as the precursor of contemporary pantomime dames, first appeared in this role at Drury Lane in 1888 as the naughty aunt. Later, he often worked as a double act with Herbert Campbell, which meant that he sometimes played male characters to Campbell's dame. In 1894, in *Dick Whittington*, Campbell played Eliza the Cook to Leno's Idle Jack. This pattern was reversed in *Bluebeard* in 1901, when Leno played dame (Sister Anne) to Campbell's Bluebeard (Baker 1994 and Frow 1985).

What becomes apparent from descriptions of Leno's dame is that he was both an excellent comedian and an observant actor. A contemporary critic wrote that Leno's dame was not a burlesque but a well-observed representation that relied on the speed and absurdity of the comic patter (Baker 1994: 173). At this point, the dame was still a working-class woman in ordinary working clothes with grey hair firmly tied back in a top knot. This look pre-dated Dan Leno and lasted well into the twentieth century. Pictures of Arthur Askey as dame in the 1960s conform to this identity, and some contemporary dames such as Jack Tripp show this derivation in their interpretation of the dame. See, for example, figure 21 in chapter 6, in which Les Dawson wears the mid-calf-length skirt, apron, mob cap and hair in a bun derived from this tradition. At the same time speciality clothes were introduced for particular moments in the pantomime. For example, in *Mother Goose* a glamorous costume is needed as Mother Goose steps out of the magic pool, and there is usually a more extravagant costume for the walkdown finale as in figure 23 which shows Widow Twankey in her finale costume at Salisbury Playhouse (2003).

Arthur Askey, as dame, wore only a base make-up rather than the exaggerated female make-up of other dames. He believed very strongly that the comedy came from identification of the man in drag and that the dame should make no attempt to impersonate a woman (Wood 1982). Other pantomime dames throughout the century have varied opinions about the costume, although most agree that there should be no attempt to pretend to be a woman. However, it is general practice for the first costume to consist of a simple dress and apron as the dame establishes her role and for subsequent outfits to be increasingly outrageous. At the same time speciality or comic clothes are introduced at particular moments in the pantomime, such as Les Dawson's outfit for setting sail to Morocco in *Dick Whittington* (1992) seen in figure 24.

In the first decade of the twentieth century, Malcolm Scott, who did comedy impersonations of famous women, appeared as dame. His appearance was more realistic than the comedy grotesques of other dames. This represented a new image for the dame as pretentious dowager, sending up contemporary fashion or famous beauties. Douglas Byng, who presented upper-class interpretations of the character,

Figure 23: Widow Twankey in *Aladdin* (Salisbury Playhouse, 2003). Photographer Robert Workman

Figure 24: Les Dawson as Sarah the Cook in *Dick Whittington* (Plymouth: E&B Productions, 1992). Photographer Eric Thompson

wore elegant gowns and lots of jewellery. In *Snow White* he preferred to play a governess rather than a nurse (Wood 1982). This separation of the working-class and the upper-class dame has led to two main types of interpretation based on the physical build of the comedian and his style of comedy. These two groups are the working-class, knockabout dames, from Dan Leno, George Robey, Billy Dainty to Chris Harris,[2] Ian Good[3] and many others, and the rarer, more glamorous dames who are much closer to female impersonators, such as Malcolm Scott, Douglas Byng and more recently Lily Savage. Even Danny La Rue, who fell into the 'posher' category, was known as a female impersonator, though he always maintained that he was 'playing a woman knowing that everyone knew it was a "fella"' (Baker 1994, p. 202). The important element whether the character is glamorous or down-to-earth is that the comedy relies on the double representation of a man playing a woman rather than the uncertainty about gender that true female impersonation or drag attempts to invoke.

The most successful drag artist in pantomime at the moment is Lily Savage (aka Paul O'Grady) whose role as the Wicked Stepmother in *Snow White* (Bristol 2003) was reprised at the Victoria Palace Theatre in London in 2004, marking a return to the West End for pantomime. However, it is notable that Paul O'Grady/Lily Savage chose to play the evil queen rather than the dame role. The role of villainess allowed him to use the persona of Lily Savage, an ex-hooker with a sharp tongue, rather than conforming to the maternal attributes and flirtatious complicity of the dame. The presence of a male stepmother meant that the nurse, normally the dame role in that pantomime, was then played by a female comedian doing stand-up but not physical comedy and in a much reduced role. This created an anomaly in the pantomime, which lacked the complicitous and playful link between audience and performer normally led by the dame.

The double layer of representation is made plain in costume, make-up, hair and dialogue. Dames generally wear outrageous and grotesque costumes and in some cases each entrance is the opportunity for a new costume. Those dames who are in the knockabout tradition tend to have fewer and more practical costumes although they will still be bright and incorporate clashing colours, large spots and stripes and often striped stockings and boots. Brightly coloured wigs with plaits, buns, Afros or beehives are also a feature. The appearance of the dame and the ugly sisters parodies current fashion. For example, the ugly sisters in *Cinderella* at Eastbourne (2004) took part in aerobic exercise in brightly coloured lycra costumes with miniskirts that displayed their figures in the worst possible way. Mrs Crusoe in *Robinson Crusoe* (Guildford 1990) appeared for a Madonna song in a parody of the metallic futuristic pointed bra Madonna had worn in the video. Costumes will tend to exaggerate and make grotesque the physical differences between men and women; breasts and bottoms are generally padded. Make-up is also often a parody of that worn by women with false eyelashes, raised eyebrows, bow lips, and sometimes a red spot on the nose of a drinker. Here again the ugly sisters tend to be more extreme than a dame who has to maintain a greater degree of empathy with the audience. Figure 4 (chapter 2) shows the ugly sisters in the Hairdressing Scene in *Cinderella* (1990). The outrageous wigs and make-up, the physical comedy and the grotesque parody are all apparent in this photograph.

The physical appearance is designed to parody contemporary fashion, but the outrageous, inelegant costumes, flat boots or difficulty walking on heels, deliberately butch gestures and walking style make plain that this is a man. Asides to the audience confirm this double representation with lines like:

Feed – Marry me, you'll get a surprise
Dame (To audience) Not half the surprise he'll get

Feed – You could be the mother of my children – wouldn't that be marvellous?
Dame – Marvellous? It would be a miracle. (Wood 1982)

It is clear in design and in dialogue that the audience and performer share a secret, unknown to the other characters, because the dame is play-acting a role in the story as a woman but is also interacting with the audience as a male comedian. Most important according to Senelick is the licence for physical comedy allowed by the presence of a man in drag. Because the men in dresses are cartoons of feminine beauty, they cannot be taken seriously so that when they take part in physical comedy and slapstick routines they can 'throw up their skirts in the skirmish' (Senelick 2000: 238). Senelick argues that

> A real woman on the nineteenth century stage was automatically eroticized by a predominately male audience; the best means to deflect that gaze back to the play was the avoidance of beauty. The more physical the comedy, the more the need for a woman to be played by a man; hence the scarcity of female clowns (Senelick 2000: 238).

While I might argue with the fact that women are unable to take part in physical comedy, this does raise the question of how far society has changed in the intervening years. Although the dame builds a strong relationship with the women in a family audience, and although there have been a few successful female dames, such as Hilda Baker, there remains the sense that the flirtatious sexuality is more problematic with a female Dame, since instead of teasing the King, Emperor or audience with an impossibility, the tease could develop 'real' and therefore unwanted sexual undertones. The double presence of both male and female in the character of the dame that is taken advantage of in the comedy and in the flirtatious complicity with the audience, rather than any question of the ability to play physical comedy, might be a stronger reason for the continued importance of the dame.

There are some drag performances in pantomime that contrast with the dame. In *Mother Goose* in Aberdeen in 1989, Mother Goose was played by Matthew Kelly, with Dave Lynn (a successful drag artist) as the evil demon. The demon appeared in male dress in Act I, but after Mother Goose bathed in the magic pool and appeared in glamorous evening dress, the demon did the same, changing clothes to appear in full drag make-up as a glamorous woman rather than the comically unsuccessful version of femininity of the dame. There is a similarity here with the presentation of Lily Savage as the villain rather than the dame that seems to suggest a link between drag performance in pantomime and villainy or bitchiness.

Presenting the other side of this argument, The Spirit of the Northern Star, the Fairy character was played by Dr Evadne Hinge[4] in the 1990 production of *Robinson Crusoe* at the Yvonne Arnaud Theatre in Guildford. Dr Evadne Hinge is a character created by George Logan. Even the publicity announced the part as played by Dr Evadne Hinge, so that the male presence was almost entirely absent. This introduced a second dame, or more precisely a drag act, to the pantomime in the role of the Fairy who is supposedly pure and ethereal. This double presence altered the interaction between the characters and the immortals, although it had less impact on the balance of the pantomime than unsettling the role of the dame might.[5] Figure 25 shows Dr Evadne Hinge in an earlier performance as the Evil Queen in *Sleeping Beauty* (1989). The difference between the dame's hair, make-up and costume and the drag performer's appearance is clearly apparent here. The male presence of the dame allows sexual innuendo and flirtation without any sexuality at all. Some people are uncomfortable that children might perceive homosexuality in the flirtations between dame and King or Emperor, but the absence of any pretence of femininity and the absence of sexuality or sensuality in these scenes is important to the

Figure 25: George Logan as Dr Evadne Hinge playing the Evil Queen in *Sleeping Beauty* (Plymouth: E&B Productions, 1989). Photographer Eric Thompson

innocence of pantomime. Moreover, the absence of genuine sexuality, but the possibility of sharing a joke between dame and audience is important to the relationship between audience and performer, and, ultimately, the complicity between audience and performer is as important to the pantomime as the relationship between the characters.

John Morley equates the humour of the dame with naughty seaside postcards and the bawdy, silly old jokes associated with them (Wood 1982). They are funny because the reader recognizes the accuracy of the character and the situation, but in order to create comedy the characteristics and situations are exaggerated to a broad parody. Within the framework of the story the dame is flirtatious with men and presents herself as comically sex-starved and man-mad.

Dame   Quite right. Leaving me locked in the dungeon with this dirty old man. Bless you Rowena (Hudd 1998)

In *Babes in the Wood* at Sadler's Wells in 1994 Jack Tripp as the dame had the following exchange with the villain.

Sheriff   What's cooking good looking?
Nurse   Nothing spectacular, Dracula.
Sheriff   You've got to see it to believe it
Nurse   Well you'd better believe it because you're not going to see it (winks at the audience)
Sheriff   Let's talk of love
Nurse   Of love? Love reminds me of riding a bike – use any old thing to learn on, but once you've learned, get a good 'un.
(no writer credited on video at Theatre Museum)

Although there is consistent play on the double presence of the dame as both male and female, and the comedy is flirtatious containing many double entendres, the body parts are always kept covered so that the illusion, such as it is, is maintained for the children in the audience and the characters in the story. Pantomime's innocence is not undermined.

There are two comedy routines that play on the audience's desire for the man beneath the dress to be revealed. Most famous is the striptease routine in which, to the tune of 'The Stripper' (David Rose), the dame takes off her dressing gown to reveal a bodice, corset and long bloomers. She dances around removing various articles, though always being completely covered in huge bra, body stocking and long, coloured stockings, before pulling off the bloomers only to reveal many more layers of bloomers, each with a different symbol or word on the back until her frilliest knickers are revealed as she poses at the proscenium and the lights go out.[6] The other teasing routine occurs when the dame goes behind a screen. She throws garments onto the top of the screen, a blouse, a skirt, a bra. It appears she is undressing. The screen is removed to reveal her fully dressed, ironing. These examples perhaps most clearly exemplify the fun the dame has with her interaction with the audience, flirting with them, teasing them with the reality of her gender, but always maintaining the character's illusion of femininity.

It follows that as society changes so will the dame, providing a barometer of society's attitudes. In a Victorian society where unmarried women were a financial drain on their fathers or brothers and an embarrassment in society, this portrayal set a different light on the situation. It forced society to consider the woman as a person rather than as an object. But why do we still accept this in a supposedly more equal society? Perhaps because society is still not equal. Single mothers still have to support their children, whether through work (in which case childcare is an issue) or on benefits, and are still among the poorest people in our society. The changing situation of women is reflected in how the dame is presented.

Dame   Anyway this is where I live – on my own, on me tod and on me uppers. But I've been blessed – huh! Blessed she says! – lumbered more like, with my two boys. Yes girls. I'm a single mum. I put the Social into the Social Services and I put the Ginger into Gingerbread! (Rayment 1997)

Baker argues that drag acts are not mocking women but the mores and rituals of the dominant culture. Because of this and because of the relationships they set up, women identify strongly with the dame and often feel themselves represented in the pantomime, which encourages them to be complicit in the comedy and participation. Chris Lillicrap has discovered that dressed as the dame, even in the dressing room or eating in the canteen, he has different relationships with women and becomes

privy to conversations I would not have been privy to. I've sat in an auditorium with chorus girls who are having private conversations, and I've disappeared into the background because I've got boobs and wig. (Lillicrap)

The trick, however, is to keep men engaged with the fun of the ungainly and inelegant dame too.

You're doing all the things that are essentially female not very well: the walk, the pushing out of the boobs, the hairdo, the make-up, but they need to know the Dame is really a hairy-chested bloke with boots on. (Lillicrap)

Children find the dame maternal and enjoy the physical comedy, the silliness and the slapstick. A good dame balances all these requirements to appeal to all parts of the audience.

More fundamentally, Chris Lillicrap identifies how the dame figure, exposes the pretence and the mask of femininity that society expects of women:

I remember when I first started to put the make-up on [....], women will give you, free, all sorts of amazing advice – 'You ought to try this lip gloss, you ought to try doing this with your eyes, you want to do this, that, that...' And I thought 'This is extraordinary' [...] because I'm thinking, 'Just a minute, there are an enormous number of women who get up every morning and put on a mask, and they present a mask to the world.' And you know the phrase, 'Oh, I didn't have a face on. I've got to go and put my face on.' You hear women say this all the time, don't you? And I put a face on and become a character when I'm a Dame. And the minute I have that face on, people tell me I walk differently, I talk differently. Women do that. If you want to get deep into it, why is it funny? It's because maybe a bloke is not terribly good at hiding behind the mask, and so he actually exposes bits of that mask which women would love to do. Why is that funny? Because you don't expect a woman to – you're exposing the mask, the veneer of being an elegant woman. (Lillicrap)

What Chris Lillicrap is starting to explore here in relation to the dame and the social masks people wear has been developed by Judith Butler in *Gender Trouble* (1990).

Lillicrap identifies the masks people wear in order to conform to society's stereotypes. Butler goes further than assuming that a mask hides an 'authentic' identity and suggests that identity, and particularly sexual identity of both male and female, is performed and constructed through the signifying codes of the body (in Counsell ed. 1990: 72–76). Society requires conformance to heterosexuality and reproduction as the normal modes of behaviour. Other forms of gender construction such as cross-dressing challenge the separation of male and female and parody the conformity of society to patterns where anatomical sex and gender identity are assumed to be unified. Since male or female impersonation reveals that gender is a social construction, it could be argued that all forms of cross-dressing mock the notion of a true gender identity and expose the fact that gender is performed. It follows that playing the dame as an imitation of a woman supplies a double representation of both male and female, which reveals the social construction of gender, and implicitly critiques the gender stereotypes to which society conforms.

More importantly, all my interviewees have insisted that the dame must never be mistaken for a woman. What is revealed is a third space, a fantasy 'other' that erases the boundaries between the dualism of masculine and feminine, that is simultaneously neither and both.

Naturally, the same potential reading could be argued in relation to the principal boy, since there is a potential critique in the cross-dressing of the character of the stereotyping and social construction of male and female roles. However, the relationship here is between woman and boy. There is no man present but a boy striving for manhood and using the stereotypical gestures of the idealized, heroic man. But the male heroic figure is absent. The presence of a woman playing a boy striving for manhood allows the audience's imagination to be released to create for themselves the representation of the ideal man. The presence of a male principal boy removes illusion and imagination from the representation, and the actor may not live up to expectations.

Played by a woman, the principal boy wears tights, high boots and a tunic, decorated in accordance with the status of the character. Prince Charming's tunic is likely to be in gold or silver with decoration and embroidery; Dick Whittington is likely to have a tunic of rougher cloth in earthy colours, possibly with patches and pockets (this might be a trace of Harlequin from whom the hero is descended). Although the derivation of the hero is from Harlequin, played by a man, the history of breeches parts for women is older than British pantomime.

Sandra Richards, in *The Rise of the English Actress* (1993), dates the introduction of 'Breeches parts' from about 1660. Actresses had appeared before then in male clothes, for example, Moll Frith, alias Moll Cutpurse, appeared at the Fortune in 1605, but the rise of Puritanism delayed the widespread employment of actresses until the Restoration period. The tradition of displaying women's legs in tight pantaloons began during this period (Richards 1993: 1–2). By 1820, when Madame Vestris played a breeches part in a short after piece called *Giovanni* in London and her legs became famous, the sight of a woman showing her legs in breeches had been commonplace for a century and a half (Frow 1985: 91). Madame Vestris was regarded as a gifted performer and a noted singer, and she was also the first woman ever to manage a London theatre. Other performers highly regarded for their appearances in breeches parts were Mrs Anne Bracegirdle in the seventeenth century, Peg Woffington who arrived in England from Ireland in 1740 and Mrs Dorothy Jordan in the early 1800s (Frow 1985: 107). Despite this history of breeches parts in many types of theatre performance, Madame Celeste, who played both Jack and Harlequin in *Jack and the Beanstalk* in 1855, is thought to be the first principal boy (Frow 1985: 106). There were already examples of women playing the hero in the pantomime opening, such as Eliza Povey, who played the role of Jack in 1819 but not only refused to climb the beanstalk (a double was employed) but didn't go into the Harlequinade which was still extremely acrobatic. Elizabeth Poole played 'young boy' roles for Charles Farley at Covent Garden from 1831 and Miss Saunders in 1841 at the Marylebone, but they were also replaced for the harlequinade (Frow 1985: 108). Senelick dates the first female principal boy in 1815, 'played by a teenaged girl capable of conveying a sense of androgyny; the effect was all but asexual' (Senelick 2000: 262). As Gerald Frow states: 'By 1865 "Principal Boys" were general' (108), with the tunic replacing the breeches by the 1930s.

The practice continued, though with occasional male musical comedy stars appearing, such as Wilfred Douthitt as Prince Auriol in *Sleeping Beauty* in 1912, 1913 and 1914, Randolph Sutton in 1916 and Fred Barnes in 1920 (Frow 1985: 182). Norman Robbins notes that the demand for men in the armed forces may have influenced the return of women as principal boys (Robbins 2002: 186). Then in 1956–7 the principal male character in *Aladdin* at the London Palladium was played by the comedian Norman Wisdom. A series of male principal boys followed including Frankie Vaughan, Cliff Richard, Frank Ifield, Engelbert Humperdinck (all pop singers), the young comedian Jimmy Tarbuck and the National Theatre actor Edward Woodward (Holland 1997: 197 and Frow 1985: 183). In 1971 Cilla Black restored the tradition, followed by Barbara Windsor, Anita Harris, and in the present we have Bonnie Langford, Michaela Strachan and Toyah Wilcox. But since the 1950s the part of principal boy has been interchangeably played by men and women.

In the Victorian era love scenes were kept to a minimum, especially since the sex drives of women were not acknowledged, and audiences appeared 'more alert to its absurdities than to any lesbian undertones' (Senelick 2000: 262). However, the fetishism of the female leg was important in the Victorian period; although the principal boy was soberly dressed until the twentieth century, female gymnasts, acrobats and dancers revealed their legs and added to the popularity of pantomimes. The principal boy, with her male attire and confident boldness, was provocatively androgynous rather than vulnerably feminine, important given the stereotype of women of the era.

The style of the principal boy has changed considerably over the years reflecting the fashion as well as the expectations of the female form. Victorian pantomimes featured a 'big-bosomed, broad-buttocked, butcher-thighed race of principal Boys' (James Agate quoted in Frow 1985:183), followed by the more severely masculine style of the 'New Woman' before the First World War. In the post war years the style was softer and more feminine and over the intervening years the principal boys have slimmed down considerably reflecting the changes in society's tastes. The performance has not changed however, and the principal boy still maintains a sense of androgyny despite the revealed legs and high heels.

Like the pantomime dame, there is no sense that the principal boy is a man. The costume makes this absolutely clear, revealing a shapely figure and long legs in high-heeled shoes or boots extending the appearance of 'legginess'. Hair is often long and tied in a ponytail, make-up is feminine though restrained. David Pickering in the *Encyclopedia of Pantomime* states:

Such actresses are most definitely not male impersonators and retain their femininity in the role, generally wearing flattering costumes showing off their legs – to which they draw enthusiastic attention by giving them an occasional hearty slap – despite the fact that the character they play is generally of the strapping, undaunted, even chauvinistic, masculine variety (Pickering: 159 quoted in Holland 1997: 198).

Figure 26 shows Bonnie Langford, regarded as one of the best principal boys of contemporary pantomime, as Jack in *Jack and the Beanstalk* displaying her legs in tunic and short boots. Interestingly, Gary Wilmot mimicked the thigh slap of the

Figure 26: Bonnie Langford as Jack in *Jack and the Beanstalk* (Plymouth: E&B Productions, 1993). Photographer Eric Thompson

female principal boy when playing Dick in *Dick Whittington* at Plymouth Theatre Royal (2003), marking the pantomime tradition and drawing attention to the absence of the female in the role.

The principal boy stands with legs akimbo, fingers clenched and hands on hips establishing a posture that might signify some lost vision of 'manliness' that in no way attempts to create an illusion of genuine manhood (Frow 1985: 183–4). Like the dame's version of femininity, the principal boy uses postures as a parodic imitation of manhood that point to the absent masculinity of the character, but, also, as Peter Holland points out, to the absent male in pantomime. 'The heroic male is a heavily marked gap in panto performance' (Holland 1997: 198).

Attention is drawn to the female presence in dialogue as well as through dress. Dandini describing his job as valet to Prince Charming in *Cinderella* says:

> Dandini: A valet deals with all affairs of state, treasury, laws of the land [..] and an awful lot of ironing.
> (*to the audience*) Although not as much ironing as there might be. This Prince doesn't seem to bother much with trousers. (Jordan 2003: 2)

Jack in *Mother Goose's Silver Jubilee* comments on the entrance of the principal boy as follows:

> Jack: It really is a pantomime and to prove it here comes a handsome stranger. Well, that's what I call a man! (Kaler 2003, from memory)

The introduction of the male principal boy alters this situation and reduces the opportunity for comedy at the expense of the cross-dressed character. At the same time it introduces the 'heroic male' presence which means that there must be a representation based on societal expectations rather than an idealized gap. So instead of a female presence that in the imagination of the observer implies an idealized heroic male, the male principal boy is expected to embody those virtues and win the princess because of his physical appeal. The reduction of the reliance on imagination means that the male hero, who is unlikely to fulfill the dreams of all parts of the audience, may be less widely regarded as the heroic male. Also, the effect of the more realistic sexual relationship is to change the focus of the story from an adventure or quest as the boy journeys to adulthood, into an adult romance that has a distinct sexual agenda. Interestingly, Kate Edgar separates the 'quest' pantomimes (*Dick Whittington, Jack and the Beanstalk, Aladdin*), where the majority of the story is an adventure and the love relationship is secondary, and where a female principal boy is still widely acceptable, from the 'romance' pantomimes (*Cinderella* and *Sleeping Beauty*), in which the principal focus is on the relationship of the hero and heroine, which she believes now need a male prince because of audience expectations of sexuality and romance.

There are two issues raised by Marjorie Garber in her discussion of cross-dressing in *Peter Pan* (Garber 1997: 165–185) that are relevant here. Firstly, as discussed above, the imaginary or fantasy 'other', represented by the principal boy, allows girls not only to imagine the heroic male, but to identify with and explore their own masculine side; the tomboy, free to do what Victorian women could not. The third sex, the 'betwixt and between' of the cross-dressed character demonstrates the power of transvestism in the imaginary world of the viewer. But equally significant in this argument is that the principal boy, as in *Peter Pan*, will not grow into a man, the female presence always denies that potential. Garber regards this denial of the male in the conflation of child and woman as a castration of the male, noted as the absence of the male in pantomime. Again there is evidence here of the innocence of pantomime in the presence of a boy/woman striving for adulthood and therefore presenting another asexual relationship to the family audience.

The principal boy being played by a woman is more controversial than the male dame. It is strongly challenged by some producers as a confusing practice that leads to children misreading the relationship between principal boy and girl as lesbian. In the majority of my interviews with practitioners and production staff children were not credited with the ability to understand the separation of character and performer which they appear to understand in play.[7] I was especially bemused by the acceptance of the dame but not of the principal boy since one can make similar arguments about both. There was also no sense that any potential misreading that might give a positive representation of a homosexual relationship might be acceptable in a popular theatre form. Be that as it may, the argument here is that the presence of the male principal boy introduces sexuality to the relationship, altering the interaction between principal boy and girl from one of romantic, innocent love to one of lust and sexuality and altering the story from a quest for transformation and adulthood to the more specific one of sexual awakening. In our sexualized society this appears to be more desirable than the innocence pantomime had maintained despite its flirtatious and erotic double entendres.

The second most frequent comment was that the principal boy was only there to be sexually titillating for the poor fathers who were dragged along by their families and that this was no longer politically correct. This certainly appears to be a factor in the development and popularity of breeches roles and may still be so, although, with the appearance of topless or naked women daily in the tabloid press and the presence of figure-hugging and leg-revealing costumes worn by the pantomime dancers, there are much greater opportunities for male titillation elsewhere. Interestingly, some principal boys are now dressed in breeches and some male principal boys are regarded as titillation for the mothers (figure 27 shows Aladdin on the right, wearing trousers in Salisbury Playhouse's 2003 production).

The sexual implications of the romantic roles aside, the principal boy might be read as a positive role model for girls, as it is a woman who plays a leading active role in the pantomime, defeats evil and wins the day (albeit with the help of the fairy). To counter the perceived difficulties caused by female principal boys, many pantomimes now employ male principal boys. This raises issues of gender balance in the pantomime; the only remaining women are the fairy and the principal girl, both of whom are represented as pretty, sweet and largely passive, although both parts generally now have a little more street credibility both in the writing and the performance.

In the end, all the arguments about cross-dressing the dame and the principal boy are to some extent interchangeable. Both roles are transvestite roles which remove

Figure 27: Widow Twankey, Aladdin and Wishee Washee in *Aladdin* (Salisbury Playhouse, 2003). Photographer Robert Workman

the possibility of heterosexual relationships, even as the heterosexuality of the characters is highlighted in the story. The dame is represented as man mad, though lacking in sex appeal, exposing society's repression of overt sexuality in women, especially women of a 'certain age', as well as its anxieties about homosexuality. The principal boy is represented as sexless, but able to form a loving relationship while presenting a deliberately provocative appearance, which exposes the double standards in society's expectations of women, while the frequent replacement of the principal boy with a male performer exposes homosexual anxiety.

Two things are gained by the presence of the cross-dressed characters. First, the iconicity of the actor is removed and the audience is distanced from identification with the character so that social issues can be exposed through laughter. What this means is that rather than character and performer being seen by the audience as united, they are clearly seen here as separate. Elin Diamond argues that 'a gestic feminist criticism would "alienate" or foreground those moments in a play-text in which social attitudes about gender could be made visible' (in Counsell and Wolf 2001: 83). By the separation of character and performer and, more importantly, the juxtaposition of gender between character and performer, society's rules and values are exposed. In the case of pantomime, I don't suggest any serious or political intent and certainly the presence of comedy and laughter to some extent deflect any potential effects, but pantomime remains subversive and transgressive even as it is commercial and institutionalized. Secondly, the fantasy of transgression, of breaking out of the restrictions of society, is given full rein. This is an aspect of pantomime that has parallels with the carnival traditions of reversal and transformation.

Notes

1. Probably written by Ralph Higden (Hartnoll 1972: 376).
2. Chris Harris has written, directed and played Dame in many pantomimes. For a number of years in the late 1990s he was a regular at Bristol Old Vic. For the last three years he has played Dame at Bath Theatre Royal. He provided two interviews for this work.
3. Ian Good was the regular Dame at Eastbourne for three years before moving to Brighton in 2004. He was interviewed in the course of research for this work.
4. Hinge and Bracket are played by Patrick Fyffe and George Logan. They are a double drag act who found a niche in the mainstream as two genteel middle-aged ladies who played piano and sang mostly Victorian and Edwardian songs.
5. Baker (1994) and Senelick (2000) refer to straight plays and musicals that have been attempted by drag artists in their alter egos, including Hinge and Bracket and Danny La Rue. These have been largely unsuccessful because of the introduction of gender confusion to the plot, although Baker reports that Dame Hilda Bracket was more successful as Katisha in *The Mikado* in 1993. This is particularly interesting given Baker's supposition that Katisha is essentially a Dame part.
6. Jack Tripp's version of this routine can be seen on video at the Theatre Museum Covent Garden.
7. My own experience and that of several interviewees (including Jordan) is that quite young children have no difficulty in moving between states of involvement in a story and instructions about that story in their own play and in watching performances. It is predominantly adults who worry that children will not understand or will misconstrue events.

8

Audience Participation, Community and Ritual

During moments of audience participation the performers and the audience work together as co-conspirators in the development or completion of the story. As argued above, the moments of participation between audience and comedian are a reflexive reminder of the performance frame. These moments are therefore times when the emotional distance between audience and story is increased, but that between audience and performer is reduced. A relationship is established that gives the audience members a sense of involvement in the pantomime and encourages them to believe they have shared a unique experience with the performers.

There is also a physical space between performer and audience that is challenged: the comics do not simply speak to the audience, they also throw things at the audience, chase through the audience, involve audience members in the comedy, and in the songsheet invite several young volunteers onto the stage. Just as with the emotional distance, the involvement of the audience in the performance is closer, but the distance from involvement in the 'story' is greater. In this way, the distance between performers and audience is constantly shifting not only towards and away from the story, but towards and away from involvement with the performers in 'pantoland'. But the breaking of the physical barriers between performer and audience also allows the audience to feel that it is more fully a participant and not separated from the world of the performers. However, the opportunities for breaking down the barriers, whether physical or cultural, between audience and performer could lead to anarchy and are therefore carefully controlled.

One way that the performers, particularly the comics and the immortals, have of controlling the distance between performer and spectator is by controlling the participation and therefore maintaining authority over the performance. The audience is vocally or physically involved as a participant in the performance, while the performers maintain control of the events, and, at different moments, the audience is emotionally involved in the story in scenes played out without participation. Audience participation, led by the performers is important in providing a bridge between the worlds of the story, 'pantoland' and the real world of the audience.

The comic's first job is to encourage the audience to respond vocally when required. This requires him (and it usually is a 'him') to build a relationship with the audience, but particularly with the children in the audience and lay down the rules of participation. The Dame also builds a relationship with the audience but she tends to relate more closely to, and achieve empathy with, the adults in the audience.

During the opening spot by the Silly Billy character, the young comic sets up the rules of participation for the audience. If Dick Whittington or Jack (of the Beanstalk) is being played by a male comic the separation of roles between comic and hero may become confused and overlap so that Dick or Jack lead the participation, but it will always be the younger comic with whom the children are expected to identify. Generally the rules take the form of 'when I do x, you must do y' and any other instruction includes a start and end point. So, for example, 'whenever I say "Wotcher Kids" I want you to shout "Wotcher Billy" (or Wishee or Jack or Simon), shall we have a practice – after three – one two three – Wotcher Kids'. Here the comic has given clear instructions about what to do and when. At that point it is mostly the children who participate. The comic will then berate the adults and try again. He will usually be satisfied by the third attempt, by which time the majority of the audience is participating.

The comic must have the audience members on his side before he can ask for their help, and having an interactive exchange is a way of building that relationship. The comic will also tend to use the language of contemporary teenagers, will sing their style of music and dress and behave as older children might, so he might be lazy or stubborn, will have street-cred and will probably disobey his mother (in minor ways). In these ways he builds empathy with the children in the audience and encourages them to join in, but he also lays down the rules of participation and creates a controllable situation. Inexperienced performers struggle to direct and control the audience until they realize how it must be done. There are tried and tested patterns that work, simply expecting the audience to join in or giving unclear or confusing instructions, or not following through on rules you've set up, leads to chaos. This is noteworthy because what appears to the spectator to be the opportunity for anarchy or transgression is, in fact, carefully controlled and orchestrated. One set of rules, 'join in according to my instructions and as required in the genre', is established in place of another, 'sit passively, silently and attentively'.

As argued above, before arriving at the performance the majority of the audience is already aware of the outer frame of performance that is established by awareness of the genre and knowledge of expected patterns of behaviour. A type of community is already present in advance of the performance that has similar expectations of the performance and that will provide a collective response to the experience. The interpretative and behavioural patterns of a particular theatre experience are established by what H. R. Jauss identified in literary theory as a 'horizon of expectations' (developed in relation to performance in Carlson 1990: 11 and Bennett 1997: 139ff). In performance this means that if a theatre form is known within a culture the audience will be able to predict to a large extent the content of that experience and, in this case, that participation will be required, and what types of participation will be required. The pre-performance signs, such as the venue, the advertising material, the date and time of performance (in this case, daytime or early evening performances around the Christmas period) will provide the information necessary for the audience to identify the genre of performance and therefore understand what is expected. It is therefore already an 'interpretive community' (Stanley Fish cited in Bennett 1997: 40 and Carlson 1990: 16)[1] bringing a horizon of expectations to the performance, for as Herbert Blau says: 'An audience without a history is not an audience' (quoted in Bennett 1997: 140).

The expectations of the audience are open to confirmation or revision during the course of the performance, but substantial alteration of the expectations leads to confusion for the audience. In most cases these arguments, drawn from reader-response theory, apply to how the audience might interpret the text, but this sort of pre-performance information also informs the audience about expected behaviour patterns. In the case of pantomime, unlike many contemporary forms of theatre in traditional spaces, the audience expects not only to interpret the text, but to participate in the performance according to particular pre-determined conventions.

One of these conventions is the framing of the performance by the Immortals using rhyming couplets and involving the audience in opportunities for participation. Another is the entrance of each of the principals in turn, giving each the opportunity for a song directly addressed to the audience or a comedy routine involving the audience. The order in which the comics (Dame, Silly Billy character and sometimes Broker's Men/Chinese Policemen) enter depends on several considerations. In commercial pantomime the top of the bill will generally enter later and will choose which of the participatory activities to include leaving other activities for the other comic. These might include comedy interaction with particular audience members or the setting up of running gags, the giving away of sweets or the announcement of parties and birthdays so identifying audience members and their groups specifically. Where the order of entrance is not a contractual issue the pantomime itself might provide an order. For example, Mother Goose normally enters early in *Mother Goose* because there is not much that can happen before Mother Goose and Priscilla (the goose) meet. Sarah the Cook is a relatively minor character in the plot of *Dick Whittington* and so will probably not be introduced until Dick has met the Fitzwarren family. In *Aladdin* Wishee Washee generally does an audience warm-up before the Dame's entrance and after Aladdin and the princess have been introduced, but in *Jack and the Beanstalk* the Dame will enter earlier to establish the poverty and desperation of the family.

The Immortals, fairy and villain, also encourage the audience to participate, either by booing the villain or cheering the principal boy and his helpers. These four characters, comic, Dame, and Immortals are the characters who have the most interaction with the audience. However, all rules are made to be broken, especially in pantomime, and the principal boy or girl may ask the audience for a response or for help at some stage in the pantomime, and, occasionally, other characters may interact with the audience. It is fair to say that the immortals speak directly to the audience and that the comedians set out the rules for participation and carry out the majority of the interaction.

Participation requires a number of things: empathy with a grotesque character, involvement with the events of the plot, but most fundamentally, it requires the audience members to involve themselves in the performance, to act as a community, to transgress the behavioural patterns associated with certain types of theatre going, but to conform to the expectations of this genre and the authority of the performers.

Many writers now include controlled tasks for the audience so that it is directly involved in the performance. The first task for the audience is set up, usually by the comic, who will often leave an item on the stage for the audience to guard. It might be a gift for Cinderella or a box with the rent money. If the audience sees anyone approaching the box they must shout for the comic as loudly as possible. This is practiced and subsequently provides a running entrance motif for the comic. Wishee Washee's entrance routine at Salisbury Playhouse included all the events outlined above.

> Wishy Washy: .....but I do do everything! (Aw) I do more than that (bigger aw). And I do the shopping too, I've just been to the shops because I was hungry and d'you know what I bought? A big bag of peanuts! They are just scrummy, yummy in my tummy, but I'm a bit full now, so I'm going to leave the rest on this shelf till later, but coz we're pals, will you keep an eye on them for me while I'm folding these tablecloths? And if anyone comes to steal them, will you tell me? Thanks...oh, but we need a signal. I know. If you see anyone go near my nuts will you shout 'Wishy, they're nicking your nuts!' Let's have a practice.....
> (Reid and Thomas 2003)

This ploy can occasionally backfire if someone accidentally gets too close to the box and the audience calls for the comic at the wrong time. This happened at the Yvonne Arnaud Theatre, Guildford (2003), on the night I was there. In a dance routine the Fairy kept getting too close to the box, so the children obediently shouted for Jack, but he couldn't respond to the children because of the dance routine. The children then felt that they were being ignored which upset the relationship with the comic.

There are moments when the audience is given a stronger role in the plot, without the completion of which the performance cannot continue. The most famous moment when audience participation is required in order to complete the plot is in *Peter Pan* (Barrie 1929). When Tinkerbell is dying, having drunk the poison left for Peter by Captain Hook, Peter tells the audience that she can recover if the audience believes in fairies. To prove that the audience members believe they must clap their hands, 'Clap if you believe in fairies'. Nowadays, this action is usually accompanied by shouting and stamping from the audience, but the premise remains the same, without the direct participation of the audience the plot cannot continue. This device of giving the audience a task, the completion of which allows the plot to continue is used in many pantomimes across the country. For example, towards the end of *Cinderella* the Ugly Sisters often imprison Cinders in a cupboard before the shoe-trying scene. The audience has to alert the Prince to her presence (*Cinderella* Manchester, 2003 and *Cinderella* Birmingham, 2003). In *Mother Goose's Silver Jubilee* (York, 2003) the cast require someone who has never done anything bad to save all of Yorkshire from corruption through greed by saying 'Ah Bisto'. A child from the audience performs this task.

In Jeanette Ranger and Chris Lillicrap's version of *Cinderella* the running gag and the requirement for the audience to help the characters complete the plot are linked. Buttons plants the master key on the proscenium arch for the audience to guard.

BUTTONS   (HE SITS DOWN ON THE HAMPER LAUGHING AND THEN SHOOTS UP. HE HAS SAT ON THE KEY HANGING ON HIS BELT OR IN HIS POCKET.) Oooh! I'm always doing that. (HOLDS UP LARGE KEY) That was painful in the extreme. This is the master key of Stoneybroke Hall, it opens absolutely everything. And I'm in charge of it. The trouble is it's so big. I tell you what; I'll put it over here for safekeeping. (GOES TO PROS ARCH WHERE HE HANGS KEY ON HOOK). Oh dear, what if somebody should come and steal it? I know, will you keep an eye on it for me? Will you? Great! And if anybody goes near it, you shout BUTTONS! just as loud as you can and I'll come running. Alright? Let's have a practice. I'll pretend I'm someone trying to take the key. (HE DOES SO A COUPLE OF TIMES UNTIL THEY ARE SHOUTING LOUDLY ENOUGH) Wonderful! I can see the key will be safe with you lot.
(Ranger and Lillicrap)

In the final part of the story, Cinderella is locked in a trunk by the sisters using the key, while the audience screams for Buttons. Buttons appears and finds out from the audience what has happened, retrieves the key from where the sisters have thrown it and frees Cinderella to try on the glass slipper, giving a concrete purpose to the audience's participation throughout the performance.

In pantomime there is a pattern of events that is followed during the opening scenes, during which the main protagonists are introduced and the plot is outlined. As we have seen, the fairy and the villain open the performance speaking directly to the audience and invoking some response from them. The audience already knows that it is expected to boo the villain and cheer the fairy and the good characters, but audience participation is included in the opening scene to reinforce the convention and begin to build the audience's involvement by declaring a need for assistance or, in the case of the baddie, hatred of children.

The Genie of the Ring in *Aladdin* (Potters Bar 2002–3) says to the audience:

And I live somewhere magical
That I bet you'll never guess
But as it's you, I'll give a clue
Can you keep a secret? (Audience: Yes)

So I can be the winner
In this goody – baddie duel
I have to hide so I reside
Inside a royal jewel.
(Jordan 2002)

She has already encouraged the audience to speak to her and given them some information they may need later about her hiding place. She then introduces Abanazar before enlisting the audience's help as follows:

It is he who starts our story
But friends, do not be scared.
Good will always win the day
If you are all prepared

To help me stop this wicked man
His quest will be denied
His evil ways should fail him
With you, friends, on my side. (Jordan 2002)

The villain will generally include some abuse of the audience to stimulate hissing and booing. In *Jack and the Beanstalk* (Plymouth 1998–9) the Giant's accomplice, Roach, includes the following lines:

Roach: But what care I? I really love this job
It's so fulfilling to be paid to be a slob!
Tonight he dines alone within his lair
So I'll need a plump young maid, perhaps a pair!
For fricassee of maiden is the dish
(*He scans the audience*)
No there's nothing here, just lots of wish-
Ful thinking and a fluttering of hearts.
Although for pudding I had planned some raspberry tarts! (Davies 1998: 1)

Or Abanazar in *Aladdin* (Potters Bar 2002–3) begins:

Sand from the Sahara, water from the Nile
Frozen, Flemish fennel from a phosphorescent phial.
Leave it on a low light, to summon up a spell
For global domination. (*To audience*) I'm a baddie. Can you tell?

Hang on a minute, what are you lot doing here
I'm not at home to visitors, I thought I made that clear.
(*Peering at the audience*)
It's children, horrid children, and worse than that by far
They're puny and they're pasty and they come from Potter's Bar. (Jordan 2002)

There is a very clear distinction between the fairy who asks for help and encourages positive responses and the villain who abuses the audience and laughs at the children to inspire booing. Participation is not the main focus of the opening scene which has stronger functions in relation to outlining the plot and characters, but already the opportunities for participation establish the framework for the performance and clarify for the audience that participation and response to direct address are welcomed at this performance and confirm the audience understanding of this genre.

There are also certain catchphrases associated with performance that the majority of the audience knows from previous experience, such as 'It's Behind You' and 'Oh No it Isn't'. Audience members expect to participate in particular ways when they come to the pantomime, and new audience members soon learn what is expected from the rest of the audience and from the surrounding material. The 'Oh No it Isn't' and its variations are often the opportunity for the villain to interact with the audience, since s/he is most likely to disagree with and taunt the audience.

Rowena: That Idle Jack is the key – he's a rotter isn't he?
Audience: No
Rowena: Oh Yes he is
Audience: Oh no he isn't
Rowena: Oh – shut your faces or I'll fillet your furbees.
(Hudd 1998)

'Oh yes he is, Oh no he isn't' is a pattern that could go on forever. It is often concluded by shortening the length of the phrase and so increasing the pace. For example, 'Oh yes he is' might be shortened, after a couple of iterations, to 'Is, Is, Is,' to which the response is 'Isn't, Isn't, Isn't'. An example from *Cinderella* by Ranger and Lillicrap demonstrates the changing rhythm, but doesn't include the audience, although the audience might well have been encouraged by Buttons to back him up in the performance.

BUTTONS: (REALISING THE HAMPER IS EMPTY) Oh you don't want to look in there.
SALMONELLA: Yes we do.
BUTTONS: (WALKING THEM FORWARD) Oh no, no, no you don't.
LYST/SALM: (WALKING HIM BACK) Oh yes, yes, yes we do.
BUTTONS: (WALKING THEM FORWARD) Oh no, no, no you don't.
LYST/SALM: (WALKING HIM BACK) Oh yes, yes, yes we do.
BUTTONS: Don't.
LYST/SALM: Do.
BUTTONS: (SITTING ON HAMPER) DON'T
LYST/SALM: DO! (THEY OPEN IT TIPPING HIM OFF) AAAAAARGH!
(Ranger and Lillicrap 1999: 9–10)

The performer will have to end the participation by introducing verbal abuse as in the Hudd example above, or with a punchline or visual gag as in the Ranger and Lillicrap example. The villain may try to catch the audience out by inverting the phrase (i.e. switching his part from 'Oh yes it is' to 'Oh no it isn't') so that the audience, without thinking, disagrees and says the opposite of what it means. The villain then laughs at how stupid the audience is to be caught out. Whichever device is chosen, it is the performer who starts, controls and finishes the moment of participation, but the moment allows enjoyment of the direct interaction between performer and audience in which both know their parts.

The other well-known opportunity for audience participation is the ghost gag or the 'It's Behind You' routine. This is a routine that occurs in the majority of pantomimes and which audiences expect and relish. A group of characters, including the Dame and the comic, discuss the thing they're scared of; a gorilla in the woods, a ghost in the dark etc., then decide to sit on a bench and sing a song to forget their fears and keep cheerful. As they sing, the scary animal appears behind them to the accompaniment of excited screaming from the audience. The audience tries to warn the characters who suddenly become rather deaf, but eventually the characters hear and follow the audience's pointing hands to look for the ghost. There is always a walk round with the ghost following the characters, but the pay-off is that each character in turn sees the ghost, is scared and runs off. Finally only one character remains. The Dame and ghost come face to face, only for the ghost to run off in fright at seeing the Dame's face. This routine is totally implausible but is loved by audiences, to the extent that 'It's behind you' is as well known a catchphrase associated with pantomime as 'Oh no he isn't'.

Other audience participation opportunities are controlled within rhyming couplets, so that it is not only the convention and the character that exerts control, but the verse pattern imposes rhythm and pace (in practice, this doesn't always happen as planned). The script for *Dick Whittington* by Roy Hudd (Barnstaple 1998) includes the opportunity for the audience to complete occasional lines by Rowena Ratface, but the lines are in rhyme so that only one response is possible.

ROWENA   I'll give you a clue what I plan to do
                It's bad and <u>beelzebubbish</u>
                I'll get Dick and that Tom cat thrown out of the town
                What do you think of that?
AUDIENCE <u>Rubbish</u>
(Hudd, 1998 p. 1.4.2)

ROWENA   Excuse me now, I must embark
                Soon I'll create <u>high panic</u>.
                I'll turn their pleasant sunny cruise
                Into a trip on the ......(signals to audience to join in)
AUDIENCE <u>Titanic.</u>
ROWENA   Oh, very good, very good.
(Hudd, 1998, p. 2.2.10)

In other scripts, too, the audience responses are written in and any deviations by anarchic audiences would be adapted by the actor or ignored, the action would not be affected.

DICK   Would you like to come to London with me?
AUDIENCE Yes
DICK   Then hold on to your hats, we'll be there before breakfast.
(Elliott and Davies 1991, p. 1.1.4)

The audience will look forward to such moments, possibly without noticing the control that is exercised over it.

The longest section of participation happens just before the walkdown at the end of the performance. The songsheet is flown in and the audience, led by one or two of the comics, engages in a singing competition to see who can sing the song loudest. The songsheet occurs, in practical terms, so that the walkdown set can be built and the performers change into glamorous outfits for the finale, but it also occurs after the story has been completed. As Kate Edgar pointed out, you can only do the songsheet when the audience is relaxed.

> It's about a community singalong. Everybody knows where they are, we're all friends, we've been through the story together, we've rescued the princess, we've defeated the giant, now let's have a little singalong for 10 minutes, then we know we'll get the finale, walk down and we'll be ready in time for the bus. (Edgar)

This is the culmination of the participation opportunities, and the longest and loudest. The performance begins with hissing and booing at the immortals, then the comic and Dame warm the audience up, introducing the rules of participation and activities and events for the audience to participate in. There are regular opportunities for participation throughout the performance so that the audience remains aware and active. Then, just before saying goodbye, there is one final opportunity for noise and mayhem. In a sense it is the audience's finale, its last moment of participation before returning to everyday behaviour. Cynically one might also acknowledge that the audience also claps and cheers much louder in the finale if it has just been extremely vocal in the songsheet.

In performance there is communication between performers, between audience and performers and between audience members. The third of these implies that there might be individual responses to the performance, which may be true to some extent in terms of interpretation. However, it is generally accepted that despite the variety of cultural values and experiences brought to the theatre by individual audience members there is a homogeneous response (Elam 1980: 96). Laughter, participation and applause are all infectious and confirm for the audience members that they have responded correctly within the genre (Elam 1990 and Ubersfeld 1981). In this way an audience community, with a shared experience of the performance, is created. Individuals at a theatre performance are led by the majority to a particular response. Marvin Carlson describes a *New Yorker* cartoon which 'showed a theatre-audience member, having paused to wipe tears from his cheeks, looking around in some consternation to see that everyone around him was laughing uproariously. "Hey, wait a minute" he says. "Is this satire?"' (Carlson 1990: 13). This effect means that new audience members will soon understand what is expected of them and will generally go along with the majority or will dislike the experience sufficiently to leave.

The devices and the types of rule-setting outlined above are apparent in audience participation in comedy performances and especially in children's theatre. The effects of this participation are to encourage the audience to act as a body and therefore to take part in a communal experience, to become a community for the time and place of performance. This is an area studied by theatre anthropologists such as Victor Turner and Richard Schechner, who identify certain patterns of behaviour as ritual. Rituals take place in special places and times, where particular behaviour is required. Simple actions and responses are repeated that transport the participants from their everyday life to a different mental and emotional place. These activities help create a sense of 'communitas'[2], 'a feeling of group solidarity, usually short-lived, generated during ritual' (Schechner 2002: 62).

There are activities in contemporary societies that take the place of rituals, and performance is one of these activities. The separation of the activity to a particular time and place, framed by the attendance at a theatre and away from everyday life is one aspect of ritual. The involvement of the audience as participants in the creation of the performance is another aspect that channels behaviour into rhythmically co-ordinated responses performed on cue to become mass action. Participation can be used to induce mass action for ideological reasons, but the purpose of ritual is simply to mark the calendar or to transport people from one life phase to another (Schechner 2002: 57). It is significant that pantomime has been phenomenally successful at Christmas but not at other times of the year, and so has become not only a ritual activity as performance but a part of the Christmas ritual for many people.

Chris Jordan raised an interesting point about this when interviewed. He described how, after Christmas lunch, people will ask, 'Did you enjoy your Christmas lunch' and his response was 'Well, it was turkey!' What he is suggesting is that whether the turkey was well or badly cooked became less relevant than the participation in the ritual event. This has interesting consequences when applied to performance. When asked how they enjoyed the pantomime most people will say 'It was fine'. This might be the effect of a lack of comparison for many people who only go to the theatre for pantomime, but it might also imply that some other aspects of the ritual performance are less relevant than its efficacy as ritual. This is particularly apparent in amateur and community performances where participation with the community is more important than the production values. Although the producers I spoke to while researching this book are all immensely professional and are proud of the quality of their productions, it may be that for many audience members, being there and taking part in the ritual of pantomime with the family at Christmas has as much importance as evaluating the quality of that performance. Despite this, I have no doubt that the audience is more affected by, and involved in, a good performance, but this does indicate the importance of balanced and appropriate participation to the success of the pantomime.

Performance can be theorized as a ritual for the performers and attendance at performance can be theorized as a ritual for the spectators. However, audience participation in performance and identification and complicity with characters on the stage provides the opportunity for unusual ritual behaviour that is a combination of ritual and transgression or play. According to Turner's definition, transgression within the safety of defined boundaries leads to 'normative communitas', the audience is returned to life having experienced a transformation for a limited time and place, within safe boundaries. Thus, the joining in with, and familiarity with, the events of the performance (often referred to as the pantomime conventions) is part of the ritual and creates a sense of community identity. At the same time, the shouting and responding in a place where passive behaviour is normally expected is transgressive behaviour or playfulness, although one might argue that this is pseudo-transgressiveness, since we have seen that it is controlled and rule-bound. The fluidity of performers' roles, moving from identification with the audience to involvement in the plot contains elements of playfulness. Richard Schechner suggests that this combination of ritual and play allows people to temporarily experience a reality separate from their ordinary lives (Schechner 2002: 45). Freed from the constraints of daily life and allowed to engage in playful or transgressive behaviour, people are uplifted and experience camaraderie. In fact, it may be possible to understand pantomime as one of the last vestiges of the licensed carnival in Britain. Carnival depends on a balanced tension between the allowed ritual and transgression. The balance in pantomime may be skewed towards ritual with very little real transgression, but there remain opportunities for play, for participation and for the establishment of a community identity.

Notes

1. Stanley Fish developed this term, which referred to the literary communities and sub-communities in America. Such groups share interpretative strategies which exist prior to the reading of a text and therefore the interpretation is informed by the expectation within the community and genre. Bennett and Carlson develop the term in relation to performance texts.
2. This is a term that Turner used that has several categories within it, including normative or spontaneous, official, ordained or imposed (Schechner 2002: 62).

9

Topical Reference and the Unique Event

In the previous chapter I argued that the pantomime audience member has two experiences of community. Firstly, the audience is part of a community that anticipates and understands the expectations of the genre as predicted by the pre-performance materials. Secondly, the audience member becomes part of an audience community that takes part in the communal activities of that performance. Those activities include the opportunities for participation as well as the more passive responses of attentiveness, laughter, applause, reading the performance and conformity to the homogeneous behaviour that might be required at any performance event. However, there is a third type of community that has not yet been explored. This is the wider community of the time and place of performance, whether that is Barnstaple 2001 or Birmingham 2004.

The performers refer to events and places in the town as well as wider political and cultural events in the country to establish a shared community with the audience in the experience of living in contemporary Britain. The shared community between audience and performers reinforces the sense of identity of the audience members. Richard Schechner describes seven interlocking spheres in his analysis of the functions of performance. In his list are included 'to mark or change identity' and 'to make or foster community' (Schechner 2002: 39–39). He also includes 'to entertain' which I will argue in subsequent chapters is also an important feature of pantomime. For the moment, however, I will focus on the interaction of the two spheres that allow the audience to be reinforced as a community and as individuals. The performance is signified as unique and particular to the audience community because of the references to the shared life experience of this performance (in the relationships established between stage and audience) and of the shared cultural references and values (local and intertextual reference). Finally, the comics take every opportunity to signify the performance as unique, special to this moment and to this relationship with this audience, by the inclusion of satirical and ironic comments on current events and the inclusion of ad-libbing, corpsing and cod-corpsing. These all contribute to the sense of shared life experience and therefore to the empowerment of the individual for a brief period.

Topical references to local or community events or difficulties widens the performance frame so that the performers present themselves as part of the same community as the audience. *Aladdin* at Salisbury Playhouse (2003–4) incorporated references to St Mary's shirts (the uniform of a local football team) and a reference to the difficulty of parking, 'which is a big thing in Salisbury' (Reid). When Aladdin became rich Dame Twankey became Fabrezia Lenoria Comforta Persilia Twankey the 27th Duchess of Fisherton. This combines comic reference to household products for doing the laundry with local reference (the theatre at Salisbury is just off Fisherton Street). Occasionally these references may allow for sponsorship opportunities as well as the comic reference, as can be seen in figure 28, in which a local estate agent is identified. In Birmingham, Julian Clary combined a reference to Daz (a laundry detergent) with awareness of the pantomime conventions by pointing out that he had just made a 'topical reference'. In these asides and many more in most pantomimes across the country, references are made to real events and material goods so that the onstage and offstage worlds collide and entwine. The effect of these asides is to give a sense that the performance belongs to the community, strengthening the relationship between performer, performance and place, and reinforcing the individual identity of the audience members by acknowledging shared experience between performer and audience.

For example, at the Yvonne Arnaud Theatre, concern was expressed that Cinderella might get stuck in the one-way system on her way to the ball. The

Figure 28: A local reference in *Jack and the Beanstalk* (Salisbury Playhouse, 1987). Photograph by Robert Workman

incongruity of this image created a comic moment, but the shared experience of being stuck in that particular one-way system produced a particularly strong identification with the situation and the performers. There is therefore a strong sense of empathy with the performers produced from this example of shared knowledge and experience.

The political life of the country that is shared by audience and performers is frequently referred to in topical gags, and allows the possibility that pantomime can remain up to date and respond to current events, albeit in superficial and humorous ways. For example, in Barnstaple (1998) on the night of Peter Mandelson's resignation from the government when Dick was pointed out to the Alderman as 'needing a job', the Alderman introduced the question 'you're not Peter Mandelson?' to a delighted response from the audience. This sort of immediate response to current events gives the audience a sense that it is attending a unique performance that relates to its everyday lived reality. The recent production of *Aladdin* (2004–5) at the Old Vic included numerous references to contemporary politics and politicians, but also, and particularly, to Kevin Spacey the international film star and current artistic director of the theatre. Audiences recognize the reference and feel themselves to be 'in the know'. The pantomime is geared to their reality and speaks to them. It is imperative that the producers know their audience, therefore, and the Old Vic pantomime was clearly speaking to a more theatrically literate audience than many local or repertory pantomimes, although it also included references to *Lord of the Rings* since Ian McKellen was playing Widow Twankey.

Chris Lillicrap suggests that one of the reasons for pantomime's continued success is that it has the flexibility to adapt in this way, even if only in a one line aside.

> The year there was that scandal about Cherie Blair's flat in Bristol, we used that in *Aladdin*. Widow Twankey had got a brand new laundry but she hadn't been able to afford time to look for herself because she was a working mum. We included a whole piece from Cherie Blair's speech. [Widow Twankey] got a friend to [buy the laundry], but actually she ended up finding somebody who could get it for half price. So that was a satirical, popular joke (Lillicrap).

On the day Saddam Hussein was found, in a performance of *Snow White* the cottage of the Red Dwarf was discovered,

> And the Principal Boy said, 'What do you mean, it's hidden in here by magic?' And I said 'Oh there's lots of things been found in here, love! They found Saddam Hussein here this morning.' A huge round of applause followed (Lillicrap).

These sorts of immediate responses, adapting to current events gives the perception that the performer and audience are looking at the world together, 'as mates' (Lillicrap) and sharing a unique experience. Lillicrap believes that by joking about current events, sexism, racism and so on, pantomime exposes political correctness and can be satirical. This is similar to *Commedia* and street theatre performances through the ages, which have always retained the flexibility to be satirical and 'to take pot-shots at the government' (Lillicrap). More important than the satire, although that produces the laugh, is the immediacy of the comment, which highlights the sense of a shared experience and a unique event in which comedians speak directly to the audience and ad-lib freely. Although pantomime comments on and refers to current events and can be satirical, it is not really subversive, but it allows the expression of popular feelings and ideas and sometimes the expression of politically incorrect sentiments. It makes the audience feel represented by performers living in the same political world and sharing the same lived experience.

There are several features of pantomime performance that develop this sense of a shared world view, and they vary in different types of performance. In the commercial field the use of star performers from television or sports personalities creates an intertextual association[1] that reinforce the audience's sense of sharing in the comedic reference to a world it knows. The audience recognizes an actor or personality from another situation. The reading of the pantomime character is overlaid with knowledge of the actor and his/her famous roles or knowledge of the achievements of the personality in another sphere. Pantomime plays on this complexity by including reference to the other roles of the actor in the script and on the posters. There are commonly references to the programmes with which a particular actor is associated, catchphrases are used and the theme music from that programme may be used to introduce the actor.[2]

In Redhill (1997), Kathy Staff, who is known for her role in *Last of the Summer Wine*, sang 'Nobody Loves a Fairy When she's Forty' as 'Fairy Kindheart' but wearing the wrinkly stockings and slippers of 'Norah Batty', the character from the television series. The entrance of Tessa Sanderson (Olympic gold medallist in Javelin) as 'Friday' in *Robinson Crusoe* (1990) was presaged by a javelin being thrown into a target. In the same performance Doctor Evadne Hinge (a popular drag character played by George Logan) was booked to play The Spirit of the Northern Star. On this occasion there was reference to the programme *Dear Ladies* in which George appeared as Doctor Evadne Hinge, but in the programme for the pantomime it was the doctor, a comic drag creation who was credited as the performer, not George Logan, the man. So the performer was playing a character, playing a character. A more recent example of a performer stepping out of his role into a celebrity persona happened in *Cinderella*. On entering to deliver invitations to the Ball, Julian Clary remarked to the audience, 'It's me again. I'm never off – you're getting your money's worth!' (Birmingham Hippodrome 2003–4). This meant that for this moment he stepped out of character and reminded the audience of his celebrity and status.

These intertextual slippages can cause confusion too. Dave Benson Phillips talks of an experience in *Cinderella*:

> I was trying to set up I was Buttons, I work here, I'm in love with Cinderella. This child was adamant I was not Buttons, I was Big Dave from the telly and wanted everyone to know. He waited until it all went really quiet and he shouted, 'But your name's really Big Dave' (Benson Phillips).

Despite the possibility for confusion there is huge comic potential in the juxtaposition of texts. Pantomime writers and directors incorporate such juxtapositions not only in the casting and reference to performers but in references to other elements of contemporary culture.

In repertory performance continuity of casting from one year to the next replaces the incorporation of known personalities, so that the reference is from one pantomime to another, or to different performances within the repertory season. Unless the performer concerned becomes strongly identified these references are generally less clear and effective. There are significant exceptions: Granville Saxton is a recognizable and frequent villain at the Nuffield Theatre, Southampton; Ian Good appeared as Dame in Eastbourne for four years; both Salisbury Playhouse and Theatr Clywd have developed identifiable cast members over a number of years. The King's Theatre Edinburgh has played host for several years to the same group of four performers as the core of its pantomime, despite this being a commercial production. Most notable, however, is Berwick Kaler's reign as Dame and writer at York Theatre Royal which has so far continued for twenty-five years. This allows many opportunities for intertextual reference between pantomimes, which include reference to continuities of casting referred to in the performances, but also running gags such as the inclusion of, for example, references to 'Mrs Ackersley' and the designation 'babbies and bairns' in each of Kaler's shows. Each new production includes discussion of previous performances so that each new production exists not only as itself but as a compilation and continuation of the previous material.

Reference is also made to the wider cultural fields of film, television, celebrity and politics within pantomime performances. Joanna Read and Stuart Thomas, who wrote *Aladdin* for Salisbury Playhouse (2003–4), created a series of references to film and television that ran through the performance. The villain entered to a James Bond theme 'it's a wonderful way of sending up a character, with the villain thinking he's brilliant and the music – every time he comes in – it undercuts him' (Reid). Comedy is created by the different readings made possible by the intertextual reference. The Chinese Policemen in the same pantomime had a section exploring references to *Dixon of Dock Green* and Abanazar's final disguise was a costume (poncho and hat) and musical accompaniment reminiscent of the tough action hero in *A Fistful of Dollars*. Abanazar told the audience 'there wasn't much of a budget' to explain the costume. In all these cases the association of the film or television reference was set against the characterization for comic effect.

In the same production there were references to the *XMen* and *The Matrix*.

Wishy   Don't worry mum! I saw this in a movie. The X men are here! *(He crosses to Pong)* Beware my lethal adamantium claws *(claws to Pong)* my highly dangerous laser beam eyes *(stares at Pong, nothing happens, crosses to Ping)* my fearsome frosty breath *(breathes on Ping)*. Don't make me angry. You won't like me when I'm angry. *(crosses to centre)*. It's not working mum.

Dame   Try another movie, son.

Wishy takes out Matrix glasses. Ping and Pong do the same. Matrix sequence into Chase.

These references use a shorthand understood by audience and performers, providing a connection with lived experience and a juxtaposition of images usually for comic effect.

However, topical media references date quickly, and are constantly updated. Looking back at the 1992–3 script for *Aladdin* at the Yvonne Arnaud Theatre Guildford, I discover references to Jeremy Beadle, who fronted a programme called *Beadle's About*, and to Joan Collins who had recently appeared in *Dallas* and Sue Ellen, a character from the same television series. While in *Robin Hood and the Babes in the Wood* at the Northcott Theatre, Exeter in 2003–4, Harry Potter and Hermione appeared in the school scene.

Music plays a particularly important part in the use of intertextual or incongruous association for comic effect. The reference to another situation that can be caused by the use of well-known music can undercut a character or situation, or make an ironic contrast that alters the reading of the events happening onstage. For example, in *Robinson Crusoe* (Davies 1990) the theme from *Superman* underscores the entrance of the Dame to rescue the other characters from the Stockade where they have been imprisoned before being cooked. The incongruity here is between the image of Superman and the visual presence of the Dame which are juxtaposed as a result of the musical reference. The music undercuts the Dame's attempt to be heroic and creates a reflection of her visual image, in brightly coloured dress and wig and bold make-up, with bust and bottom accentuated as a female grotesque, set in contrast to the sleek muscular figure of Superman, albeit he is also dressed in bright, strange uniform. Another example exists in *Jack and the Beanstalk* (Rayment 1997), in which the theme from *Chariots of Fire* accompanies a slow-motion chase sequence making a connection between the slow motion of the heroic figures in the film to undercut the comedy figures in the slapstick chase. Other examples in *Robinson Crusoe* are the placing of the themes from *Neighbours* and *Ghostbusters* as ironic comments on the action. Ghostbusters is used during the 'It's Behind You' routine as the characters are seen being scared by the ghosts, drawing comparison with the characters in the film who rid the city of ghosts. It is notable that references to film and television themes in pantomime are often used to create humour by undercutting the comedy characters or the villain by drawing an unfavourable comparison between the pantomime characters and the film heroes. The presentation of this material signifies to the audience that the comic characters are not heroes, they are 'people like us', thus creating a sense of empathy and identification, different to the aspirational relationship created between audience and pantomime hero.

Incidental music also uses known themes and intertextual reference to set the scene. The theme from *Jaws*, or *Psycho*-style string figures warn of approaching danger. Such themes are generally only used for comedy danger because of the associations with the film which cannot be matched by the situation onstage. However, there are times when comedy effect is not required. Transformation scenes require uplifting, grandiose music and fights have fast music or, as the hero starts to win, *Star Wars*-type broad themes can take over. At such moments the signifying features of heroic music are used without the direct reference. Film music, television theme tunes and music from advertisements are now more widely known than classical music, and more commonly drawn on in pantomime, but the television and film music often refers back to classical themes. The Hamlet cigar advert is accompanied by Bach's 'Air on a G String'. Now when the Air is used in popular theatre it is likely to refer to the 'cool' imagery of the advert. Orff's *Carmina Burana*, now widely known from several television commercials, was used for the 'Nightmare Ballet' in *Snow White* (Woking 1997). This demonstrates how the cultural reference and therefore the signification of music constantly changes as a result of new associations. If a film theme is directly quoted it carries the imagery of the film and points back to the film. To avoid the direct association and the potentially comic effects, the film may not always be directly quoted. The style and tone of the film music can be used to recall the emotional intensity of the film or to tap into the same cultural imagery just as John Williams used non-representational music of a specific style to create the *Star Wars* score (Flinn 1992: 152). However, in pantomime, it is generally the comic effect or the direct reference that is required, so the quotation of popular music is a common feature of the musical score even when the songs are original.

Songs are used in the same way, where the comic effect comes from the juxtaposition of the character with the known singer. Examples are the grotesque figure of the Dame singing a Spice Girls' song or one of Madonna's songs. Lily Savage as the Queen in Snow White sang 'The Female of the species is more deadly than the male', and Abanazar in *Aladdin* at Theatre Clywd sang 'Born to be wild'. Elvis Presley's performance is implicitly (and sometimes explicitly) referred to whenever the Villain sings *Evil*. The same is true of Michael Jackson's recording of *I'm Bad* which is a common reference as audiences listen to the villain singing the song and laugh at his inability to 'moonwalk' (or cheer his success at copying Jackson's moves). What you get is a wonderful parody; the villain playing Jackson or Presley, which can be further complicated if the villain is played by a well-known television personality. Then you might see Leslie Grantham, best known as 'Dirty Den' from East Enders, playing a villain pretending to be Elvis. This complexity of reading is an important feature of pantomime texts and is relevant to the choice of music for comedy situations. Some connection between all these personas is made in the minds of audience members, and the incongruity is startling and funny. Again the effect is to distance the audience from the story, but involve it with the performers in a communal understanding of, and response to, the comic reference.

All these examples draw on the audience member as part of a collective with a shared experience of life and culture, but the response to the intertextual references also relies on the spectator as an individual in their reading of the complex cultural references. The majority of the audience is likely to draw on the same body of references and arrive at the same conclusions about the juxtapositions of material and performers, but it is at this point that the individual identity of audience members begins to become important, as they are invited to actively interpret complex layers of signification. However, in a popular performance like pantomime the likelihood of misreading is slight because of over-coding and the use of widely known terms of reference.

The understanding of a wide range of cultural references relies on the audience member's shared experiences to espouse a particular ideological stance. This would generally include poking fun at authority figures and politicians and the parody of heroic feats and events as represented in popular culture, though support for genuine heroism in life or sport. So, the audience members have been required to interpret complex intertextual references through their shared experience of life and popular culture which requires individual interpretation, and at the same time the audience members are empowered by the feeling that their cultural references, life experiences and ideologies are shared. But there is another way in which individual identity is supported.

There are a number of ways in which pantomime performance is signified as being unique at each performance. In the same way that stand-up comedians interact with the audience and play off the information received so that the audience believes it has experienced a unique event, so too in pantomime during the comedy routines of Dame and comic, and in all the opportunities for audience participation, the performance is unique. Alongside the comedy and the interaction with the audience which both result in a sense of the unique live performance there are two other devices that are present in pantomime and which signify the performance as unique.

The first of these is that individual audience members are identified during comedy routines and involved to some extent in the action. It is quite common for the Dame to ask for the house lights to be raised so that she can see the audience and pick on individuals from the community. The Dame leads the majority of the interaction building different relationships with the various groups in the audience. She is maternal to the children, she acts as a co-conspirator with the adults, but one of the ways she builds this relationship is by interacting not only with the whole audience community, but also with smaller groups or individuals within that community.

Twankey: Hello Boys and Girls. Are you all alright? Alright Boys? (*Response*) Alright Girls? (*Response*) Alright Mums? (*Response*) Alright Dads? (*Response*) Oh come on Dads, make an effort, otherwise the Widow Tabatha Twankey's going to have to come down there and cheer you up. Especially you, sir. Yes, that's me, the Widow Twankey, and I live here in Old Peking where I run a struggling washeteria with my two sons. (Jordan 2002)

Chris Jordan's scripts generally include the opportunity for the Dame to identify a particular member of the audience who will be referred to throughout the performance.

Twankey: And I must say there are some very eligible young men in the audience today. (*Pointing to a man in the audience*) Now there's a fine specimen. What's your name dear? (*Hopefully he will answer*) Oh George. Where are you from George? (*he answers*) Sorry? (*He repeats himself*) No I heard you the first time, I'm just sorry. Well, George, will you be my date for the evening? Not that you've got much choice in the matter but it is polite to ask. (Jordan 2002)

The attention of the audience is being focused on one of its members who becomes both victim and star for the evening. The individual is a participant as the butt for humour and the performance is unique because of the involvement of a different audience and participant at each performance. The audience becomes a community supporting the individual as their representative, being grateful they were not chosen and complicit with the Dame in making fun of the individual. This produces a complex series of emotions, but results in the awareness of sharing in a unique, one-off interaction.

Chris Lillicrap includes the following psychic routine in the Dame's opening spot in *Snow White*:

Stay still because I don't want anyone to get hurt. Stay still so I can pick up the vibes. Oh hang on, there's a strong one over here, very strong indeed; it's a bit spooky... I'm getting it just down... (SPOTTING FEMALE AUDIENCE MEMBER) there. It's her... her in the floral do dah, here there. Now I know what's wrong with you. You have got a very severe pain in the neck, haven't you? (POINTING AT HER HUSBAND) and there he is! Hang on I'm getting a very strong one in the middle... Oh him there. I know what's wrong with you sir... you have got what we call Irritable Trowel Syndrome. It means he's useless at gardening. That's right isn't it! I'm getting a dark one over here; very dark... it's just there... (SPOTTING MAN IN THE AUDIENCE) It's him... (TO WIFE) Is he yours? Nothing wrong with your eyesight love. (Lillicrap and Ranger)

Here, it is very clearly the relationship between man and wife that is being targeted, so that the adults in the audience can identify with the humour, join in with the laughter and feel part of the event. The same audience member will then be referred to or picked on repeatedly during the course of the performance. One such audience member was Susan the night I saw *Cinderella* at the Tron Theatre, Glasgow (2004), of whom it was said 'It's a good job the plot doesn't rely on Susan'. These may be slight alterations and form a small part of the performance, but they are extremely effective devices in drawing the audience into a sense of a shared interaction. This means that the performance is necessarily unique to that evening and that group of people. That sense of sharing a unique moment of contact with performers who are highly regarded is a feature of live performance and may account for the continued popularity of live events that are signified in this way, such as stand-up comedy and pantomime.

The other device used by comedians in many types of performance, including pantomime, to signify the performance as unique is to arrange for something to go wrong and to deal with it as though it had never happened before. A missing trumpet in a ghost routine in *Dick Whittington* (Birmingham Hippodrome 1994) gave the performers and audience a great deal of fun, but was it planned? It is a feature of pantomime that comedians insert asides and play scripted lines as asides to each other and to the audience to develop this sense that the performance is anarchic, unique and original. In the Busy Bee routine at Sadler's Wells (*Babes in the Wood* 1994) the two comedians conclude a sequence of corpsing with the lines: 'Do what the script says, you're ad-libbing now aren't you'. What they're doing here is giving a sense of a unique performance because they suggest it is ad-libbed, and that they are simply having fun. I would hate to suggest that they're not having fun, nor that comedians do not ad-lib, but I would suggest that such moments are sometimes scripted or at least planned, and that they are a clever device that presents the world of pantoland in a certain, extremely entertaining, light. Whether real or not the audience reads the performance as unique and anarchic; a world they enjoy being part of for the space of an evening.

The performers join the audience in laughing, or corpsing, at the 'accident' or the ad lib that is indicative of the fact of live performance in what is in fact a cod-corpse. The point of this device is to reflexively remind the audience of the reality of the performance and to create the sense of a unique event with live, fallible performers for whom the stage is a dangerous and embarrassing place. One producer explained how a reviewer, in all innocence, described the cod-corpse in his review, describing it as one of the funniest moments of the pantomime. The problem was that he ruined the gag for subsequent audiences. In light of this, I won't give any examples, but leave it to Forbes Masson to explain the issues.

> When I first did *Cinderella*, when I was in it years ago, in the beauty scene, we did a cod corpse, which really worked every night, and the audience was really pulled in by it.....I wrote it into this script [*Cinderella* at the Tron 2004] and the actors couldn't get it, and didn't want to do it..... And I was a bit annoyed with that, because I thought it worked so well. And then when it actually came to the scene, they cut that out, but another corpse developed. As the scene played, they started doing one themselves by accident.....But again, it's a device to let the audience in. Some people think it's a bit cheap, but if it's handled in the right way it gets the audience on their side. (Masson)

These moments, if well played and believed by the audience, generally produce a really strong contact between audience and performer and the biggest laughs of the evening. The audience feels that it has experienced something unique and personal and shared with the comedian in a moment of reality. The comic repartee gives the audience a sense that it has been involved in a special 'real' moment that gives added value to the event. The audience is drawn into the shared experience which produces contact, involvement and pleasure for the audience. They have been part of something live, special and unique and that fact allows the reflected glory of being at the event to empower the individual. The reinforcement of the individual also occurs because of the perception that the experience of the world and the ideological position within that world is shared by audience and performers. There is a sense that the performers are special people, but that the audience members can identify with them and are a little like them.

Community is created, as seen in the previous chapters, by framing the pantomime as a story being told within a performance frame that reveals the personas of the actors. But the performance is also framed by references to the real world and the lived experience of the audience and performers. The audience identifies with characters in the story, but is a co-conspirator with the comedians in the telling of the story and the reflexive acknowledgement of the conventions of performance and pantomime. The audience shares with the performer the time and place of performance and the experience of contemporary life referred to in performance. All of these increase the sense that the pantomime belongs to, and is unique to, the community.

The direct interaction of audience and performers in comedy and especially in topical gags and cod-corpsing is in direct contradiction to the idea, developed in the previous chapter, that pantomime is partly a ritual. The element of play comes in here, so that the balance of play and ritual are maintained through the combination of audience participation in ritual and communal activities and the signification of the unique, anarchic event in the playful, transgressive comedy.

As Peggy Phelan says, 'performance's only life is in the present. Performance cannot be saved, recorded, documented, or otherwise participate in the circulation of representations *of* representations: once it does so it becomes something other than performance' (Phelan 1993: 146). Pantomime not only *is* a unique experience because every performance is necessarily a live event, it consciously signifies itself as unique. There is a sense of added value in the conscious experience of the live event that not only contributes to the sense of shared community and values but reinforces individual identity within that community.

Notes

1. Intertextuality is a term often applied to postmodern performances, where its use often implies a parodic intent (Hutcheon in Allen 2000: 188–9). However, the term can be used in any case where there is reference between texts, which is not confined to the late twentieth century. A useful explanation of the process by which the deconstruction, reconstruction and recontextualization of intertextuality takes place (drawing on Walter Benjamin) is included in Fischer-Lichte 1997: 285–6.

2. The attraction to audiences of television characters and 'pop' stars is fascinating. It may partly be due to the fact that theatre is live and, therefore, in theory, anything might happen, but more fundamental is the desire to be in the presence of the famous person. The star is thus accorded a stature and reverence that may be out of keeping with their achievements.

10

Artifice and Excess in Pantomime Comedy

The last few chapters have focused on those elements of the performance that draw the audience into a relationship with either the story or the performers, but there is a further aspect that has been mentioned briefly in relation to physical comedy and design. That is artifice, which I interpret as superficial or artificial, playful, excessive and ingenious. Artifice potentially allows the audience to experience a different role at certain moments of the performance, as passive observers of a more distanced entertainment. The same idea of artifice and excess, though not passivity and distance, can be argued in relation to physical comedy, but physical comedy also has a role in creating the feeling of organized chaos. Equally, pantomime design can be considered excessive, but it also supports the transformative and magical qualities of the story, and reflects utopian images in relation to contemporary culture. Verbal comedy and dance, and to some extent music, can also be argued to be excessive and playful contributors to the artifice of pantomime.

The word 'artifice' can be used to describe a fraud or a contrivance, a piece of cunning, skill or ingenuity. It relates to the word artificial and perhaps carries negative connotations of the superficial as well as an association with things that are not from nature. The term need not be considered negative, though. One might imagine the trompe l'oeil of baroque design, or the surface decoration of a neo-gothic building to appreciate artifice, its relationship to excess, and its use of playfulness and wit. It is in this sense that the term relates to pantomime, in which comedy scenes, dances and songs are ornaments, adornments added to a story to which they bear a logical if slightly surreal relationship. Truthful storytelling is pushed to excessive and surreal ends as characters get sidetracked into moments of verbal comedy; rhythmic, alliterative or surreal humour. These scenes are excessive both in the sense that they are unnecessary to the development of the plot, and in the nature of the verbiage they produce, which overflows with wit, ingenuity and playfulness. Audiences have this opportunity to become passive and admiring observers of the skill and verbal dexterity of the performers rather than participants in a chaotic experience.

The opportunity for artifice and excess is an area where pantomime differs from many forms of contemporary theatre that follow a linear narrative. The 'integrated' musical and most children's theatre performances make a point of the fact that all elements continue to develop the narrative. This is not the case with pantomime. Although all the features derive loosely from a narrative, much of the entertainment in pantomime derives from deviations that stem from the plot but move into entirely excessive, surreal or unrelated areas. Alain Masson develops the idea of artifice and excess in relation to entertainment in the musical films of George Sidney (Altman 1981: 28–40). Instead of an attempt to reduce the distance between narrative and number as in 'integrated' musicals, he suggests that Sidney heightened the contrast between the elements as a means of extending the conventional or simple narrative. 'His intention is to compensate for the simplicity of the story-line, or its absence, by the richness of the mise en scène, [...].' (Altman 1981: 37). Pantomime has some similar features to those Masson finds in these films. These are the mix of genres (which will be discussed in relation to music and dance below), and the way the plot is interrupted for moments of entertainment. The audience is expected to enjoy and be entertained by verbal excess and deviations from the plot for their own sake. The moments of excess and artifice contribute to the enjoyment of an audience unlikely to be highly involved in the outcome of a story with which it is already familiar. This relates to the idea discussed in chapters 8 and 9 above, that a combination of the familiar (the nostalgic or ritual elements) and the new (the playful or transgressive) can be at the same time safe and exciting, familiar and stimulating, and predictable and comic.

There are clear and familiar structures and patterns that verbal comedy uses, such as rhythmic patterning, the rule of three, alliteration, rhyme and repetition. These all contribute to the shaping of the dynamics of a scene, building to a climax either for a punchline or in order to be undercut. However, the content, and the placing of these tried and tested structures, has two purposes. Moments of verbal comedy interrupt and divert from the story, but they also alter time and pace, and highlight specific moments or information and so contribute to the story. In this way comedy both supports the story and features in the surreal excess of its telling in pantomime.

Patterns of tripartite repetition can be used to establish a subject ready for the payoff. Tony Allen describes the three stages of a tripartite repetition in stand-up comedy as 'establish, reinforce, surprise' (Allen 2002:42). In an interview, Joanna Reid talked about the opportunity to build up a sequence ready to undercut offered by tripartite repetitions. She identified a dynamic shape that rises and is suddenly disrupted. The disruption of the rising pattern, the disruption of the expectation of continuity is a key to the effectiveness of this device, causing an emotional release at the point of disruption. In musical terms Leonard B. Meyer suggests that 'the greater the buildup of suspense, of tension, the greater the emotional release upon resolution', and that 'the longer doubt and uncertainty persist the greater the feeling of suspense will be' (Meyer 1956: 28). This of course assumes that the stimulus continues to increase, because once the listener becomes too accustomed to a pattern its effectiveness tends to diminish. Three times appears to be the optimum repetition in verbal comedy. So there is a dynamically increasing pattern that builds up tension and is suddenly released in laughter as the pattern is altered.

The disruption of expectations is present in the following rhyme which completes a series of nursery rhymes and doggerel songs that have disrupted endings in *Jack and the Beanstalk* (Davies 1998).

Jack: Mary Mary quite contrary
       Is your garden fit?
       It is of course
       She's got a horse
       And gives it plenty of water

All: Uh?
Jack: I can't find a rhyme for that! (Davies 1998: 11)

In that case it was the rhyme scheme that set up the expectation that was disrupted, but in the following example from *Aladdin* by Reid and Thomas (Salisbury Playhouse 2003) the build up occurs over a pattern of three similar statements before being undercut and the pattern broken after the third repetition.

Ab: Thank you, but I need a boy of stout spirits
Wishy: I've got stout spirits
Ab: Ah but I need a boy with sharp eyes!
Wishy: I've got sharp eyes
Ab: I need a boy who's not afraid of the dark
Wishy: I'm not afraid.
Ab: Look I want to take Aladdin! (Reid and Thomas 2003: 22)

In this example the use of the phrase 'I need a boy' is the central motif of the repetition providing similarity even though the rest of the phrase is not identical. The repetition of Abanazar's line by Wishy adds to the build up of tension as whatever Abanazar says is directly countered. However, it is not only the repetition that builds tension in this case, but the fact that the audience knows that it must be Aladdin who goes with Abanazar as he is the only person who can open the cave and find the lamp. The disruption of Abanazar's plans by Wishy Washy's enthusiasm is demonstrated here, resulting in Abanazar's increasing frustration, witnessed by the audience, building the dynamic tension and being released by the direct statement of the last line.

Longer sequences are built up where direct repetition establishes rhythm and builds excitement as well as frustration as the same information is endlessly repeated. The following sequence is from the same production of *Aladdin* at Salisbury Playhouse (2003).

Dame: What's going on? Where's Princess Jasmine?
Aladdin: I'm afraid Abanazer [*sic*] has kidnapped her!
Dame: Oh, no!
Aladdin: And he has the lamp!!
Dame   Oh for shame, how did he get his mitts on that [......]

Enter Wishy

Wishy: What's all the commotion? Where's Princess Jasmine?
Dame: I'm afraid Abanazer has kidnapped her!

Wishy: Oh no!
Dame: And he has the lamp!
Wishy: Oh for shame, how did he get his mitts on that!

Enter Emperor

Emp: What's going on? Where's my daughter?
Wishy: I'm afraid Abanazer has kidnapped her!
Emp: Oh, no!
Dame: And he has the lamp!
Emp: Oh for shame, how did he get his mitts –
Aladdin: Give it a rest, all of you! (Reid and Thomas 2003: 51–2)

It's important in this sort of sequence that each actor plays the scene with the same rhythm and stress, which is clearly articulated in the writing. First there are two short direct questions: 'What's going on? Where's my daughter?' that each have a stress on the first word of the phrase and a rising inflection. The response: 'I'm afraid Abanazer has kidnapped her' could run straight on into the fourth line: 'And he has the lamp'. The interjection of 'Oh, no!' inspires the increased stress on the fourth line's 'And' as well as increasing the dynamic importance of the line and the pace of the exchange. Rather than one long sentence there are three short ones. The longer line at the end rounds the sequence off and, before the answer can be supplied, someone new enters and the pattern begins again, so the unanswered question adds to the tension. The rhythms and stresses of this sequence are then exactly repeated by each new character so that the tension of the audience and the frustration of Aladdin are simultaneously built to be released on Aladdin's line 'Give it a rest, all of you'.

There is a similar, but even longer, sequence in *Robinson Crusoe* (Yvonne Arnaud Theatre 1990). After the ship that all of the characters have been travelling on has been wrecked in a storm, Robinson Crusoe enters Stage Left, has an interchange with the audience and exits Stage Right. Each of the comedians enters Stage Left in turn, assuming that they are the only person who has survived the shipwreck. Each of the comedians has an interaction with the audience before exiting Stage Right to look for the others. A procession moves across the stage stopping to deliver almost the same melodramatic speech.

Mrs Crusoe: [.....] Alone!....alone! Bereft beleaguered and bewildered! The only
             one saved from the shipwreck.... I shall be left here to die....What
             do you mean I'm not alone?....[....more interaction with audience
             and she exits]
Cockle: [Comedy business with shark.....] Alone!....alone!....ditched
             dropped and dangled! The only one saved from the shipwreck.... I
             shall be left here to die.....What do you mean I'm not alone?....
             [*Same biz* ....he exits]
Billy: [comedy business with mouth full of water...] Alone!....Alone!...
             nabbed, nobbled and knackered! The only one saved from the

shipwreck....I shall be left here to die.... What do you mean I'm not alone?.. (Davies 1990: II-1-4 and 5)

Alliteration in groups of three words is used to slightly alter the pattern of the entrance speeches, and it is noticeable that the alliteration is also in patterns of three. Each comic has different business, but goes into the same melodramatic speech to be interrupted, each time at an earlier point, by the audience, whose excitement increases at each reiteration of the speech. Immediately after this sequence all three comics and Robinson discover each other to release the build-up of excitement generated by the three repetitions and they set off to rescue Polly (the heroine) and find the treasure.

All the above examples use a familiar structure to set up expectation, frustration, tension and then release in laughter. At the same time these moments of verbal excess alter the pace and dynamic of delivery and draw focus away from the story and onto the excessive verbiage that can then be enjoyed for its own sake. There are other ways the pace of delivery is altered, either to interrupt and slow down the delivery of information, or to increase speed for comic competitive or rhythmic repartee and verbal excess. The insertion of repetition, as in the following exchange, has the effect of slowing down the Dame's speech, allowing time for the audience to gather and assimilate the information which it will be expected to remind Aladdin of later.

Dame: Not just any old ring. There's an old family legend that says should the wearer of this ring find him or herself in mortal peril
Wishy: Peril! Peril! Peril!
Dame: Then turning the stone around three times
Wishy: Times! Times! Times!
Dame: Will save the day!
Wishy: Day! Day! Day!
Dame: (To Wishy) Oh shut up!
Aladdin: Are you nuts, mum? (Reid and Thomas 2003: 28)

Wishy's lines interrupt the Dame to give this section of the scene a dynamic build as the Dame rides over the interruptions in a crescendo. Each phrase is therefore played louder and more deliberately, as the Dame demonstrates her increasing frustration with Wishy. The effect for the audience is to enjoy the silliness, but to have its attention drawn to the repeated and clearly placed information. At the same time the repetition is cod melodramatic which adds to the heightening of emotional energy, but also provides a comic atmosphere to be mirrored later, and remembered when Aladdin is in 'real' trouble. It is noticeable that in all these comic sequences the lines are short and the pace of delivery is rapid so that the conversational rhythm between the comics remains constant and the pay-off or undercutting of the moment is never delayed long.

The other types of wordplay that contribute to the verbal excess and have an effect on pace are the pun and the gag. Both distract comics and audience from the plot for a short period, although the pace of delivery remains fast. In other words, the verbal excess is allowing time to pass in the plot and for plot information to be delivered gradually. These sorts of exchanges could be regarded simply as time-fillers, but they serve a significant purpose in contributing to the enjoyment and excess of pantomime. They distract from the plot in familiar ways, but contribute to the originality of the production.

The following two exchanges occur in Chris Jordan's *Aladdin*.

Emperor: What's your name boy?
Wishee: Don't tell him Aladdin.
Emperor: Ah, Aladdin. A-lad-in trouble.
Pong: Soon to be A-lad-in jail.
Emperor: And then A-lad-in need of a new head.
Aladdin: But right now, just A-lad-in a hurry! (Jordan 2002: 12)

Or:

Emperor: A couple of dawn raids and Aladdin will be captured and in clink before you can blink.
Pong: In jail before you can wail
Emperor: Inside before you can hide.
Pong: Doing time before you can rhyme.
Emperor: Doing porridge before you can.....go to Norwich. (Jordan 2002: 17)

The scenes above are brief asides in the midst of chases. They represent breather moments when the constant movement of the chase is interrupted. Such moments can be extended as the comedians get carried away with their witticisms, as in the following sequence in which Wishee Washee acts as the straight man to PC Pong:

Pong: We're very busy in the station at the moment. There's been a spate of burglaries.
Wishee: Really?
Pong: Yes, it's been terrible. Last night two burglars broke into the razor blade factory.
Wishee: What happened?
Pong: They got nicked. And then someone vandalised the Palace lift.
Wishee: What happened to them?
Pong: Sent down for six months. And would you believe it someone broke into the Tequila shop.
Wishee: Don't tell me.
Pong: Straight in the Slammer! And finally...
Wishee: You have had a busy night.
Pong: There was a break in at the Peking poodle parlour. Someone stole all the dogs.
Wishee: Have you caught anyone?
Pong: No but we've got plenty of leads (Jordan 2002: 36).

These exchanges are all pure verbal excess. They are not developing the plot or expanding the audience's understanding of the characters. They are included for the joy of the moment, the verbal excess in playing with words and for the change of pace they offer. That might be to speed up the verbal exchange, slow down and weight the delivery of information or to change the mode from visual to verbal humour providing a step change without slowing the pace of the performance.

A very different type of wordplay, alliteration, has already been seen in some of the examples above. Each time a letter or syllable is repeated at the beginning of a word in a sequence it has the same effect as a repeated musical note. Like the use of rhyme it draws attention to itself, creating a stress on the word and an expectation that the pattern will be followed. But with alliteration the stress works more like an internal rhyme because of the proximity of the repetition. This creates a stress pattern for the phrase where the repeated letter will tend to appear at frequent regular intervals for a few, often three, words before the sequence is broken. It appeals to the intellectuals in the audience who appreciate the extended language drawn on by alliterative sequences, but who also appreciate the difference between written and performed language that allows the word 'knackered' to be linked with 'nabbed' and 'nobbled'.

Alliteration provides the opportunity for verbal excess in the second half of the scene below, in which the possibility of alliteration is built up word by word between the characters as they enjoy the wordplay. I include the first half of this exchange because it demonstrates how tension and the dynamic of the scene are built by delaying the punchline of, what is in fact, a very poor joke through rhythmic repetition. The joke's ineffectiveness is highlighted by the delivery which incorporates a dynamic build in a pattern of three followed by the release on the punchline.

Wishy:	Well, it's funny that none of us had ever heard of him, I didn't know that Dad had any brothers.
Dame:	Well, now you come to mention it, neither did I. You don't think…
Wishy:	What, mama? That he's a…
Dame:	Well he could be a….
Wishy:	You don't mean he's a….
Dame/Wishy:	Member of the Rotary Club!!
Dame:	Heaven forbid. No I was going to say you don't think he's an imposter do you?
Wishy:	What, an impersonating imposter?
Dame:	Yes, an impertinent impersonating imposter!
Wishy:	Well, mother, if Abanazar's an impotent impertinent impersonating imposter.. that means Aladdin's in trouble!
Dame:	No, My poor son! Alone in the desert with a dastardly devilish doppelganger in disguise (Reid and Thomas 2003: 39).

Yet again the characters are sidetracked from involvement with story or plot, and instead, they're playing with language, although the sense of what they say remains consistent with the plot. The alliteration sets up a rhythmic pattern that bounces through the phrase landing on any reiteration of the syllable 'imp' and later the letter 'd'. Each alliterative sequence is broken with a return to the plot and to prose from the rhythmic and therefore musical diversion. The word 'desert' sets up the possibility which is followed through in 'dastardly devilish doppelganger', but there is a hiatus before the word 'disguise' which also has the stress on the second syllable so falling out of the alliterative rhythmic pattern. The change of rhythm creates the sense of finality on the word 'disguise' that marks the end of the sequence.

Repeated words or names can also create a rhythmic pattern, even if the phrases are not of comparable length. Repetition sets up the expectation of a rhythmic pattern, but the shorter the lines and the more similar in length and content, the greater the awareness of the wordplay. In the following example the use of the names Ping and Pong at the end of consecutive lines of similar length give rhythm to the sequence. These names are also alliterative which increases the effect.

Pong: What'll he do to us, Ping?
Ping: Ooh, make us eat rice cakes till we're stuffed, then tickle us till we pop!
Pong: I don't want to pop, Ping.
Ping: I don't want to pop, Pong. (Reid and Thomas 2003: 11)

The Emperor enters and a short scene is played.

In the second half of the sequence the lines are more varied and the effect less dramatic, but the pair are building on the audience awareness of their verbal patterns and need no longer be so particular.

Pong   Goodbye your majesty. Now what were we doing before we discovered the Princess, Ping?
Pong: I think we were chasing Aladdin, Pong.
Pong: Are you sure we weren't being chased by a runaway rickshaw, Ping?
Ping: What runaway rickshaw, Pong?
Pong: That one there, Ping.
Ping: Make like Jackie Chan, Pong, and run. (Reid and Thomas 2003: 11)

The placing of the name at the end of all the lines before the last gives rhythm to the sequence even though the lines don't scan. The placing of the clear instruction 'run' at the end of the last line points to its importance and acts as a tag.

Chris Jordan, writer and director of pantomimes at Eastbourne Theatres, describes how word-order affects rhythm and therefore the effectiveness of a line. He is therefore very particular with actors about the correct learning of rhyming lines and gags.

If a gag isn't working I love it because I think 'Why? There's a reason why this gag isn't working. What's going on onstage? The audience aren't getting either something to do with the feed or the tag isn't being driven properly (Jordan).

Dame: Are you alright in the stalls?
Audience: Yes

Dame: Are you alright in the circle?
Audience: Yes
Dame: Are you alright in the upper circle?
Audience: Yes
Dame: Well you shouldn't be, It's loose. (Jordan)

To add anything after the word 'loose' upsets the way the energy lands on the word and weakens the tag. This is similar to the situation above, where the words 'and run' were placed after the repetitive 'ping' so that the finishing punch was clearly articulated. This is a musical feature of language and relies on hearing the rhythm and stresses of a phrase so that the gag is set up at the beginning and clearly finished with a punch. Joanna Reid talks about the sentence 'I'll put it in the safe for safe-keeping because it's a safe-bet it'll be safe'. She says: 'You know it's nonsense but if you play it at the right speed it sort of has a buh-doom at the end of it that gets you the laugh' (Reid). It is the repeated word that creates the rhythm and builds up the expectation which is released in the punched ending. It is also notable that most of such phrases use masculine endings to create a clean final punch.

In some cases it is essential to insert 'padding' into phrases so that the rhythmic stress falls correctly. This is particularly noticeable in writing song lyrics, and Stewart Lee and Richard Thomas talked about the way they inserted expletives as metrical padding to enable the gag lines in *Jerry Springer the Opera*.[1] The same devices are necessary in pantomime writing so that rhythm contributes to the awareness of repetition and the build of a pay-off, as well as to the sense of artifice.

Internal rhymes have the same effect as alliteration in setting up internal stresses and rhythms and allowing the characters to play with words rather than simply getting on with the story. These sorts of distractions are one of the joys of pantomime, adding energy to the scene, but also, since the story is known and the outcome expected, these deviations are what the audience becomes involved in.

Pong: Let it be known by Royal decree, there is to be no peekin' in Pekin'.
           Anyone with the cheek this week to sneak a peek at her eke shall hear
           me shriek, squeak and be up before the beak, or in a creek in less than
           a week.
Aladdin: Pardon?
Pong: Don't you be funny, sonny.
Aladdin: Well one of us has got to make an effort (Jordan 2002: 5–6).

These nonsense patterns of wordplay can grow into some quite extended sequences and have direct musical references alongside the use of musical features such as rhythm, rhyme, motif, dynamic shape and pace. Chris Jordan's *Cinderella* contains the following exchange:

Dandini: Now what's your name my dear? (he turns face to face with the Brokers
          Man and jumps back in horror)
Ron: Ron
Dandini: Do I know you, Don?

Ron: Ron, Ronald Whippet of Whippet and Run Brokers Ltd.
Dandini: Dandini, Valet to the Prince Charming.
Ron: Pleased to meet you Dan.
Dandini: Likewise Ron. So if you're Mr Whippet of Whippet and Run, where's Mr Run, Ron.
Ron: Well, my former associate Dennis Run, couldn't stand the stresses and strains of the brokerage business so Den Run ran Dan.
Dandini: Did you run Don?
Ron: Ron.
Dandini: Did you run, Ron?
Band: 'Mena Mena'
Ron: Weeelll... No. I've decided to go it alone as a one man band. I've even changed the firm's name from Ron and Den the Brokers Men to Ron Ron the Brokers... Mon.
Dandini: I see (plainly not seeing at all) (Jordan 2003: 3)

This builds on mishearing character names and the rhythms of the song 'Da doo ron ron'. It is totally irrelevant to the plot, but provides a divertingly surreal interchange.

The longest example is from Chris Jordan's *Aladdin* but he remembered the sequence, in true oral tradition, from a pantomime in which he performed written by Berwick Kaler. In this the musicality of repetition, altered repetition and alliteration comes into play again, as longer and longer sequences are built in a competitive game, before reducing to three syllable phrases at great pace and almost sung. The whole is an example of the artifice and wit of verbal comedy.

Twankey: Wishee. It's time you learned the truth about your dad.
            Dad was a sailor, Dad was.
Wishee: Was dad a sailor was dad?
Twankey: Dad was. Dad sailed the seven deadly seas dad did.
Wishee: Did dad sail the seven deadly seas did dad?
Twankey: Dad did sail the seven deadly seas dad did.
            Dad sailed to Baghdad dad did.
Wishee: Did dad sail to Baghdad did dad?
Twankey: Dad did sail to Baghdad dad did.
            Dad picked up this old bag in Baghdad dad did.
Wishee: Did dad pick up that old bag in Baghdad did dad?
Twankey: Dad did pick up that old bag in Baghdad dad did.
            Dad died of a deadly duodenal in Baghdad dad did
Wishee: Did dad die in Baghdad did dad?
Twankey: Dad did die in Baghdad dad did.
Wishee: Did dad die?
Twankey: Dad did die.
Wishee: Did dad die?
Twankey: Dad did die.
Wishee: Die

Twankey: Die
Wishee: Die
Twankey: Die
Both: Die Die di didly I diddly I ti ti (etc.) (Jordan 2002: 19–20)

During the final moments the two characters dance to the rhythm of their words.

This scene is notable for the use of alliteration, rhythm and internal repetition. Many lines have a reflective structure internally, with, for example, 'dad did' or 'did dad' at the beginning and end of each line. This is compounded by the consistent use of those two syllables throughout the whole sequence. The two syllables are augmented by very few unrelated words, and those that are added are often alliterative, such as 'deadly', 'die' and 'duodenal'. Beyond those words there are 'sailed' and 'Seven Seas' which make intertextual references to other tongue-twisters, and to 'Baghdad' which contains the word 'dad' and introduces the word 'bag' which then appears separately. Altogether, this is an extremely tight piece of writing that demonstrates the use of rhythm, repetition and alliteration to produce a surreal, musical and excessive comedy moment.

In all the above there has been no suggestion of humour that is not fit for children. However, with the use of wordplay and puns there are bound to be some *double entendres* that could be read differently by adults and children, especially since the pantomime aims to entertain all age groups. All the producers, directors and writers I spoke to take the issue of what is acceptable to a family audience very seriously. Chris Jordan writes jokes into the script but then has discussions with the cast about what can be used. When trying to push one of the Chinese Policemen through the mangle in the slosh scene there is the following exchange:

Wishee: I can't get it in!
Dame: Oh you're so like your father sometimes, he could never manage the
          mangle. (Jordan 2002: 38)

The lines could be misconstrued, although the tag line suggests that any misreading is in the mind of the hearer not the intention of the speaker. The difficulty of getting a person through a mangle provides the reason for the children to laugh at the same time as the adults and so doesn't lead to the children asking what was funny.

Paul Elliott describes a scene in *Jack and the Beanstalk* (Edinburgh 2004) in which the Dame, King and Jester are all transported back to childhood in the nursery together. They're all wearing nappies and one says

'I don't know whether I'm a boy or girl' so they look down his nappy – nothing. And they work out why he's a little boy – because he's wearing blue bootees, which is sweet because all kids know, so everybody will get the joke. (Elliot)

More commonly an Ugly Sister may say on arrival at the Palace, 'Oh the Prince's balls get bigger every year', which, of course, refers to the event but is expected to be misconstrued since it is spoken by one of the man-chasing Sisters. Some people regard that as too near the knuckle, but judging what might be acceptable is a difficult issue.

> Some characters can get away with it better than others. Often the Dame can get away with it, and that's great, the adults have a giggle and the kids are thinking, 'What on earth was that all about?' They don't get it at all, and that's fine. But it is very easy to get very crude with it. I had a big debate with my cast when I first wrote *Jack and the Beanstalk* …. In the milking scene, Jack wasn't around to help with the milking,….so Jack comes in late. And the line was, 'Jack, you're late!' And I said, 'We're not going to get away with it if we say, "Ee, Jack, you're late".'….. A lot of them would say, 'They [the audience] won't even spot it.' But if they do spot it, it's not on. Or if you say it with a totally straight face and don't reference it at all, you can get away with it, because people don't want to believe it. Those who spot it go 'Cheeky, they got that in.' (Jordan)

This issue is part of a continuing debate among pantomime creators and producers about what is acceptable, for whom, said by whom, in what context. Each case must be judged according to the context, but the reputation that some pantomimes have of introducing blue material at evening performances appears to be unjustifiably applied to all pantomimes, and largely untrue. However, what is acceptable in society is constantly changing and there can be no hard and fast rules. In any case, it is the delivery of double entendres that is vital to the perception of the material; some performers can make a telephone directory sound filthy. At the same time, some adults in the audience appreciate the wit that allows adult material, by which they are entertained, to be referred to over the heads of the children. It seems that the 'adult' humour that is allowed is hidden behind acceptable situations and comments that can be 'misread' by some parts of the audience, but direct reference to anything sexual or any swearing, common in everyday life, is not acceptable in a family show.

In conclusion, pantomime writers and comedians use all sorts of wordplay and all the musical possibilities of language; alliteration, repetition, rhythm, rhyme, dynamic change and alteration of pace, to create a web of fast verbal exchange that contributes to the pantomime by giving a sense of artifice and excess. Comedians take every opportunity to briefly deviate from the plot to provide moments of gratuitous laughter, where the musical aspects such as pace, delivery and structure are often the key to tension and release and what makes it funny. The verbal comedy in pantomime contributes to the enjoyment of the audience through its artifice and the opportunity for excess. At the same time the audience is given a period of respite from involvement in chaotic activity, a change of pace and an increased distance from the story. These are moments of skill, ingenuity and excess that allow audiences simply to sit back and be entertained.

Some final quick examples demonstrate the potential for very silly comments that contribute to the sense of surreal verbal excess in pantomime. First from Joanna Reid:

Ping: Do you think we'll get the sack?
Pong: Well, maybe a small holdall (Reid and Thomas 2003:15).

Aladdin: D'you know Uncle, it's funny that no one in the family ever mentioned
           you –
Ab: I was the black sheep!
Aladdin: In what way, Uncle?
Ab: I was a sheep and I was black, now shut up and keep walking! (Reid
           and Thomas 2003: 30)

And from Chris Jordan:

Pong: But remember, if 'ifs' and 'ands' were pots and pans, frying an egg would
      be a messy business (Jordan 2002: 41).

Notes
1. This was discussed at the *Soundings* Symposium at Rose Bruford College in 2003
   and brought to my attention by Dominic Symonds.

11

MIXING GENRES IN PANTOMIME MUSIC

The use of music in pantomime is extremely complex if one questions whether it creates distance or supports the integration of all elements of the story, because at different times music does each of these things. Comic percussion crashes, bumps and whistles highlight moments of comedy business, frame the slapstick as comic rather than painful, and offer opportunities for competitive interaction between drummer and comedian, all of which act reflexively and distance the audience. Songs and dances are often musical interventions or diversions that might start from a point in the story but that don't really move the story forward as they would be expected to in 'integrated' musical theatre. In this sense they contribute to the artifice of the entertainment and provide distance from the story, respite from the relentless pace of comedy and action, replaced by passive contemplation of visual and aural stimulation. As Alain Masson says in relation to songs and music in Hollywood film musicals, '…music and dance are not exclusively a function of revelation or commentary in relation to the narrative; they are not content just to illustrate the story told by the narrative. Their role is rather that of a challenge to the plot in its more conventional moments' (Masson in Altman 1981: 37). This is not to suggest that music has a dialectical function, although its incongruity is often used for comic effect, but that musical numbers and the artifice of mixing genres exposes the pantomime's refusal of 'integration' and the importance of reflexivity to its capacity to entertain.

At the same time, incidental music and some aspects of songs and dances maintain the emotional level, and contribute to the pace, location and stereotyping of characters in support of the story. Although the pace of delivery and the relationship between performers and audience alters, the energy doesn't falter. Melodramatic incidental music encourages or inspires a heightened, over-the-top style of acting that sometimes contributes to the comic effect and sometimes becomes emotionally charged and involving. Music also suggests the atmosphere of the scene, suggests changes of location and mood during scene changes, and raises the volume, pace and excitement during fights and chases, thus manipulating the audience response. Moreover, some songs support character archetypes through intertextual associations of genre and lyric.

There is no sense of musical continuity, but rather a use of music to serve these disparate functions within the pantomime, all of which support other aspects of the performance. Therefore it is the variety of the musical contribution to the performance, and the importance of the mix of genres to comedy and to artifice that is the focus in this chapter.

In the largest commercial companies, such as QDos Productions Ltd (formerly E&B productions), music is regulated by a musical supervisor who produces the scores for all their pantomimes. The majority of the music used in the largest pantomimes comprises well-known songs and dances in arrangements that are used from one year to the next, with perhaps twenty-five to thirty new arrangements per year. The supervisor attempts to provide a sense of unity in each score by using themes from the principals' numbers in fanfares, playout, entrance and exit music and incidental music but this is not always possible. Because of the large number of productions and the short rehearsal period, if directors, principals or musical directors change their minds about solos during rehearsals the best intentions have to be modified. However, the importance of using existing music is the familiarity the audience has with it, which provides a point of reference for the character.

Martin Waddington has worked for commercial companies and repertory theatres. For some of these he has adapted or arranged existing songs and dances, while for others he has composed an original score, although the likelihood is that the original scores would be requested by repertory theatres. He believes that the best strategy, even in original scores, is to write pastiche or well-known musical styles. 'People are not sure whether they know it or not, and it sounds comfortable and familiar, but that's the art of theatre, you present certain stereotypes that people can be comfortable with and then you play with them' (Waddington). This idea of giving a sense of comfort and familiarity in musical styles and atmospheres, but having fun and playing with expectations, correlates with many other aspects of the performance already discussed.

Whether the music is original or a compilation of existing songs, dances and themes, the completeness of the score varies from company to company, with the musical director filling in the gaps in incidental music and the drummer creating the effects. Individual musical directors employed by repertory theatres or smaller commercial companies will usually be expected to provide scores for the pantomimes they are working on, whether as a compilation of existing songs or as original music. In the commercial field QDos Productions generally produces the most complete scores containing songs and dance arrangements (drawn from popular music), entrance and exit music, fanfares and stings.[1] Some companies supply the musical director with only melody line and chord symbols for numbers, and no incidental music, dance arrangements or band parts. Even less information is available for many published pantomimes. The published script for *Goldilocks* (Morley 1981) contains a music plot suggesting extant songs for the various situations and characters in the pantomime but with the proviso '[t]his music plot does not include incidental music such as drum rolls, circus entrance music etc.' (p. vi). *Cinderella*, written by David Cregan with original music composed by Brian Protheroe, performed at Stratford East in 1998 is also released with no incidental music. In many cases in both repertory and commercial theatre musical directors are required to provide incidental music, but to conform to standard practices. Although there are differences in interpretation, the requirement to be unobtrusive and the lack of power of the music staff means that conventions are closely observed (Taylor 1999: 156).

Pantomime scores, like many theatre music scores, do not have a formal structure of their own. Individual music cues such as songs and dances have an identifiable formal structure and incidental music cues follow patterns that have become culturally ingrained as a result of consistent use in many forms of popular theatre and media for many years (Taylor 1999). However, the musical score as a whole is dependant for structure on the narrative that it accompanies. The overture may contain two or three of the songs from the show, as might the entr'acte and playout. Playon or playoff music for principal characters may reprise a theme song sung by her/him in the performance or a theme tune identifying the source of a celebrity's fame, which will be repeated whenever that character needs identification. When necessary incidental music will be used to heighten tension or underscore high emotion and may contain references to themes from the show. In other words the musical score is not worked out as a formal structure but simply put together as it serves the plot. This means that the score is a collage of musical numbers which have no connection to each other except through the alliance with the action.

Although there are pragmatic and economic reasons for the structure of the pantomime score, the result is a mixing of genres in a loose configuration of diverse but largely familiar materials that contributes to the sense of artifice. Thus, the musical score is an ornate complement to the story and the character stereotypes that offers a symbolic representation of the emotional direction of the characters. A principal boy would never express true love in anything other than a song in an appropriate musical language. He certainly wouldn't physicalize love, though, of course, this is partly the result of cross-dressed characters, it is also the result of the symbolic approach to storytelling. Equally, the villain is certain to have a moment to express his villainy in a song with a strong beat and low in pitch so that the music as well as the words and the vocal delivery symbolize a cliché of evil ('I'm Bad' in the list below). The principal girl's goodness and her love will be symbolized in lyrical ballads ('Somewhere Out There' in the list below).

The following complete list of musical cues from E&B's production of *Robinson Crusoe* (Davies 1990) illustrates the way the music score is constructed.

ACT I

1.	Overture		
2.	Fairy entrance music	(based on Somewhere Out There)	
3.	Opening Chorus	The World must be Bigger	Polly and Chorus
4.	Dame's entrance	(based on There's Life in the Old Girl Yet)	
5.	Dame's Song	There's Life in the Old Girl Yet	Mrs Crusoe
6.	Principal Boy's entrance	Fanfare	
7.	Dame's Playoff	(based on There's Life in the Old Girl Yet)	
8.	Evil entrance	Heinkel (a musical sting)	
9.	Entrance of girl's father	Hornpipe	
10.	Incidental music	Drama (a musical sting)	
11.	Evil entrance	Heinkel	

12. Billy's entrance	(based on D'You Wanna be in my Gang)	
13. Billy's Song	D'You Wanna be in my Gang?	Billy Crusoe
14. Evil entrance	Heinkel	
15. Sailors and Cockle	Hornpipe	
16. Incidental	Drama	
17. Principal Boy's Song	I want to be Free (to the tune of Wherever he Ain't from *Mack and Mabel*)	Robinson Crusoe
18. Incidental	Swelling Music as boat leaves harbour	

(end of Scene 1)

19. Song	I Should be so Lucky (Spice Girls)	Mrs Crusoe and Cockle
20. Comedy Playoff		

(end of Scene 2)

21. Underscore and song	Somewhere Out There (Disney)	Neptune, Fairy, Robinson, Polly

(end of Scene 3)

22. Dance	Sailor's Hornpipe	Mrs Crusoe, Dancers and Babes
23. Comedy Biz	Drums, Rumba and military drum playoff	
24. Evil entrance	Heinkel	
25. Incidental	Several drama chords.	
26. Chase	Medley of tunes timed to chase and projection of Power Boat Race	

(end of Scene 4, Scene 5 is projected chase)

27. Ballet	The Underwater Palace of Atlantis Comedy Ballet Entrance of Neptune	
28. Song	Somewhere Out There (Reprise)	Neptune

ACT II

29. Entr'acte	segue Cannibal Dance Theme from *Shaft*	Dancers, Robinson, entrance of Friday
30. Song	Friendship	Robinson and Friday
31. Incidental	Comedy creeping and sting	

32. Fight (Cannibal's win)
33. Incidental   Theme from *Superman*

(end of Scene 1)

34. Evil entrance   Heinkel
35. Song   I'm Bad   Bluebeard
36. Fairy entrance   Fairy Music
37. Comedy Playoff

(end of Scene 2)

38. Limbo dancing   Drum rhythm
39. Comedy biz   Percussion and Theme from
                              Neighbours
40. Song   Where did Robinson Crusoe Go?   Mrs Crusoe, Billy,
                                                   Robinson, Cockle
41. Chase

(end of Scene 3)

42. Fairy entrance   Fairy Music
43. Song   It Takes Two   Fairy and Billy segue
                                                   continue chase

(end of Scene 4)

44. Comedy biz   Squeaky Shoes gag
45. Comedy biz   It's Behind You routine
                              (using *Ghostbusters* theme and
                              'Strangers in the Night')
46. Comedy biz   Misterioso
47. Production Number   Dancers, Neptune as
                                                          Sun God
48. Evil entrance   Heinkel
49. Duel   Chase Music   Robinson and
                                                   Bluebeard
50. Song   Where did Robinson Crusoe Go?   Mrs Crusoe, Billy,
                              (Reprise)   Robinson, Cockle,
                                                       Polly, Friday

(end of Scene 5)

51. Songsheet   Yellow Polka Dot Bikini
52. Walkdown   Where did Robinson Crusoe Go?
53. Fanfare for the Happy Couple
54. Playout

This list shows that, as in most productions, most characters sing. The songs are drawn from a range of popular sources: 'Somewhere Out There' is a Disney song, 'Shaft', 'Ghostbusters' and 'Superman' are film theme tunes, 'Neighbours' is a television signature tune, 'Yellow Polka Dot Bikini',[2] 'I Should be so Lucky', 'Bad' and 'D'You Wanna be in My Gang' are all contemporary chart songs. The rest of the music is drawn from traditional songs or from older musicals and music hall. This sort of mix of genres is apparent in the majority of commercial and amateur pantomimes and some repertory pantomimes.

Elsewhere in this list it is possible to identify the opportunities for dance routines, entrance and exit music, chases and some stings. The amount of music in pantomime performance is phenomenal, with at least one song in every scene, and often many more. Most songs have some movement or dance that requires an instrumental section and set-piece large-scale dance and transformation scenes provide climactic moments. An important structural factor is that there is music at the end of every scene, which 'buttons' the scene if applause is required and may be reprised for the scene change unless a new theme commences. The end of Scene 1 has 'Swelling Music as the boat leaves Harbour', Scene 2 has a comedy playoff followed immediately by the introduction of the song 'Somewhere Out There', Scene 3 ends with 'Somewhere Out There' followed by 'The Sailor's Hornpipe' to open Scene 4 and so on. The music covers the scene change, but does not run across from one scene to another, thus music is helping to articulate the change of mood from one scene to another and signifying a change of geographical location or anticipating the entrance of a character. At these moments music is supporting the development of the story and creating the illusion of integration.

The tempo and style of songs relates to character types; the hero and heroine might sing a slow ballad, the comedy characters sing either an uptempo song or 'point number' or an ironic rock/pop number. Arrangements for songs and dances may use jazz, rap, rock or pop, but the genres and musical language draw from mainstream popular music. The result of all this is that although the score is not unified in a traditional musical sense there is a sense of unity created in the reference to known and expected music, the popular language and the restatement of themes and songs. There is also a fulfilling of expectations, that although the collage of elements in the pantomime may be a mish-mash, it is an expected and familiar mish-mash.

On a few occasions the music is themed for a particular pantomime; Martin Waddington has composed pantomime music based on Gilbert and Sullivan, on English folk tunes, on ABBA, while on other occasions the score is 'a complete mish-mash of all sorts of things' (Waddington). *Dick Whittington* in Guildford (2003) included a lullaby from *Chitty Chitty Bang Bang*, a medley of sailor's hornpipes and sea shanties including 'What shall we do with the drunken sailor' and 'Bobby Shaftoe went to sea', and another medley of traditional London songs including 'Oranges and Lemons', 'Pop goes the Weasel', 'Let's all go down the Strand' and 'Knees up Mother Brown'. King Rat (Sylvester McCoy) sang 'Jailhouse Rock' as an Elvis impersonation, Dick Whittington (Bonnie Langford) sang an arrangement of 'On the other side of the tracks', while the Finale of Act One included an arrangement of 'One Day More' from *Les Miserables* with new words as the cast prepared to sail to Morocco.

The music of pantomime is an area that has changed to reflect the period in which the work is produced, and this can be seen in the list above, but also in the majority of other pantomimes that include pop music as well as songs from variety, musical theatre, films and traditional music. However, there is a particular difficulty with using pop songs in pantomime as 'it's not particularly theatrical music' (Waddington). Kate Edgar develops this idea further when she says:

> My objection to using pop music in panto is that you stop for three minutes and sing a song. The difference between pop and musical theatre is musical theatre will take the story forward and by the end of a song you can be in a completely different place…you can reveal something and keep the story going, whereas in a pop song it's usually a statement of an emotion which is then repeated for three minutes. (Edgar)

On the other hand, given the suggestion that 'music acts as a relief from the relentlessness of the comedy' (Waddington) the fact that very little happens for three minutes is sometimes important. Edgar relates this to the derivation of pantomime from variety performance, but also to the enjoyment of pantomime: 'Curiously enough, I find that pantos that are all story and no stopping for songs are terribly dull.' (Edgar)

There are two reasons generally suggested for the range of materials used in pantomime scores: first that there needs to be something familiar to every part of the audience, from grannies to grandchildren; secondly that the place in the plot suggests the music and the pantomime tradition drives the inclusion of music that is recognizable, thus narrowing the possibilities. However, there is a third reason that cropped up in conversations with both Kate Edgar and Martin Waddington; that the music should be fun. Kate Edgar gives the following example:

> You can have Widow Twankey and Wishy Washy at the top of Act Two [in *Aladdin*], and we know that he is rich, but they're sad because they don't know where Aladdin has gone. We wrote a comedy cowboy lament with coconuts. The incongruity of the Cowboy lament in Ming Dynasty China, and the recognition of the style is tremendous fun. (Edgar)

The use of clear styles gives Edgar a template for writing original but generically recognizable music, but also allows her to have fun and play with the expectations of the audience in this case by writing a rhythmic, comic number to express sadness. She often includes Latin American style numbers 'because they're festive and they're celebratory… At the end of the day pantomime should make you feel happy and there's happy music from around the world' (Edgar). Martin Waddington also identified the fact that audiences respond to certain rhythms and will clap along to recognizable music and genres in the right situation. This sense of fun, playfulness and ingenuity in compiling the musical score from diverse, but accessible materials, is clearly a feature that contributes to pantomime's ability to entertain people from all generations.

The influence of large-scale musical theatre has had an impact on a small number of recent pantomimes, in which the opening scene has become a continuous musical fabric with short danced cross-overs as punctuation between the songs and the music underscoring throughout the scene. These large-scale productions are increasingly using music from the contemporary musicals known from London productions such as 'Putting it Together' from *Sunday in the Park with George* (Sondheim) at Plymouth Theatre Royal, which segues into a jazz dance during which everyone is introduced and then continues into 'Let the Good Times Roll' for Gary Wilmot's opening spot. A similar pattern was evident in *Cinderella* at Manchester Opera House. *Dick Whittington* at the Yvonne Arnaud Theatre in Guildford used a similar format to build to the end of the first act. An impressive vocal and dance arrangement of 'One Day More' from *Les Miserables* with the words 'Sail Away' provided a spectacular musical and visual climax to the act.

The use of continuous music underscoring the opening scene was also present in *Red Riding Hood* at Stratford East which had mostly original music. In this production a musical vamp linked the entire scene at the fair. This included Granny's entrance, 'Coming Round the Mountain' and 'Happy Birthday' with audience participation, a number about the Funfair, a 'stomp' feel number and the introduction of all the other characters. The music finally stopped only as the fair was being packed up, about twenty minutes into the performance. The excitement generated by this continuous musical fabric and the increased pace of the scene moved this minority of pantomimes towards musical theatre.

Even in pantomimes with less complete or continuous music, when there is a desire for a number to appear integrated, as in sad scenes or love scenes, underscore is introduced shortly before a song begins to prepare and heighten the emotional atmosphere for the song. In *Robinson Crusoe* (Davies, 1990) the whole of Act 1 Sc. 3 is underscored as 'a grand tableaux' [*sic*] where first the fairy speaks in rhyme over music then sings with King Neptune. The music continues under the scene between the lovers, Polly and Robinson Crusoe, swelling at the end to a quartet for the lovers and the immortals. Rather more common practice in modern pantomime, however, is to start the musical introduction at an appropriate point, two or three lines before the love song. This serves two purposes: it builds the intensity of the scene so that the characters can break into song, it smoothes the introduction of the music so that, rather than a sequence of cue, musical introduction, then song, which would draw attention to the start of the music, the music enters unobtrusively. This use of underscore is similar to that in 'integrated' musical theatre, as, for example, the balcony scene in *West Side Story* (Bernstein and Sondheim 1957, pp.60–61) is underscored with a variation on Tony's love song 'Maria' which builds into the lovers' duet, 'Tonight'.

Underscore and incidental music can be used to support the energy and tension of a scene or act as a punctuation mark. Incidental music draws on patterns and codes that have been prevalent in theatre and film music for many years. This means that atmospheres, geographical locations and character types are easily communicated to an audience imbued with the same popular cultural traditions. So, for example, there are two or three common phrases used to highlight particular dramatic moments or the entrance/exit of the villainous character. These generally involve the use of the tritone or the diminished seventh chord, low pitch, dark sonorities and loud dynamic. In the list above, 'Heinkel'[3] is the name given to a short, very recognizable phrase that is often used for the entrance of the villain.[4] Equally the fairy has identifiable musical signifiers. High-pitched, bell-like sounds in the major key or using the whole tone scale anticipate her entrance or underscore her spells.

All the incidental music uses similar signifiers to communicate through the traditions of theatre and film music. Pantomime music is not innovative in this respect, but reinforces the use of conventional musical signifiers in association with the expected visual correlate. The music that accompanies comedy chase sequences, for example, has had similar features for the past hundred years in melodrama, silent film, cartoon and pantomime (Taylor 1999). Each time the music and action are observed together the understanding of each is reinforced and the relationship, and our reading of it, appears more 'natural'. The point is that audiences take for granted their ability to understand the musical signs to the extent that they are not even aware that they are hearing them.[5] In this way music acts to draw the audience into emotional engagement with the story and characters.

On the other hand, and creating distance, music is used to punctuate scenes and to cue applause. This is a particular feature of melodrama and pantomime texts and is rarely found in more naturalistic works. For example, the end of a comedy routine may have either a comedy playoff or a comedy chord, either of which is a cue to the audience that the scene is complete and that applause or laughter is expected. The comedy chord is rarely now a simple major triad, but a ninth or thirteenth chord on the root with the start and finish punctuated by the percussion (for example, a bass drum start with a tom-tom roll and a cymbal button). The harmony of the chord gives a sense of finality produced by the root in the bass and the percussion, but the extended chord gives a sense of mutability, not a complete closure. Other uses of single chords are known as sting chords and are used to highlight an event or a word that has just occurred. They can show tension, fear or triumph, evil or good, and affect the style of acting they accompany.

In the melodrama *The Dumb Maid of Genoa* (Anon, 1828) chords are used to stress a spoken word and to build tension through the sequence.

THE SHADE: Blondel – there thy friend was foully murdered! (music in a terrific chord) Blood for blood! (chord more terrific) Revenge! (chord) Revenge! (chord) Revenge (chord – thunder). (Smith 1973: 31)

John Morley's draft of *Goldilocks* is held in the Theatre Museum, Covent Garden with handwritten production notes specifying the following example of a sting chord:

RONNIE: That horrible man has been to see her again. (Dramatic Music Chord)
GOLDIE (gasping): Benjamin Black? Oh no. (Morley 1981: 6)

In a more recent production (Rayment 1997) chords were used in a very similar way. The following is from *Jack and the Beanstalk* at Redhill, Surrey:

FLESHCREEP: So you must be Princess Jill (chord), and you live on the hill, (chord) and your hair hangs down in a plait (chord – *tremolo* building under)

FLESHCREEP PRODUCES A SACK AND PLACES IT OVER JILL'S HEAD. SHE
SCREAMS. HE HOLDS HER.
Oh Master, now transport us back, I've got the girl, she's in the sack. (Thunder
and Rumble under)
GIANT (off): Good work Fleshcreep, come up above.
And bring the girl, my joy, my love. (Thunder and Fleshcreep exit music).
(Rayment 1997: 34)[6]

The make-up of the chords in *The Dumb Maid of Genoa* is not known, although in
Anne Dhu McLucas's edition of *Monte Cristo* (1994), written by Charles Fechter
around 1883, there is a scored example of a C minor chord in root position. It was
used to highlight the dramatic and unexpected entrance of the evil 'Noirtier'
(McLucas 1994: 25 and 114). A second chord marked into the libretto does not have
musical scoring, but rather it is suggested that this was replaced with underscore and
curtain music (McLucas 1994: xviii and 67). In the course of a hundred years the
make-up of the chords has changed to reflect the development of harmony in
popular music, but the position of the chords to highlight and punctuate words or
phrases in the text or to cue applause has remained constant.

The following example, taken from *Dick Whittington* by Roy Hudd (1998) and for
which I was musical director, demonstrates a fairly recent use of sting chords and
underscore. This example shows sting chords punctuating the action as a theft is
discovered, followed by a change of mood led by sad music reflecting Dick's mood
when it is decided that he must be the thief. Finally, the music builds to a climax as
Dick vows to prove his honesty and return. The scripted stage and music directions
are underlined, the italics are my additions describing the music that was played.

	Fitz goes to the safe and finds it empty.
FITZ	What's this?
ORCHESTRA	Chord and Dramatic Music under (*unison octaves descending from D flat to C with Timp followed by quiet Timp Roll and Tremolo rumble*)
FITZ	Where's the money? Someone's had it away with the wages. (..........) Alright. I'm sorry. Perhaps I didn't put it in the safe. Everybody search. Everybody does It may be behind this bundle.
ORCHESTRA	Dramatic Chord (*G+ , A flat/G flat and continue rumbling under*)
FITZ	Whose bundle is this?
DICK	It's mine
FITZ	– and what's this? He takes the gold from behind the bundle.
ORCHESTRA	Further Dramatic Chord (*A flat/G flat, F dim7, keep rumbling*)
FITZ	Dick Whittington you're a thief!
DICK	It's not possible.
FITZ	You of all people.
DICK	I never went near the safe.
ORCHESTRA	Sad Version of 'London' (*Minor key version of song that had opened*

> *the show talking of the joys of London.)*
> FITZ   I trusted you Dick Whittington
> And now you've let me down
> The proof is here, I think it best
> If you left London Town.

(There follows an underscored section where gradually each person turns their back on Dick, except Alice whose father holds her back and Tommy the Cat who prepares to leave with Dick.)

> DICK   I haven't a friend in the world
> <u>Tommy nudges him</u>
> Except you Tommy.

<u>Tommy and Dick stand centre in a spot.</u>

> Although you all despise me
> And my appeals you spurn
> One day I'll prove my honesty
> Dick Whittington will return

> <u>ORCHESTRA</u> <u>Music swells to a big finish</u> (*Music switches to major key before final speech and gradual crescendo and rise in pitch to perfect cadence at medium pitch held until cloth in*)
> <u>Dick and Tommy stride out of the store.</u>
> <u>BLACKOUT</u>
> <u>Frontcloth in.</u>

(Hudd 1998: 1.4.16 – 1.4.18)

Despite the potentially distancing and comic effect of the melodramatic sting chords, the emotional heightening caused by the use of underscore music manipulated the atmosphere so that the speed of emotional change and decision making by the characters was rendered possible. However, there are practical difficulties in the provision of this sort of music for live performance. As Martin Waddington says:

> Panto actors are notorious, they can do one thing one night and if they feel like doing something different the following night, they will, and there you are with your incidental music all carefully written out, which then becomes an elephant the second night because it doesn't fit. (Waddington)

What often happens is that sections of music are repeated before moving on to the next section on cue, as in the example above, but that is less effective at closely mirroring the scene. 'The more you can Mickey Mouse something, make the music appear to be the expression of what's on stage, the more effective and fun it is' (Waddington). And that statement brings us back to the playfulness of the music, though it is dependent on the time being available for its development and the performers being aware of the links being created and maintaining consistent timing.

Without music melodramatic excess is comical, but with music the actors need to slow the pace of speech for audibility and will be encouraged by the slowness and by the musical expression to increase intensity. In both theatre and cinema, in scenes of emotional agitation and little dialogue, its role is doubled. As Gorbman puts it, 'film music alleviates the anxiety of silence' (Gorbman 1987, p. 57) and at the same time it articulates the emotions. In the theatre, underscore can be used in a similar way but, because of the different degrees of volume control, it is generally more sparsely used.

Underscore music is also used in some comedy scenes to fill the silence. The 'Mirror Routine', performed by Jack Tripp and Roy Hudd in Plymouth (1996),[7] is accompanied by 'easy listening' background music. The music avoids the tension of silence and gives the actors space for physical work, but it also frames the routine as part of a variety entertainment. This type of music is also used, for example, by magicians with chords at certain cues to highlight the 'applause points'. The same device is common in circus where wordless acts always have atmospheric music either to excite or calm the audience, raise or lower the tension. This framing of the routine within a variety tradition contributes to the separation of the moment of physical comedy from the plot, and to the artifice and mix of elements in the pantomime.

The other area of music that contributes most clearly to the framing of the performance is the use of percussion to highlight comedy bumps and crashes. If a pantomime cow bumps into the Dame there will be a bass drum with a rim shot, hooter or swanee whistle. If someone is hit over the head there might be a Rim Shot, Wood Block or Temple Block.

> a pratfall is usually a drum roll with a bass drum, a knock on the head is usually a cow-bell, a hit on the side of the face would be a rim-shot. Other things I expect use of are the swanee whistles and the sirens and claxons. There's usually some kind of fart joke somewhere, or somebody gets goosed. It's all pretty broad stuff. (Waddington)

The choice of percussion would be determined by volume required and how sharp an object is being used to hit the person. All of these effects are designed to have an affinity with the type of sound that might be made but removed from reality and amplified many times. So, the cow bumps into the Dame and a loud percussion sound focuses attention on the action, defines it clearly and removes it from reality. The moment of the bump might be ill-defined visually because of the dimensions of the pantomime, the cow costume and the Dame's large bouffant skirts but the percussion effect articulates a moment of impact to which actors and audience can relate. Small effects can be made larger by focusing attention on them; the Dame walks across the stage, if her shoes squeak, an effect from the pit, attention immediately goes to her feet and the audience waits for the pay-off (she takes off her shoes and her feet still squeak). All of these sounds, which are not present or are different in life, show that this is a constructed theatrical situation, the sounds create reflexivity and distance.

The use of percussion is also imperative in removing pain. In *Peter Pan* the lost boys are all captured by Captain Hook, usually accomplished by them being hit over the head with a truncheon. A temple block (or other sound effect) accompanies the moment of impact so that the striking of a child is seen as a comic moment and a theatrical trick rather than a real event.

I think what music does is tells you it's a routine, it tells you it's planned, it tells you it's been orchestrated, therefore it's meant to happen. This is not an accident, no-one's been hurt, we've rehearsed this and you know we've rehearsed this because there's music that goes with it. (Edgar)

This is comparable to 'mickey-mousing' in film scores, particularly cartoons but also melodramas.[8] Percussion acts to delineate and focus on moments of 'business', it removes any sense of a 'real' world that might linger in a pantomime and articulates comedy. Importantly, however, it needs careful rehearsal because the drummer needs to have picked up the right stick or instrument and have his eyes on the stage to catch the trick. However, with a good comedian and drummer this is the opportunity for fun between drummer and comedian which is shared by the audience.

In conclusion, it appears that music provides opportunities for distancing the audience from the performance, either by the choice of recognizable music or genre which renders an image incongruous, or by over-coding or mickey-mousing activities that are happening onstage, and rendering them both playful and painless. Music can frame moments in time, provide intertextual reference to variety theatre, circus or pop music videos,[9] and it can cue applause. The mix of genres creates many intertextual references, as well as a disruptive combination of musical numbers. These features of the musical score distance the audience from its involvement with the story and the comedians through the creation of a comedic interaction between musical genres and between familiar musical numbers and their better known representations. At the same time, music draws the audience into an emotional engagement with the performance by signifying geographical location, providing atmosphere, raising the emotional level of a scene and affecting the acting style. In these ways music contributes to the constant fluctuation or alteration of distance between performer, character, story and audience, and to the artifice of the entertainment.

Notes

1. Stings are chords or short musical phrases that interrupt or highlight particular lines of script or provide a full stop at the end of a dramatic or comic scene.
2. A 1950s song that had been recently re-released.
3. Heinkel is sometimes the name given to the villain in the pantomime *Goldilocks*. Gary Hind who showed me copies of the music from the E&B / QDos archive could only speculate that the musical motif was called that in the company's archive because of having been used in that pantomime.
4. I have explored the derivation and pervasiveness of such signs across popular culture and over the last century in Taylor (2001). The semiotic analysis of musical codes in multimedia work draws on Tagg (1979) and Cook (1998).
5. Claudia Gorbman develops this point in relation to film music in *Unheard Melodies* (1987).
6. These music cues are not all written in the printed script but were added to the score by me as MD. They are an example of what may be added by the musical director during rehearsals at the director's request.

7. This routine has been performed by them in several pantomimes including at Plymouth Theatre Royal in 1996–7, after which Jack Tripp retired. Fortunately, it is also recorded on a video of *Babes in the Wood* at the Theatre Museum, Covent Garden. Versions of this routine have been performed on television or film by, among others, the Marx Brothers and Spike Milligan and Eric Sykes.

8. This term is used in the sense defined by James L. Smith (1973, p. 7), who suggests that tragedy is where the combatant is divided in his purpose and development of character is required and melodrama is where the combatant has a single purpose and no inner development is required to defeat the demons. It can thus be used to describe many television series including *Batman and Robin* whose fight sequences were illustrated with 'Kerpoww' etc.

9. There are examples of this in chapter 9 above.

12

A Utopian Community of Dancers

I think you've got to make pictures and the simpler the pictures, so that you're making almost kaleidoscope shapes, the better... I like to put a picture up there onstage so it's like a picture book for a child. (Lynn)

Pantomime dance has similarities with the music that accompanies it in the playfulness engendered by the combination of styles that each pantomime encompasses. The separation of the moments of dance and spectacle from the narrative drive of the plot also contributes to the artifice and the entertainment of the performance. However, there are two further functions of dance in pantomime. Firstly, the dancers represent a stable community, never represented as individuals but as a unified group in a utopian society. Secondly, watching dancers dance stimulates a somatic understanding and enjoyment of the physicality of movement. This theory suggests that mirror neurons in the brain are activated by dance (as they are by music and voice) so that the watcher's brain responds as though the watcher were in fact mirroring or reproducing the physical activity. All these features together contribute to the appreciation of dance and the audience's enjoyment of pantomime.

Although there is a lot of dance in some British pantomimes, it could be regarded as the least important element and certainly is one area that is in decline in repertory pantomimes as the numbers of dancers are reduced. As Gerry Tebbutt says:

It is the least important element...you've got to have the boys and girls there because they're going to be your crowd scene, they're going to be your fishes in the under-water ballet, they're going to help out with the ghost gag and they're going to be there for the school-room scene. If you like, in lots of ways the panto chorus are supernumeraries, so I think dance is the least of anyone's worries. (Tebbutt)

In commercial pantomime in particular many types of dance and movement are present, and it is the eclectic mix of genres of dance, as with music, that is the most significant single feature of pantomime dance. The first part of this chapter, therefore, will explore the types of dance present, and where they occur within pantomime. As with music, the eclectic mix draws on popular culture and so changes as society's tastes alter, mixing familiarity and nostalgia with contemporary or topical allusions.

In the early days of British Pantomime, the early eighteenth century, 'Entertainments' contained farcical or grotesque parts, serious vocal parts that derived from Italian *Opera Seria*, and dances in the style of the French *Ballet de Cour* (Grove Music Online 2004). Added to this were the English Masque that provided scenic decoration and extravagance and the *commedia dell'arte* for the knockabout. Dancing performances, such as *The Tavern Bilkers* (1703) and *Loves of Mars and Venus* (1717), both by John Rich, contained a story in mime. These entertainments were similar to the French *Ballet d'Action* or pantomime ballet which later developed into the Romantic ballet. In the popular entertainment that grew into contemporary pantomime the Harlequinade section grew and developed, though still retaining elements of the opening, such as the immortal characters who speak in rhyme and the presence of song and dance. Gradually the pantomime developed into a comic play in which vocal music and underscore rather than dance music dominated, but the transformation scenes and spectacular moments of display remained.

The cost of employing a troupe of dancers has led to drastic cuts in the forces employed. Norman Robbins reports that *Robinson Crusoe* at Drury Lane in 1881 employed over one hundred adults and two hundred children in the cast. The pageant in *Sindbad the Sailor* (1882) 'involved three hundred "supers" and took six minutes for them to cross the stage' (Robbins 2002: 158). By contrast, many repertory pantomimes now have no dancers but employ actors who can 'move' for the song and dance numbers and local children for speciality and production numbers. Some commercial companies follow the same pattern as the reps, but the larger pantomimes retain a small troupe of dancers who also work as understudies. *Robinson Crusoe* at the Yvonne Arnaud Theatre, admittedly a much smaller theatre than Drury Lane, employed a cast of nine in 1990, plus seven dancers (five girls and two boys), an orchestra of five musicians and sixteen children who appeared as two groups of eight on alternate nights. At a larger theatre (Plymouth Theatre Royal) in 2003, a cast of eight was supplemented by eight dancers (four boys and four girls), eight musicians and two teams of ten juveniles. The size of the troupe and the level of specialism and dance training obviously impacts on what is possible in different venues. A general rule of thumb is that smaller productions will have more song and dance routines and staged[1] musical numbers with an occasional speciality or featured dance, while the larger companies can still mount several featured dance numbers as well as the other types of dance.

Like the music of pantomime, the incidences of dance are dependent on the structure of the plot, and the first occasion for dance in the performance is the opening chorus. In the musical list from *Robinson Crusoe* (Davies 1990) in chapter 11 above, the opening chorus is the song 'The World must be Bigger' sung and danced by Polly (the principal girl) and the chorus. The relationship between some parts of the pantomime and musical comedy is most evident in the opening number, which remains similar to the opening numbers of early-twentieth-century European musical comedies such as *White Horse Inn* or *The Student Prince*, in which idealized, happy peasants or villagers are presented. Gerry Tebbutt also relates the opening happy village scene to the Princess Theatre shows at the turn of the nineteenth century in New York, which opened with a chorus of boys and girls doing a number 'that bore no relation to the rest of the evening' (Tebbutt).

Despite the fact that the opening number may not be closely related to the plot, both Tebbutt and Lynn stress the importance of the opening number to present a scene about happiness. Other opening numbers that remain popular are 'On a Wonderful day like today', or 'Gee, but it's good to be here', which lead to dance routines that incorporate musical theatre dance movements, lifts, spins, high kicks and a fair amount of unison movement and spatial patterning. The overall appearance is designed to be impressive, bright, energetic, and constantly moving. The purpose of the opening company number is to establish the pace of the production, which will be visually fast, bright and energetic, and to present the opening equilibrium of a happy community, full of life, youth and vigour in an energetic, utopian village scene. Figures 29 and 30 depict this sort of movement and energy, though the photographs were not actually the opening scene of the pantomime. The same type of choreography occurs in other village scenes which show this style of company routine

Figure 29: Dancers at the County Fayre in *Jack and the Beanstalk* (Plymouth: E&B Productions, 1993). Photograph by Eric Thompson

Figure 30: Dancers in *Dick Whittington* (Plymouth: E&B Productions, 1992). Photograph by Eric Thompson

that presents constantly changing spatial patterns, aesthetically pleasing pictures and high energy movements in a crowded, busy scene.

In repertory performances without a troupe of dancers some of the principals and children present the opening number. In this case the dance is far less intricate but still signifies energy and happiness and the unity of the company (fig. 31).

Some pantomimes have specific locations that can be identified in the opening scene, such as *Dick Whittington*, which is often introduced with a London medley. The type of music then suggests the type of dance movements, with London medleys likely to have 'knees up' type music hall dance movements. Alternatively the pantomime might have themed music as described by Martin Waddington above, and Lorelei Lynn talks of a pastiche of Old Hollywood for a version of *Dick Whittington* at York Theatre Royal, the Rock 'n' Roll theme for Peter Rowe's *Aladdin* at Theatr Clywd and folk music in *Sleeping Beauty* at Keswick[2] which all inspired different dance styles.

Figure 31: The Company in *Aladdin* (Salisbury Playhouse, 2003). Photograph by Robert Workman

I think it just depends on what music you've been given and the situation. All of that courtly business at the end of Sleeping Beauty has to be English folk, courtly type dancing...they were all dressed in medieval costume so you can't do a knees up really. Whereas with York it started off with a big Cockney number....the Lionel Bart school of choreography. (Lynn)

Gerry Tebbutt talks particularly of Roy Hudd's pantomimes, which tend to use more variety and music hall songs and dances, as an influence on his own ideas of what to include in pantomime: 'I try to do songs that are of a similar type and feel so that the whole thing knits together much more'. This also demonstrates the influence from musical theatre in his desire to see pantomime 'knit together'.

In many of the large-scale pantomimes the choreographer will introduce acrobatic tricks or modern dance styles within the framework of musical theatre routines or in dance routines specially designed to be contemporary. In the Robinson Crusoe list above, the theme from *Shaft* as music for a Cannibal Dance provided that opportunity. More recently the dancers and babes all dressed as rats to perform the Rat Rap in *Dick Whittington* directed and choreographed by Carole Todd (Birmingham Hippodrome 1994).

Although the music inspires a range of movements appropriate to the genre, which is comfortable and familiar for the audience, other movements are introduced that have become popular through mainstream pop music and dance. So, in the Rock 'n' Roll *Aladdin* at Theatr Clywd, there were movements alien to the 1950s and 1960s of the music, with body-popping and isolations more associated with urban music of the 1990s and beyond. Familiarity and nostalgia with certain types of movement are interspersed with contemporary movements that have topical associations. As in other parts of the pantomime this combination provides comfort and familiarity for people of all ages, while the genre continues to develop in line with popular culture, draws the audience into an association with the world of the pantomime through the shared experience of topical references, and maintains the distance engendered by the artifice of dance.

Song and dance routines for the principals draw on a similar mix of genres, and combination of the familiar and the contemporary, but there is a strong association with the music hall traditions, especially in the Dame's numbers, as in figure 32. Here the number is addressed to the audience and the performers work in lines facing the audience performing simple steps mostly in unison. This type of choreography results from the requirement to sing and dance at the same time, from the experience of the performers concerned, from the type of music used, and from

Figure 32: Jack Tripp and the Babes in *Babes in the Wood* (Plymouth: E&B Productions, 1991). Photograph by Eric Thompson

the importance of maintaining the direct relationship with the audience that music hall routines allow. A short dance break, perhaps half a chorus long, is often inserted into the Dame's numbers which she can dance but which more often involves the babes and produces the 'Aah factor'. The Dame is seen as maternal because of the relationship established between her and the children in this routine, and the children never fail to be sweet, attractive and appealing.

When the desire of the production team is for a more integrated approach, social dances, particularly the waltz, the polka and other partner dances, are a useful starting point as the dance then appears to grow out of the dramatic situation, such as a ball or festival. However, unless the movements of the social dance are developed and staged spatially it can be less interesting to watch than other forms of dance. This is particularly true in pantomime where the majority of the performance is addressed directly to the audience, but a partner dance is not. Choreographers then introduce spatial patterns so that dancing couples create interesting shapes and movements, or will begin with the social dance movements, but very quickly incorporate an extension of those movements that allows the couples to separate and move individually.

Roy Hudd uses social dance as the starting point for many of the dance sequences in his pantomimes in order to maintain the narrative drive, so that the dance grows out of the situation. In *The Legend of Mother Goose and the Golden Eggs* (Theatre Royal Plymouth 1995) there is a grand scene in the Hall of Gold as the conclusion to Act One. This is introduced by an extract from Grieg's *Norwegian Dance No 2* which breaks straight into the 'Trisch Trasch Polka' for the entrance of the dancers in a social dance. Here there is a sense of the dance growing out of the plot, but it is still a moment of artifice that is not entirely necessary to its development. Later in the scene there is a second social dance, a waltz, before the evening is ruined by the revelation that Mother Goose is not beautiful and by the entrance of the villain, Vanity. The social dance restarts, in a feverish spellbound version at increasing speed as Vanity transforms the dream into a nightmare. In this case, as in much of Hudd's work, the dance develops from social dance styles, but the social dance form is altered or extended to represent the dramatic events. In this case, too, the social dance is associated with happy communal situations, just as ballet tends to be associated with idealized country images of anthropomorphic birds and animals or beneficent magic spells.

Other dance styles draw on many theatrical traditions. Broadway and the musical theatre provides a source for tap numbers, large company numbers, and jazz dance, while music hall and variety provide the source for many of the song and dance routines of the principals. Added to this are references to contemporary pop videos, rock and roll movements and disco styles, so that there is an enormous range of movement to choose from. The movements will be inspired by the choice of music, the character of the performer and the place in the plot, but the combination of genres contributes to the ability of pantomime to provide something for people of all ages and the mix of genres that causes a momentary disruption.

As Chris Lillicrap eloquently describes it:

It's a bit like a pudding, there's got to be a bit in there for everybody. So there's something in there for mum, there's something in there for dad, there's something in there for the kids. There's some proper singing for grandma and granddad, because they like proper singing, not some of this modern rubbish. So we always try and get somebody to do a proper song, and the same with dance, there's some proper dancing. (Lillicrap)

The combination of genres serves the same purpose as the musical combination and is directly related to it. It provides appeal and familiarity for people of all ages, and nostalgia for the older members of the audience. At the same time choreographers constantly update and incorporate new fashions not only to appeal to the young, but to provide cultural reference and topicality. In this way pantomime continues to change and develop in line with the society it entertains. The identity of the world of the performance established through the comedy and topical references as overlapping with that of the audience is extended into the choreographic and musical performance providing continuity of experience across the whole performance, even as the audience is distanced from the story by the disruptive mix and sits back to watch the moments of visual ornamentation.

Dance and musical staging also offer opportunities to weave magic and paint pictures. As Lorelei Lynn explains, 'I think we're very lacking in magic these days and probably the pantomime is still the place that you can do it with integrity'. The use of magic and illusion in design was discussed above, but certain types of dance alongside appropriate music can create atmosphere and contribute to the sense of distance, artifice and a utopian world. The most important place where illusion and magic are required is in the transformation and its ballet sequences. In contemporary pantomime the transformation scene generally features scenic excess as gauzes rise to reveal fantastical images, clothed in glitter, dry ice and atmospheric lighting. The scenic excess is almost always supplemented by the dancers, whether as sprites (near the Pool of Beauty in *Mother Goose*), jewels (in the cave in *Aladdin*), civic dignitaries (in the Dream sequence in *Dick Whittington*) or just about anything else the writers, designers and directors dream up. The situation being presented often inspires the movement style and the type of dance routine. For example, the upright stance of civic dignitaries processing to award Dick Whittington the mayoral robes and badge of office limits the amount of upper body movement, and suggests the stately pace of the dancers in that scene, whereas the sprites or spirits around the Pool of Beauty are likely to be floaty creatures wearing chiffon and using graceful arm gestures, running patterns and arching, swaying and curving of the upper body. Jewels, goblins or skeletons in Aladdin's cave could dance in any style appropriate to the music chosen, but good sprites are more likely to be balletic or graceful (as in fig. 33), bad sprites or rats might use angular or acrobatic moves (fig. 34).

Chris Lillicrap comments on the importance of moments of dance, and particularly ballet, in transformation scenes.

We do occasionally put ballet in...For example, in *Jack and the Beanstalk* during the growing of the beanstalk we would feature dancers doing a speciality... We did it in *Snow White* with the animals covering Snow White with leaves and turned it into a complete mimetic dance sequence. (Lillicrap)

Figure 33: Dancers in *Robinson Crusoe* (Plymouth: E&B Productions, 1988). Photograph by Eric Thompson

After the magic beans are thrown into the garden in Tudor Davies' *Jack and the Beanstalk* (Plymouth Theatre Royal, 1998), the Cosmic Fairy summons the Fairy Queen who casts a spell for the Transformation.

MUSIC: TRANSFORMATION ONE
As the COSMIC FAIRY and THE FAIRY QUEEN move into the main body of the set the cottage splits, and exits left and right.

FLOWER FAIRIES enter and begin the;
BALLET 'Midsummer Nights Dream'

During the ballet, beanstalks are seen to grow.
One USC – one in Orchestra pit L – One in orchestra pit R (climbable)

Towards the end of the ballet a cock crows to herald the dawn. The FAIRY QUEEN gathers all her minions to exit the scene, leaving DAME TROT'S garden a very different place.

END OF SCENE (Davies 1998)

Act Two of the same production begins in the Land of Clouds which is revealed through a gauze at the end of the Entracte. The music segues into the Cloudland Ballet danced by dancers and babes. Both these scenes use ballet in association with metaphysical events inspired by the fairy's good offices.

Ballet has a particularly important place in pantomime as the moment of high culture which has direct associations with spells and magic transformations. There is a clear relationship between the grace and beauty of ballet as a 'higher' art form to good and beneficial magic, while some contemporary popular forms such as street dance and acrobatics are related to evil characters. However, the seriousness and elitism of ballet is also undermined and mocked.

On John Morley's video *Pantomime Dames*, Billy Dainty, as the Dame, appears in a pink tutu and performs his attempt at ballet, which is of course a travesty. *Robinson Crusoe* features an Underwater Ballet which is subverted by a comedy parody of ballet (Davies 1990: 1-6-34). The scene is the Underwater Palace of Atlantis.

Figure 34: King Rat and his Crew in *Dick Whittington* (Plymouth: E&B Productions, 1992). Photograph by Eric Thompson

The lights come up on a Sea Gauze to establish that we are under the water. We bleed through to see a beautiful underwater seascape. Sea Anemones (Babes) surround a large undulating Coral (Dancers). Robinson Crusoe is discovered – he is helped through the underwater and exits.

Toward the end of the main Ballet the Music becomes grander and we enter the COMEDY BALLET (Mrs Crusoe and Cockle) – they are resplendent in full ballet costumes (I-6-34).

Chris Lillicrap describes a scene in his 2003 production of Mother Goose:

We had the dance of the baby geese at the entrance to Gooseland. We actually do a very straight ballet – and the baby geese are doing this very straight ballet, with proper pointe stuff. Nobody says anything, but suddenly, in the middle they have a look round and realise nobody's looking, and so they burst into the Birdy Song. So suddenly these very elegant young ladies get down and do it, and then there's a huge 'Oi!' from the wings and they go back to being proper. So it's dance used to take the piss out of dance, basically. (Lillicrap)

The same format of the juveniles breaking out of a serious balletic moment when not observed is present in some of Roy Hudd's pantomimes.

The use of ballet in association with metaphysical elements, the heroic characters or the heroic quest, while the Dame and comics send up the 'higher' art forms, plays a part in the separation of the characters as heroic or comic, base and worldly or destined for higher things. Society's associations are highlighted here, as ballet, often regarded as an elitist or higher art form, is used to represent heroism and magical events, while popular forms are used for commoners and contemporary urban movements inspire the evil and villainous characters.

Other dance numbers may contain multiple narratives, jokes and comic moments that contribute to the sense of fun that is strongly featured elsewhere in the pantomime. As has become clear in the course of this study, all the parts of pantomime contribute to a whole that is anarchic fun but remains essentially truthful to the story though often reflexive and excessive. Dance contributes to the sense of play, and of fun, which is apparent throughout the performance. Lorelei Lynn describes the fun she had creating the opening street scene of a pantomime she had choreographed: 'When I did York [the Theatre Royal] I put in these little street urchins who were pickpockets and a flower girl and everything'. Here she is describing a street scene in which, rather than choreographing a company number, she introduced little moments of narrative within the plot. This is extended in comedy numbers in which she includes comic or knockabout elements that develop, or at least continue, the relationship between characters. So the Dame might put out a foot to trip people up. She goes on:

When you're doing the Dame's number, she's got to get one over on the baddie, so he's got to be kicked up the bum, she's got to be pushed over, he's got to have his head covered up by her skirt....You're bringing all those funny elements to dances such as the camp tangos and the camp ballet. (Lynn)

She also described a scene in which she incorporated Morris dancing so that Abanazar could keep getting knocked about, while Aladdin tried to mesmerize him with a Morris dancer's handkerchief. These examples demonstrate the continuation of characters and relationships through dance numbers performed by the comic or villainous characters, but also the use of dance to introduce narratives and relationships and flesh out the story. This is a feature that is perhaps more common in musical theatre performances, but the influence of popular forms on each other, as production teams cross over between them, remains and so pantomime's development continues.

The final example of the mix of genres is the occasional incorporation of actor musicians into the performance in some productions. Figure 35, from *Sleeping Beauty* at Theatre Royal Winchester (2003), shows the cast engaged in a musical number and playing instruments. This severely limits the movements they are able to perform, but provides a different sort of physical engagement with the singer and the number. The activity of playing becomes the mainstay of the relatively simple choreography, though there is some unison movement that creates a sense of framing the event. Figure 36 is from the Rock 'n' Roll *Aladdin* at Theatr Clwyd (2003) which also used actor musicians. In this case, since the musical instruments are set

Figure 35: The Company in *Sleeping Beauty* (Winchester: Hiss & Boo Productions, 2003). Photograph by Robert Workman

up around the stage throughout the performance, the performance frame is that of a high-energy bizarre concert played by the pantomime characters who also perform a pantomime story. The limitations of playing and the need to hold a hand-mike both contribute to the reading of this production as both pantomime and concert and affects the type of movements possible. However, the energy and the framing of the performance are consistent with the reflexivity in the majority of pantomime performances.

Dance serves several purposes within the plot of pantomime, creating atmosphere and developing comedy moments and relationships. The consistency with other parts of the pantomime is apparent in the play with distance from involvement with the performers or with the story. The moments of magic, illusion and transformation, often using balletic movements, encourage the audience to engage in passive contemplation of the beautiful pictorial effects, while comedy moments encourage the audience to laugh and be involved with the characters. Just as in the presentation of the story there is constant movement between interactive engagement with comedy and passive contemplation of romance. So sometimes dance contributes to the atmosphere and mood setting and at other times distances the audience from involvement with the story but engages it with the contemplation of illusion and pictorial imagery, or contributes to the genre mix, the excess and playfulness of the event.

Figure 36: Aladdin and Company in *Aladdin* (Theatr Clywd, 2003). Photograph courtesy of Theatr Clywd

There is a third feature of pantomime dance, which is that it is presented through communal activity, representing the community of dancers clearly as part of a greater whole. This is a significant factor in the ability of pantomime to construct a utopian fantasy world. Dance numbers, because they require the performers to move together, remove any sense that the performance is spontaneous. All the performers know the steps and there is uniformity to the movement that denies any sense of spontaneity. On the other hand, the energy of music and movement replaces the lost spontaneity, drawing the audience into kinaesthetic engagement and enjoyment of the spectacle rather than involvement with the story. The solos and duets attempt to maintain the illusion of spontaneity even though the presence of a band of musicians playing the correct arrangement undermines that position. In the end, though, however much there is an attempt to integrate some numbers or maintain the illusion of spontaneity,[3] the very fact of singing and dancing removes that possibility, and in a form where the movement between story and performance is highlighted, the songs and dances merely add to the artifice, through the reflexivity and distance from the story.

Instead of presenting either the illusion of realism or the illusion of spontaneity, the company dances in pantomime contribute to the representation of community. This idea is developed from Richard Dyer's extension of Enzensberger's vision of a utopian society in which community is one of the defining features, rendered visible in film musicals by company numbers, collective activity and communal interests (Altman 1981: 183–4). In pantomime the unison movement, the uniformity of dress for the chorus members, and the effectiveness of company dance is created by the whole team working together to create a single performance that is eye-catching and vibrant. The dancers are not named, they are not presented as individuals, and even in village scenes they are presented as a group with a shared experience of the world. The principal characters are presented as different from the group, the comedy and metaphysical characters are completely different, but the principal boy and girl are similar enough to be seen as the exceptions who become the heroes of the community.

The pantomime world is presented as bucolic and happy, an idealized community threatened by poverty, hunger or a giant. The Utopia presented is not a political framework for a new society, but an idealized 'other' place where all the villagers are young, attractive, energetic, and have the ability to sing and dance as one, where music accompanies action and everyone lives happily ever after. The representation of an idealized community through the use of unisons in movement, singing and costume is one of the features Richard Dyer points to in his article 'Entertainment and Utopia' (in Altman 1981: 175–189). In this article Dyer develops an argument in relation to film musicals that attributes the ability of popular musical entertainments to represent a utopian view of the world to five non-representational features as much as to the events of the narrative. In his list Dyer includes Community, Energy and Abundance, the last of which Dyer defines as 'Conquest of scarcity; having enough to spare without sense of poverty of others; enjoyment of sensuous material reality' (ibid.: 180). Community can be seen in communal dancing, singing and appearance. Energy has been identified above in the opening number, and is also present in other dance sequences, in the pace and dynamics of musical accompaniments, playoffs etc. and in the pace and physicality of verbal and physical comedy. Abundance is revealed in the excess of colour and energy in dance numbers and in the spectacle of transformation scenes, and in the genre mix of music and dance. All these elements contribute to the sense of a community established by dance and dancers in pantomime performance, and to the utopian fantasy that is projected.

There is a further aspect, though, and that is the way mirror neurons in the brain of the watcher allow her to do more than watch the spectacle, rather the watcher experiences the physicality of the movement. Part of how humans learn is by imitating others, and part of how we understand is in terms of our own experience of making the same or similar movements and sounds (Cox 2001: 195). What this suggests is that the passive contemplation of spectacular dance scenes is not really so passive in the brain of the observer, who somatically understands the bodily movements of the dancers, even if she has never danced in exactly that way. Since many of the dances in pantomime are joyous or celebratory, this physical engagement with movement and voice can contribute not only to the understanding of the mood, atmosphere or emotion of the moment of dance, but also to the enjoyment of the audience through the direct physical transmission of mirrored physical and emotional states.

In the end, the dance, like the music of pantomime is comprised of a series of unrelated dances in a range of styles. The numbers are only rarely fully integrated into the plot, scenes at balls and festivals, which generally incorporate social dances, are the exception, but, as discussed above, the scene will rarely contain just a simple social dance. For the most part, dance numbers will be an enjoyable interruption to the narrative. Alain Masson argues that inserting dance numbers that are not integrated into the story and the use of a range of different dance styles both contribute to the artifice of an entertainment (Altman 1981: 30). The dance numbers are not realistic but are part of the artificial world in which the pantomime story exists. The artificiality of the range of dance styles and the incongruity and fun of the interaction of genres all contribute to the creation of distance between narrative and number and between the story and its framing. The dancers do not step out of the world of the story, but they contribute to a world of excess, of community and of entertainment. The dance contributes to a richness and abundance in the visual world that is a complement to the simple, predictable story, and a means of extending the transformative and utopian vision.

The incorporation of dance numbers that take the spectator on new journeys at a fantastical tangent to the development of the story can frustrate the spectator as well as releasing them from identification with the story.[4] As with the music, the framing and the comedy, the pantomime dance is constructed of elements that spring from the telling of the story, but are essentially superfluous to the story. Rather the dances contribute to a sense that fantastical events are taking place in an unreal and artificial utopian world. The dances and the spectacular transformations contribute to the artifice of the work, providing colour, life, energy, a sense of community and a sense of embodied joy in the mimetic awareness of physical energy. It is ultimately through the combination of artifice, reflexivity, abundance and excess alongside the story and the audience involvement, in a constant play with distance, that the joy and entertainment of pantomime is produced.

Notes

1. 'Staging' is a term used to describe the process of adding movement and possibly some dance steps to songs where the words and music are the primary features. It also describes the situation in both repertory theatre and commercial pantomime where the principal performers are predominantly 'actors who move' so the numbers tend to be 'staged' rather than 'choreographed'.
2. This was not a pantomime but a children's musical.
3. Jane Feuer describes the 'myth of spontaneity' as one of the three myths of entertainment in film musicals, the others being the 'myth of integration' and the 'myth of the audience' (in Altman 1981: 163ff).
4. This idea is developed from 'Patterns of meaning in the musical' by Martin Sutton in Altman 1981: 190–196.

THE EPILOGUE: WHAT'S ENTERTAINMENT?

The word 'entertainment', like the words 'illusion' and 'artifice', sometimes has negative connotations in the arts and in academic life. There sometimes appears to be a correlation between the commercial world and entertainment, while the subsidized or the experimental arts seem to have different objectives. This provides the potential for a debate that I won't enter into here, although it is clear that pantomime exists in both the commercial and subsidized sectors of popular arts. However, Rick Altman identifies further confusion when referring to popular entertainments which can simultaneously relate in a positive sense to a folk ethic or negatively to commercialization (Altman 1981: 7). The same is true of pantomime which develops through an oral tradition using stories from folk and fairy tradition, and exists in a commercial world where its development is subject to economic realities, even in the subsidized sector. The fact that both positions can be argued in relation to the same work points to a problematic positioning of the idea of entertainment within the arts.

The verb itself, 'to entertain', can be variously interpreted as 'to amuse', 'to occupy', 'to please' or 'to divert'. As Rick Altman writes in his editorial introduction to Richard Dyer's article (in Altman 1981), the derivation from the French term 'entretenir' suggests a holding of attention. The use of this term for entertainment in France has disappeared to be replaced by the verb 'divertir', which suggests a diversion or a turning of attention away from something. It is my contention that pantomime does both of these things. The ways in which the story is told to draw the audience into an engagement with the hero, and an empathetic attachment to the success of the quest holds the attention. Attention is also held by the familiarity of the event, and the comedians hold the audience in a relationship of complicity as they join in to create the unique experience of the live performance. At other times in the performance the audience is diverted by the artifice of dance, the illusions of transformation and the surreal playfulness of physical and verbal comedy, as well as by the distance created through the reflexivity of the performance. Richard Dyer's article explores the possibility that musical films of the Hollywood era engage with both these possibilities philosophically through the production and reaffirmation of values. This is also apparent in pantomime in the notions of community, morality and the utopian ideology that the pantomime promotes.

So pantomime is entertaining, certainly. It is entertaining through a combination of trickery, illusion, artifice and deception that promotes in the audience a feeling of goodwill, spontaneity, playfulness and the illusion of sharing a unique moment that is genuinely 'real'. And in many cases it succeeds and remains hugely popular. But there is also real skill and artfulness in mastering the balance between diverting and drawing in. Pantomime is an art that requires training, practice and skill, in which it is important not to underestimate the value of 'A talent to amuse'.[1]

Several features of pantomime might account for its continued popularity, whether performed by comics, actors, singers or local people. These might include the groan of recognizing the old gag, song or routine, but the enjoyment of joining in with the punchline, or of listening to it adapted and delivered with joy, self-awareness, and infectious enthusiasm; the safety of slipping on the old cardigan of the story, knowing its comfort, warmth and familiarity; the excitement of the roller coaster ride in that live moment of terror as the egg flies over your head, and the unique experience that you share with the rest of the audience on this particular occasion; the joy of suspending disbelief and accepting the world of magic and fairies and believing in the utopian idyll of the characters; enjoying the reflected glow of happiness in believing in a transformative future where anything is possible; singing and shouting and throwing off the constraints of vocal restriction to share the communal experience, to breathe deeply and to release sound; and finally, to release your child-like self to enjoyment, frivolity and enthusiasm.

An area of particular interest to me has been the means by which audiences are encouraged to engage with this experience, so that they are temporarily transported or transformed. It is in this area that, I believe, pantomime excels through a number of features of its relationship with its audiences. These are the ways in which pantomime defines itself as part of a community and creates an interaction with a community in order to entertain and inspire; the ways pantomime draws its audience into relationships whether with the story, with the comics, or by allowing it to enjoy spectacle and danger in an ever-changing kaleidoscope of artifice and ingenuity; the ways pantomime reflexively reminds the audience of the theatrical present and the illusions being presented in a unique interaction; the utopianism of the transformative story, the communal situations and the ritual activity; and most fundamentally, the constant interaction between familiarity and novelty, ritual and play.

The pantomime community on the stage is represented as idyllic and bucolic. The dancers move and perform as one group and people are clearly good or bad, love each other or hate each other. Relationships are not complex. All these things might suggest that the world of the performers is distant from that of the audience, incredibly simple and straightforward and rather childish, and that the audience would not be able to share an empathetic relationship with the performers. But the pantomime encourages the audience to share in that world if only for two hours, to engage with that utopian, unattainable, impossible dream. And it does it not by directly inviting the audience to share in that utopian dream, but by making clear that the performers in this idealized world also share the world of the audience. Pantomime asks the audience to identify with the fallible comics, who repeatedly use topical and cultural reference, cod-corpse, comedy and play to present themselves as people of the contemporary world, and to provide the bridge between performance and audience. The comics make mistakes, are duped by the villain, and get covered in slosh; they are embarrassing and real. Even the Dame's costume which distances identification with the story contributes to this engagement, as the Dame speaks to both men and women, mocking and appreciating the qualities of each and the relationships between the two.

Interestingly, it is in the relationship between audience and performer that amateur and community pantomimes are so successful. The performers are already known to be the fallible real people, members of the local community, who are putting on a performance. They are what the pantomime comics represent themselves to be. So the audience is engaged by the same framing and intertextuality as in professional performances, caused by their previous knowledge of the performers, and the bridge between performer and audience is easily opened.

Then the audience is asked to recognize that fallibility and embarrassment are things we all share, by releasing its inhibitions and joining in with the playfulness. Yet there is safety; the audience takes part in ways that it expects because the performance has a long history and a relatively slow pace of change. Similar routines and catchphrases, stereotypical characters, relationships and stories mean that the audience can cast off some inhibitions in the knowledge of what will be expected and of how great the danger really is. It can partake in ritual activities and seemingly anarchic laughter and response from a position of security. It can appear to rebel against conformity within defined boundaries. So the balance between ritual and play comes into focus and allows the audience the experience of mass action, group solidarity, the fear and liveness of comedy interactions, and the separation from its everyday reality. This short-lived transformation of the audience, while watching a story about transformation of the individual that contains scenic illusions and transformations all point to the possibility of transformation for the audience. However illusory one may believe that to be, that combination is uplifting and entertaining; it makes the audience feel good.

It sounds from this as though pantomime is easy. Just get the audience joining in with the comedians and they'll be entertained and uplifted. It's not so simple, however, firstly because generating the conditions for the safe playfulness and controlled anarchy requires skill. Secondly, because finding and maintaining the balance between being truthful to the melodramatic story and the comic situation, and interacting and engaging with the audience with a clear purpose, is extremely hard, as evidenced by the many less successful performances most people have seen. What becomes clear, however, is that there is a successful formula for pantomime within which the performers approach the audience to draw them into an interactive engagement. This allows the audience to become involved in the heroic quest and the potentially transformative experience.

Paradoxically, having spent so much time exploring the methods employed in pantomime to involve the audience in the performance, it is important to stress that the elements of pantomime that distance the audience from involvement are equally important. In contrast to the opportunities for involvement, there are moments when the audience is engaged in passive contemplation of songs, dances, comic interactions or plot development. These moments provide respite from activity while maintaining the pace of the performance. They focus the energy differently by drawing attention away from the story and the characters, to the moments of ingenuity and skill, and they allow the performers to remain in control of the event by refocusing the authority of the stage. Creating an effective and dynamic balance between audience activity and passive contemplation is an important factor in the success of any pantomime.

The mix of genres, ages and geographical locations contributes to the artificiality of the performance. The performance takes place in a mythical 'everytime', the hero is an androgynous 'everyperson'. This allows the audience to be part of the performance and to identify with the hero's transformation. At the same time, the artificiality of the world of the pantomime, the mix of genres in music and dance, and the glorious excess in comedy, music, dance and design all contribute to the artifice of the piece. This artifice is not artless, however, but requires skill and expertise in maintaining the lightness of touch, the pace, energy and wit that allows pantomime to critique itself and society and yet remain, for many, simply entertainment.

That entertaining and dynamic experience is a memory shared by the audience members at each performance to which each will respond differently. Despite the communal activity of the pantomime, each memory is subtly different, recalling different moments of the performance, different responses to the event. This feeling of ephemerality has been clarified for me while writing this book. Each interview I've conducted has reminded me of another time, another place, so that the ephemerality of performance has become linked with the ephemerality of experience. The fixedness of this literary text contrasts with the ephemerality of the performances and brings me to a vastly simple conclusion. Performance and writing are media that exist in different time frames; the analysis of performance is necessarily historical, performance itself is always in the present, and pantomime represents itself as unique, live and infinitely changeable. The scripts of performances are merely traces, the video evidence captures the visual elements but of a single performance from a single perspective, and the memories of all my contributors are selective and subjective. The combination of material presented gives a snapshot of pantomime garnered from the evidence consulted and from my own experience and opinions. What is contained in any study is partial, subject to the choices made at every stage on the way and can only record a moment. This is even more apparent when dealing with a form that is still passed on within an oral tradition, that delights in changeability, topicality, and the opportunity to ad-lib, and clearly represents itself within a framework of liveness. The writing of this text solidifies and anchors a form that has been fluid and developing for hundreds of years, but only for this moment. The form will continue to develop. In the end this is an attempt to fix something mercurial, diverse and always in motion; I can't hope to capture it for an instant, but I can hope to encourage readers to look afresh at something familiar.

I have tried to present a range of examples, arguments and opinions that give a sense of what pantomime is and why it continues to be popular in Britain. There are other views and there are other possible arrangements of the material that might lead to different conclusions. There are also other books to be written; this book avoids consideration of amateur pantomimes which have a different relationship to their community; the influence of pantomime on popular performance and vice versa is another area that deserves attention; the presence of pantomimes in former colonies and the influence of early pantomime on popular forms in other countries both allow for much broader contextual studies.

In the end, I haven't written much about the stories of pantomime, but much more about the performance. The stories follow simple, defined, mythical patterns dealing with heroic quests that can be reworked by the reader to apply to contemporary life. They can represent plans for action in relation to psychological or social issues. But the pantomime is not monologic. It contains the story, but it also contains burlesque, parody and satire. Pantomime mocks itself and the society it exists in. In this sense it is subversive, both to societal institutions, but also to the idea of an over-arching monologic narrative. The polyphonic or dialogic elements in literature are regarded as having a liberating influence. The author is still in control, but there is not a single authorial voice. The same is true of pantomime, in which the story has many interpretations, and whose performance contains multiple frames and voices that subvert and support its own existence. The potential is there for pantomime to provide a dynamic and liberating experience for audiences.

In terms of the popularity and enjoyability of pantomime, it is perhaps the framing of the performance, the reflexivity and the audience participation that prompt the audience to feel that it is included in a special world. The audience becomes a community and shares the controlled anarchy that allows the conventions of pantomime and the framing of performance to be revealed and mocked. It feels it has experienced a unique event, a one-off experience, far removed from the perfect reproduction striven for in other entertainments. Even the mix of genres in music and dance contributes to the sense of artifice and entertainment. And yet the whole thing, even the anarchy, is so familiar. The same stories, frames, asides, gags, routines, characters, song and dance styles and transformations reappear from one year to the next. Does the audience forget? Or is that the point? The appearance of anarchy is reproduced in a safe, familiar, enjoyable and communal experience that is part of the ritual of many people's lives. Perhaps a slow pace of change is required by an audience who takes part in the pantomime as a nostalgic, familiar ritual and a momentarily liberating and entertaining experience rather than going to the pantomime to observe a new, original or provocative performance.

Finally, I would say of pantomime what Rick Altman says in relation to musical films of the classic Hollywood era: 'It is ironic that the most escapist of the entertainment arts should also be the most reflexive, the most aware of its status, and thus the most complex [...]' (Altman 1981: 7).

Note

1. This is a reference to the song 'If Love Were All' from *Bitter Sweet* (Coward 1929), which closes with the lines: I believe that since my life began, the most I've had is just a talent to amuse. Heigh-ho. If love were all.

BIBLIOGRAPHY

Allen, Graham (2000): *Intertextuality*. London and New York: Routledge.

Allen, Tony (2002): *Attitude: The secret of stand-up comedy*. Glastonbury: Gothic image publications.

Altman, Rick (ed.) (1981): *Genre: The Musical*. London: Routledge and Kegan Paul.

Baker, R (1994): *Drag*. London: Cassell.

Bakhtin, Mikhail (1940): *Rabelais and his world*. (Trans Helene Iswolsky 1984) Bloomington: Indiana University Press.

Bakhtin, Mikhail (1981): *The Dialogic Imagination: four essays*. (Ed. Michael Holquist) Austin: University of Texas Press.

Ben Chaim, Daphna (1984): *Distance in the Theatre: The Aesthetics of Audience Response*. Ann Arbor: UMI Research Press.

Bennett, Anthony (1986): 'Music in the Halls'. *Music Hall: Performance and Style*. (Ed.: Bratton, JS) Milton Keynes: Open University Press, 1–22.

Bennett, Susan (1997): *Theatre Audiences*. 2nd ed. London: Routledge.

Bettelheim, Bruno (1976): *The uses of enchantment*. (Paperback ed. 1991) London: Penguin.

Bial, Henry (2004): *The Performance Studies Reader*. London and New York: Routledge

Booth, Michael R (no date): Prefaces to English nineteenth century theatre. 2nd ed. Manchester: Manchester University Press.

Bouissac, Paul (1990): 'The profanation of the sacred in circus clown performances'. *By means of performance*. (Eds: Schechner, R; Appel, W) Cambridge: Cambridge University Press.

Branscombe, Peter (1980): 'Pantomime'. *The New Grove Dictionary of Music and Musicians*. (Ed.: Sadie, Stanley) London: Macmillan, 161–164.

Bristol, Michael (1985): *Carnival and the Theater*. New York and London: Methuen.

Broadbent, RJ (1902): *A History of Pantomime*. London: Simpkin, Marshall, Hamilton, Kent and Co.

Butler, Judith (1990): *Gender Trouble: feminism and the subversion of identity*. London and New York: Routledge.

Carlson, Marvin (1990): *Theatre Semiotics: Signs of Life*. Bloomington: Indiana University Press.

Carlson, Marvin (1996): *Performance*. London and New York: Routledge.

Carter, Angela (ed.) (1990): *The Virago Book of Fairy-Tales*. London: Virago.

Chapman, Clive (1981): 'A 1727 Pantomime: The Rape of Proserpine'. *Musical Times* 122, 807–811.

Clark, Katerina; Holquist, Michael (1984): *Mikhail Bakhtin*. Cambridge, Mass. and London: Harvard University Press.

Clinton-Baddeley, VC (1963): *Some pantomime pedigrees*. London: The Society for Theatre Research.

Cook, Nicholas (1998): *Analysing Musical Multimedia*. Oxford: Clarendon Press.

Counsell, Colin (1996): *Signs of Performance*. London and New York: Routledge.

Counsell, Colin; Wolf, Laurie (eds.) (2001): *Performance Analysis: An introductory coursebook*. London: Routledge.

Coupe, Laurence (1997): *Myth*. London and New York: Routledge.

Cox, Arnie (2001): 'The Mimetic Hypothesis and Embodied Musical Meaning' *Musicae Scientiae* 5/2, 195–209.

Dyer,Richard (1981): 'Entertainment and Utopia' *Genre: The Musical*. (Ed.: Altman, Rick) London: Routledge and Kegan Paul, 175–189.

Elam, Keir (1980): *The Semiotics of Theatre and Drama*. (Series Ed: Hawkes, Terence. New Accents.) London and New York: Methuen.

Feuer, Jane (1981): 'The self-reflective musical and the myth of entertainment'. *Genre: the musical*. (Ed.: Altman, Rick) London: Routledge, 159–174.

Feuer, Jane (1993): *The Hollywood Musical*. 2nd ed. Basingstoke and London: Macmillan Press.

Fischer-Lichte, Erika (1997): *The show and the gaze of theatre*. Iowa: University of Iowa Press.

Flinn, Caryl (1992): *Strains of Utopia*. Princeton: Princeton University Press.

Flinn, Caryl (1994): 'Music and the Melodramatic Past of New German Cinema'. *Melodrama*. (Eds: Bratton, J; Cook, J; Gledhill, C) London: British Film Institute, 106–120.

Frow, Gerald (1985): *Oh, Yes it is!* London: British Broadcasting Corporation.

Frye, Northrop (1971): *Anatomy of criticism: Four essays*. Princeton: Princeton University Press.

Garber, Marjorie (1997): *Vested Interest: Cross-dressing and cultural anxiety*. 2nd ed. New York and London: Routledge.

Gaylord, Karen (1983): 'Theatrical Performances: Structure and Process, Tradition and Revolt'. *Performers and Performances: The Social organization of artistic work*. (Eds: Kamerman, Jack B; Martorella, Rosanne) New York: Praeger.

Goodwin, John (ed.) (1989): *British Theatre Design*. London: Weidenfeld and Nicolson.

Gorbman, Claudia (1987): *Unheard Melodies*. Bloomington: Indiana University Press.

Harris, Paul (1996): *The Pantomime Book*. London: Peter Owen.

Holland, Peter (1997): 'The Play of Eros: The Paradoxes of Gender in English Pantomime'. *New Theatre Quarterly* xiii/51, 195–204.

Hoover, Cynthia Adams (1984): 'Music in Eighteenth Century American Theater'. *American Music* 2/4, 6–18.

Kruger, Marie (2000): 'English Pantomime: Reflections on a dynamic tradition'. *South African Theatre Journal* 14, 146–173.

Kruger, Marie (2003): 'Pantomime in South Africa: The British tradition and the local flavour'. *South African Theatre Journal* 17, 129–152.

Mackintosh, Iain (1993): *Architecture, actor, audience*. London and New York: Routledge.

Masson, Alain (1981): 'George Sidney: Artificial Brilliance/The Brilliance of Artifice'. *Genre: the musical*. (Ed.: Altman,Rick) London: Routledge, 28–40.

McLucas, Anne Dhu (ed.) (1994): 'Later Melodrama in America: Monte Cristo (ca. 1883)'. *Nineteenth Century American Musical Theater*. Volume 4. New York and London: Garland Publishing Inc.

Meyer, Leonard B (1956): *Emotion and Meaning in Music*. Chicago: University of Chicago Press.

Milner Davis, J (1978): *Farce*. (The Critical Idiom.) London: Methuen and Co.

Nagler, AM (1952): *A Sourcebook in Theatrical History*. New York: Dover Publications.

Phelan, Peggy (1993): *Unmarked: The Politics of Performance*. London and New York: Routledge.

Pickering, D (1993): *Encyclopedia of Pantomime*. Andover: Gale Research International Ltd.

Pollack, H (1996): 'Nineteenth Century Musical Theater'. *Journal of Musicological Research* 16:1, 69–77.

Propp, Vladimir (1968): *Morphology of the Folktale*. Second ed. Austin and London: University of Texas Press.

Richards, Sandra (1993): *The Rise of the English Actress*. London: Macmillan.

Robbins, Norman (2002): *Slapstick and Sausages*. Tiverton: Trapdoor Publications.

Rolfe, Bari (ed.) (1978): *Mimes on Miming*. 2nd ed. Los Angeles and San Francisco: Panjandrum Books.

Salberg, Derek (1981): *Once upon a Pantomime*. London: Cortney Publications.

Schechner, Richard (2002): *Performance Studies: An introduction*. London and New York: Routledge.

Schechner, Richard; Appel, Willa (eds) (1990): *By Means of Performance*. Cambridge: Cambridge University Press.

Senelick, Laurence (2000): *The Changing Room*. London and New York: Routledge.

Shand, John (1978): 'Pantomime'. *Theatre and Song*. Vol. 8. (Eds.: Davison, P; Meyersohn, R; Shils, E) Cambridge: Chadwyck-Healey.

Shapiro, Anne Dhu (1984): 'Action Music in American Pantomime and Melodrama 1730–1913' *Music of the American Theater* vol 2/4, 49–72

Slater, WJ (1994): 'Pantomime Riots'. *Classical Antiquity* 13/1, 120–144.

Smith, James L (1973): *Melodrama*. London: Methuen.

Sutton, Martin (1981): 'Patterns of meaning in the musical'. *Genre: the musical*. (Ed.: Altman, Rick) London: Routledge, 190–196.

Tagg, Philip (1982): 'Analysing Popular Music: Theory, Method and Practice'. *Popular Music* 2, 37–68.

Tatar, Maria (2003): *The Hard Facts of the Grimms' Fairy Tales*. 2nd ed. Princeton and Oxford: Princeton University Press.

Taylor, Millie (1999): 'Conventions in contemporary pantomime music'. *Studies in Theatre Production* 19, 139–158.

Taylor, Millie (2001): *Music in Theatre: Towards a methodology for examining the interaction of music and drama in theatre works of the twentieth century*. Ph.D. Dissertation, Exeter University. 346 .

Taylor, Millie (2005): 'Distance and Reflexivity: Creating the stage-world of Pantoland' *New Theatre Quarterly* vol XXI: 4, 331–339.

Taylor, Millie (2007): '"Don't dream it, be it": exploring signification, empathy and mimesis in relation to *The Rocky Horror Show*' *Studies in Musical Theatre* vol 1: 1, 57–71.

Todorov, Tzvetan (1990): *Genres in Discourse*. Cambridge: Cambridge University Press.

Towsen, John H (1976): *Clowns*. New York: Hawthorn Books Inc.

Turner, Victor (1982): *From Ritual to Theatre*. New York: PAJ Publications.

Ubersfeld, Anne (1982): 'The Pleasure of the Spectator'. *Modern Drama* 25/1(ed.: trans. Pierre Bouillaguet and Charles Jose), 127–139.

Warner, Marina (1995): *From the Beast to the Blonde*. London: Vintage.

Warner, Marina (1998): *No Go the Bogeyman*. London: Chatto and Windus.

Zipes, Jack (1991): *Fairy Tales and the art of subversion*. New York: Routledge.

Zipes, Jack (1997): *Happily Ever After: Fairy Tales, Children and the Culture Industry*. New York and London: Routledge.

Scripts

Anderson, Hans Christian (2004): *The Snow Queen* (adapted by Patrick Sandford) Nuffield Theatre, Southampton.

Anon. (1992): *Aladdin and his Wonderful Lamp*. Yvonne Arnaud Theatre, Guildford: E&B Productions.

Chissick, Jack and Horlock, David (1987): *Jack and the Beanstalk* Salisbury Playhouse.

Cregan, David (1998): *Cinderella: A Pantomime*. Music by Brian Protheroe. London: Samuel French.

Davies, Tudor (1990): *Robinson Crusoe*. Yvonne Arnaud Theatre, Guildford: E&B Productions.

Davies, Tudor (1997): *The further adventures of Peter Pan* Theatre Royal, Plymouth: E&B Productions.

Davies, Tudor (1998): *Jack and the Beanstalk* Theatre Royal, Plymouth: E&B Productions.

Edgar, Kate and Wakefield, Colin (2002): *Little Red Riding Hood* Theatre Royal, Winchester: Hiss and Boo Company.

Elliott, Paul; Davies, Tudor (1991): *Dick Whittington*. Yvonne Arnaud Theatre, Guildford: E&B Productions.

Hudd, Roy (1992): *Aladdin and his Wonderful Lamp: an old tale retold* Palace Theatre, Watford: Hiss and Boo Company.

Hudd, Roy (1995): *The legend of Mother Goose and the Golden Eggs* Theatre Royal, Plymouth: E&B Productions.

Hudd, Roy (1998): *The legend of Dick Whittington and his cat*. Queen's Theatre Barnstaple: Hiss and Boo Company.

Hudd, Roy (1999): *Cinderella*. Queen's Theatre Barnstaple: Hiss and Boo Company.

Hudd, Roy (2002): *The legend of Jack and the Beanstalk* Queen's Theatre Barnstaple: Hiss and Boo Company.

Jordan, Chris (2002): *Aladdin* Potter's Bar.

Jordan, Chris (2003): *Cinderella* Devonshire Park Theatre, Eastbourne.

Lillicrap, Christopher (2003): *Snow White* Anvil Theatre, Basingstoke: The Proper Pantomime Company.

Morley, John (1981): *Goldilocks*. (Author's Draft in Theatre Museum, Covent Garden.) London: Samuel French.

Ranger, Jeanette and Lillicrap, Christopher (no date): *Cinderella* The Proper Pantomime Company.

Rayment, Mark (1997): *Jack and the Beanstalk* (with additional material by Trevor Bannister) Harlequin Theatre, Redhill: London Productions.

Reid, Joanna and Thomas, Stuart (2003): *Aladdin* Salisbury Playhouse.

Video

Babes in the Wood (1994): Sadler's Wells. Directed by Roy Hudd.

Dick Whittington (1994): Birmingham Hippodrome. Director and Choreographer Carole Todd.

Wood, Elizabeth (1982): *The Pantomime Dame*. Arts Council of Great Britain.

INDEX